CISTERCIAN STUDIES SEI

£3

CW00409583

N

Bede the Venerable

HOMILIES ON THE GOSPELS

Book One

CISTERCIAN STUDIES SERIES: NUMBER ONE HUNDRED TEN

Bede the Venerable

HOMILIES ON THE GOSPELS

Book One
Advent to Lent

Translated by
Lawrence T. Martin
and
David Hurst OSB

Preface by
Benedicta Ward SLG

Introduction by
Lawrence T. Martin

Cistercian Publications

A Cistercian Publications title published by Liturgical Press

Cistercian Publications
Editorial Offices
161 Grosvenor Street
Athens, Ohio 45701
www.cistercianpublications.org

A translation made from the critical edition of Dom David Hurst OSB, *Bedae Homiliae evangelii*. Corpus Christianorum, 122. Turnhout: Brepols, 1955.

The work of Cistercian Publications is made possible in part by support from Western Michigan University to the Institute of Cistercian Studies.

Library of Congress Cataloging-in-Publication Data

Bede, the Venerable, Saint, 673-735
    [Homiliae evangelii. English]
    Homilies on the Gospels/Bede the Venerable: translated by Lawrence T. Martin and David Hurst
    p. cm. — (Cistercian studies series ; no. 110)
    Translation of: Bedae homiliae evangelii.
    Contents: bk. 1. Advent to Lent — bk. 2. Lent to the Dedication of the Church.
    ISBN 0-87907-610-0 (bk. 1). — ISBN 0-87907-710-7 (bk. 1 pbk.).
    ISBN 0-87907-711-5 (bk. 2). — ISBN 0-87907-911-8 (bk. 2 pbk.).
    1. Bible. N.T. Gospels—Sermons.   2. Church year sermons—Early works to 1800.   3. Occasional sermons—Early works to 1800. 4. Sermons, English—Translations from Latin—Early works to 1800. 5. Sermons, Latin—Translations into English—Early works to 1800. I. Martin, Lawrence T., 1942- .   II. Hurst, David, osв.   III. Title. IV. Series.   BX1756.B37H66   1990
252'.6—dc20   89-39171
          CIP

The editors of Cistercian Publications express their deep appreciation to John Leinenweber, Hermitage of the Dayspring, Kent, Connecticut, and to Professor Gerald Bonner, Emeritus Reader in Theology at the University of Durham, for their help in preparing the manuscript for publication.

The author expresses his appreciation to Sonia Dial for her great help in typing the manuscript and creating the indices.

The preparation of this volume was made possible in part by a grant from the Division of Research Programs of the National Endowment for the Humanities, an independent federal agency.

contents

pREfACE

I T HAS ALWAYS BEEN MY DELIGHT to learn or to teach or to write'.[1] *Discere, docere, scribere*, the key-notes of Bede's life, were also for him the centre and heart of christian living. As a monk, he was able to teach by his learning, above all in writing, those who would preach to others the Word of Life. He often insisted that the preacher must teach by 'word and by example', and in his writings he presented his contemporaries with both words from the Fathers and with examples of the way of life of apostolic preachers. In his last book, the *Ecclesiastical History of the English People*, he described the way of life of the great missionaries who had first preached to the English and begun the work of making the *gens Anglorum* also a *gens Christi*. He presented Gregory the Great as 'our apostle', both as concerned for the preaching of the word of life to the English and as the writer of *The Pastoral Care*, the handbook for the pastor which Bede regarded as fundamental to the work of preaching.[2] He gave vivid, memorable, pictures of Augustine, bringing to Aethelberht of Kent 'the best of news,

1. Bede *Ecclesiastical History of the English People*, ed. and trans. B. Colgrave and R.A.B. Mynors (Oxford 1972) Bk V, cap. xxiv, p. 567.
2. Ibid., Bk 11, cap. 1, pp. 107-9.

iii

namely the sure and certain promise of eternal joys in heaven and an endless kingdom with the living and true God',[3] and then living near St Martin's church and 'following the way of life of the apostles and the primitive church... they preached the word of life to as many as they could'.[4] He described with loving care the preaching of Aidan of Lindisfarne and the Irish missionaries in Northumbria, walking everywhere, praying, reading the Scriptures; 'the best recommendation of his teaching to all was that he taught them no other way of life than that which he himself practised with his followers.'[5] Above all, he wrote about Cuthbert, the ideal man of God, whose compassion led him into the most neglected and inaccessible parts of the country to preach and administer the sacraments, weeping with the penitent, patient with all, accessible even at the expense of his own deepest desire for utter solitude.[6]

The Word of God had to be understood with the mind as well as the heart, and Bede gave these pictures of the care with which the first missionaries had preached to the English partly out of thankfulness for the glory of such a past but also as a rebuke to those who in his own times neglected such preaching; many bishops and priests never visited the people who lived 'in inaccessible mountains and dense woodlands... to teach the truth of the faith'.[7] Much of Bede's work in the monastery had been largely concerned with helping pastors to be able to undertake such preaching. Himself the foremost scholar of his age, Bede had at Jarrow the inestimable privilege of a library and, what is more important, the skills to use it. Through the books brought to him from the Mediterranean world by his abbots, he was able to absorb the text of the Scriptures and the comments of the Fathers upon them so deeply that he was later regarded as one of the Fathers of the Church himself. He knew himself to have been especially fortunate, and

3. Ibid., Bk 1, cap. xxv, p. 73.   4. Ibid., Bk 1, cap. xxvi, p. 77.
5. Ibid., Bk 111, cap. v, p. 227.
6. Bede. *Life of St Cuthbert*, ed. and trans. B. Colgrave, *Two Lives of St Cuthbert* (Cambridge 1940) pp. 207-13.
7. Bede, 'Letter to Egbert', trans. D. Whitelock, *English Historical Documents*, vol.1 (Oxford 1979) p. 802.

therefore regarded it as a duty to provide compilations of commentaries on many books of the Old and New Testaments with abbreviations, omissions and additions of his own, which were to be handbooks for those who would never have access to such books and had neither the skill nor the time to use them if they had. It was necessary to 'open the Scriptures', so that the Word of God to the English might be fully known; and for this the sermons and commentaries of the early Fathers, especially Gregory the Great, Augustine, Jerome, and Ambrose were indispensable.

It was not only the official pastors whom Bede wished to help to understand the Scriptures; others also were pastors, like the shepherds after they had visited the new-born Christ:

> It is not only bishops, presbyters, deacons and even those who govern monasteries who are to be understood to be pastors; but also all the faithful who keep watch over the little ones of their house, are properly called pastors.[8]

Although not a bishop, nor ever holding any administrative position in his monastery, Bede was a priest and therefore among such 'pastors', and as well as his work to help other preachers he was at times himself required to preach. His homilies were given in his own monastery and in the context of the liturgy,[9] most probably after the reading of the Gospel either at the Eucharist or at the preceding vigil.[10] From the sermons he had preached by the time he was fifty-eight, he selected fifty, and in the list of his works he included them after his commentaries on the Gospels of Luke and Mark as his other work on the Gospels: 'Homilies on

8. Homily I.7; p. 69.
9. For a reconstruction of the order of Bede's homilies by use of the Gospel commented on in each see D. Hurst (ed.) *Bedae Venerabilis Opera: pars 111, Opera Homiletica,* CCSL 122 (Turnholt 1955) pp. ix–xvi.
10. There has been some debate about the exact occasion upon which Bede preached his homilies; these are presented by Andreas van der Walt in his unpublished doctoral thesis, 'The Homiliary of the Venerable Bede and Early Medieval Preaching' (London 1980). It is also possible that the homilies were from the first a literary composition only and were not actually preached; cf. L. Martin, *The Homilies of the Venerable Bede,* 1, Introduction, pp. xxi–xiv.

the Gospels: two books'.[11] At times, perhaps in place of one of his abbots during their frequent journeys abroad, Bede preached to his brothers and at least fifty of his sermons were written down, presumably by Bede himself either before or after preaching; perhaps he tailored the written form for a wider audience. Presumably he preached on other texts at other times of the year, but these were the sermons he collected together and revised. Each has for its text the verses read for the feast concerned from one of the Gospels, upon which he commented directly. Later editors copied sections from Bede's commentaries on Luke and Mark and set them out as if they were sermons, which in fact is what he had provided the commentaries for, but only these fifty are certainly Bede's own sermons.

Most of the homilies were related to the major turning points in the church's year, Easter and Christmas. Eighteen were grouped around the celebration of the Nativity, whose dating at 25 December Bede had popularised in one of his earliest works. Four of these were for Advent, one for the Christmas Eve, one each for the three masses of Christmas Day, one each for the feast of St John and the Holy Innocents, one for the Octave Day of the Nativity, one for Epiphany, five for the Sundays after it, and one for Candlemas. It is no surprise that the largest group of homilies centred around Easter, that central feast to which Bede paid so much attention elsewhere. Twenty-two of the sermons related to Easter, with seven sermons in Lent, with one each for Palm Sunday, Holy Week and Maundy Thursday, two for Holy Saturday, one for Easter Sunday, five during Eastertide, one for Ascension, one for Pentecost, and one for the octave of Pentecost; a sermon for the Ember Days also fell within the Easter cycle and contains some of Bede's reflections on intercessory prayer. The remaining sermons were for the feasts of the saints, especially the martyrs, who provided the earliest pattern of christian sanctity: John the Baptist had already provided the theme for two Advent sermons, and the Holy Innocents had been the subject of a

11. *Ecclesiastical History*, Bk.V, cap.xxiv, p. 569.

sermon in the week after Christmas; two sermons were given for the apostles, one for the feast of Peter the Apostle, and the other for the apostles Peter and Paul; two were for the feast of the birth of John the Baptist and one for that of his beheading, while one was for the Roman martyrs John and Paul—who may have been especially commemorated both because their names were included in the canon of the mass and because of a special devotion to them by Saxon pilgrims who had visited their supposed burial place in Rome in the church built on the Caelian hill. Another homily commemorated John the Evangelist, and contains Bede's teaching on the contemplative life. Three sermons were of more local interest, one for the anniversary of the death of Benedict Biscop, and two for the anniversary of the Dedication of the Church of Saint Paul at Jarrow.

Bede's sermons are in a more relaxed, less condensed, style than his commentaries and they are therefore more readable. He is not here helping other pastors to understand the Scriptures, to avoid heretical interpretation, to have available all possible interpretations of a text for a mixed and varied audience; he was himself preaching, and to a well-known audience, for whom the material on which he based his sermons was already familiar. In his sermon for Christmas on Luke 2:14, for instance, he addressed his 'dearly beloved brothers' directly, and drew out from the Gospel the theme of true peace, which he then urged his hearers to apply to themselves: 'may this solemnity be shared by us. . . may all our way of life be fitting to the company of the heavenly citizens'. In this sermon Bede's mastery of oratory, his understanding of those forms of rhetoric which he set out in his treatise on metre, achieves a splendid climax expressing the 'recapitulation' theology of Irenaeus directly to his hearers when commenting on 'she wrapped him in swaddling clothes and laid him in a manger':

> Here, dearly beloved brothers, we must look upon
> the great condescension of our Redeemer; here
> from the whole inmost center of our heart we
> must each of us say to ourselves with the prophet,

'what shall I deliver to the Lord for all the things
which he has delivered to me?' For he to whom
we most truthfully chant, 'Great is the Lord and
exceedingly praiseworthy and of his greatness
there is no end', was born as a little one for us
so that he might make us from little ones into great
ones, that is, from sinners into just people.
Four other such contrasting clauses lead to the powerful 'he
whom heaven and the heaven of heavens do not hold was
contained by the narrowness of a small manger that he
might bestow upon us the amplitude of seats on high'. It
is a passage which also shows Bede's mastery of the full
text of the Scriptures and his use of one part to illustrate
others. Similarly, in his homily for Easter Night, Bede com-
bined his deep understanding of patristic theology and the
spiritual understanding of Scripture with a brilliant evoca-
tion of the moment and the people gathered in the church
of Saint Paul:

Let us, mindful of our redemption, devote ourselves during this night to a worthy vigil to God
and give our attention as we listen to the prayers
and divine readings that tell of the favors of the
grace given to us.

In this sermon Bede commented on the meaning of only
the beginning and end of the Gospel contained in Matthew
28:1-10, presenting rather the great images of Easter, the
light from darkness, the deliverance from Egypt, and especially the significance of Christ as the Pascal Lamb:

The unspotted Lamb came and deigned to be immolated for us; he gave his blood as the price of
our salvation and by undergoing death for a time
he condemned the sovereignty of death forever.

It is one of the great passages of latin prose, alternating the
work of Christ the Lamb and the work of the devil, the lion,
and inevitably loses some of its impact in even the most
sensitive translation.

Bede's life and thought was shaped by the firm theology
he derived and assimilated from his reading of the Fathers
of the Church, and this gave his homilies a quality of time-

lessness so that they have become a part of the christian tradition of preaching and have been used especially as lessons for the office of Matins, along with those of the other Fathers. This does not mean, however, that they are cold and distant; on the contrary, they are full of passion and poetry, and they are also firmly earthed both in Bede's own experience and in that of the audience to whom he preached, especially perhaps in those directly connected with the founder of Wearmouth-Jarrow, Benedict Biscop, and the dedication of the church of Bede's own community. It is significant that the only one of the sermons to be replaced by another when the collection was copied by Paul the Deacon was that for Benedict Biscop's anniversary. Bede was always a practical man, eager for the Gospel to be available to all and to be thoroughly taken into the life of each hearer or reader. At the end of his life, he was engaged in a translation of the Gospel of St John into English for the use of those who could read English but not Latin. It seems entirely appropriate that in a world where Latin is even more alien than it was in eighth-century England, a translation of Bede's homilies should appear:

> thus it is brought to pass that every band of the faithful may learn how to be faithful, by what steadfastness they ought to arm themselves against the assaults of unclean spirits and that every choir of suppliants to God may understand what especially should be sought from the divine clemency.[12]

Benedicta Ward SLG

Oxford, 1990

---

12. Letter to Egbert; Whitelock, p. 801.

intRoduction

THE VENERABLE BEDE'S HOMILIES on the Gospels, one of the masterpieces of monastic literature, was probably written late in Bede's career, perhaps sometime in the 720's.[1] Bede entered the monastery at the age of seven, and he spent the rest of his life as a monk at Wearmouth and Jarrow.[2] It is therefore not surprising that his *Homilies on the Gospels* was clearly intended, as the reader will discover, for a monastic audience. Bede's main concern is with the spiritual meaning of the gospel stories, their meaning for the spiritual life of the monk. There is little exhortation about specific moral problems, as we find, for example, in the sermons of Caesarius of Arles. Bede does, however, refer to the specific details of the prayer life of the monastery, and he includes passages of direct address which speak to the concerns of his monastic audience.

If Bede's *Homilies* were originally delivered orally, it is possible that they were given at mass, but their general lack of reference to a eucharistic setting perhaps implies a more

1. W.F. Bolton, *A History of Anglo-Latin Literature 597-1066* (Princeton, 1967) 167.
2. *Bede's Ecclesiastical History of the English People* V, 24, ed. by Bertram Colgrave and R.A.B. Mynors (Oxford, 1969) 566-567.

likely delivery at some other point in the monastic horari-
um. The tenth-century Benedictine reform in Anglo-Saxon
England made provision for a daily chapter meeting, which
was to include a reading from the Rule, or on feast days,
of the gospel of the day, 'and the prior shall explain what
has been read as the Lord inspires him'.[3] If a similar practice already existed in eighth-century Northumbria, this
might well have been the original setting for Bede's *Homilies on the Gospels.*

It is far from certain, however, that Bede's *Homilies* were
ever actually preached. The 'dearly-beloved brothers' ad-
dresses and similar indications of oral delivery may simply
be conventional. If Bede did once preach his *Homilies,* in
their present form they are surely intended to be read, and
probably reread on a regular annual cycle since they lack
any topical references or other features that would cause
them to become dated. Indeed, Bede's *Homilies* have such
a universal quality that they spoke to monastic audiences
all over Europe for centuries,[4] and the present translation
is offered with the conviction that Bede's *Homilies on the
Gospels* can still speak to religious and secular as well.

Bede may have intended his *Homilies* to be used for private devotional reading *(lectio divina)* or for public reading
to the brethren. St Benedict's *Rule* calls for public reading
at meals and before Compline,[5] and in his description of
the Night Office Benedict prescribed readings from the
books of the Old and New Testaments, 'and also the explanations of them which have been made by well-known
and orthodox Catholic fathers'.[6] While it is true that at
Bede's time Benedict's *Rule* had not yet attained the preeminence it was later to achieve, and the general practice was
for each monastery to have its own eclectic rule, Bede

---

3. Milton McC. Gatch, *Preaching and Theology in Anglo-Saxon England:
   Aelfric and Wulfstan* (Toronto, 1977) 40-41 and refs.
4. The one homily which is characterized by many specific references
   to Anglo-Saxon England, I.13, on Benedict Biscop, was adapted for
   continental use in several manuscripts by the substitution of biographi-
   cal material on St. Benedict of Nursia.
5. Chs. 38 and 42.
6. Ch. 9.

reveals in his writings a great respect for and familiarity with Benedict's *Rule*,[7] and there is evidence that Bede's abbot, Ceolfrid, followed in at least one respect Benedict's provisions for the ordering of the divine office.[8] The fact that Bede's *Homilies* cover the liturgical year, and also perhaps their noteworthy uniformity in length, might be taken as support for the notion that their author intended them for a place within the liturgy. Dom Pierre Salmon believed that Bede's *Homilies* were certainly intended to provide readings for the divine office.[9]

If, however, Bede's monastery did follow Benedict's prescription of readings for the Night Office from 'well-known and orthodox Catholic fathers', it would seem unlikely that Bede would have composed his own homilies for this setting. Bede was characteristically humble about his great learning and frequently described himself as 'following in the footsteps of the fathers'.[10] In his scriptural commentaries Bede often quoted extensively from the fathers—in fact, at times his commentary is made up entirely of lengthy quotations from earlier writers.[11] If Bede thought of himself as composing texts for the Night Office according to Benedict's prescription, therefore, it seems that he would have contented himself with simply collecting patristic passages. But Bede's *Homilies on the Gospels* differ most strikingly from his scriptural commentaries in the almost total absence of direct quotation from non-scriptural sources in the *Homilies*,[12] and the abundance of such quotation in

---

7. Henry M.R.E. Mayr-Harting, *The Venerable Bede, the Rule of St. Benedict, and Social Class*, Jarrow Lecture, 1976, p. 8. See also G. Bonner in *Anglo-Saxon England* 2, p. 77.
8. Patrick Wormald, 'Bede and Benedict Biscop', in *Famulus Christi*, ed. by Gerald Bonner (London, 1976) 77.
9. Pierre Salmon, OSB, *The Breviary through the Centuries*, trans. by Sister David Mary (Collegeville, MN, 1962) 67. Professor Gatch agrees with Salmon on this point—see Gatch (note 3 above) p. 191, n. 31 and p. 186, n. 12.
10. CC 121: 3, 9/10; for other refs. see Paul Meyvaert, 'Bede the Scholar' in *Famulus Christi* (see note 8 above), pp. 62-63, n. 7.
11. See Meyvaert, p. 44.
12. The only non-scriptural direct quotations in Bede's *Homilies on the Gospels* seem to be that from Rufinus' translation of Eusebius' *Ecclesiastical History* in *Hom.* II.21, and that from Cyprian's *De unitate* in *Hom.* II.22.

the commentaries. This feature of Bede's *Homilies*, then, might point toward an original setting which was non-liturgical, viz., private devotional reading. Alternatively, the lack of patristic quotations might be taken as evidence that Bede in fact delivered his *Homilies* orally and later wrote them down for either public or private reading, perhaps revising them somewhat for the sake of a wider reading audience.[13]

Whether or not Bede himself intended his *Homilies on the Gospels* to be read in the liturgical context of the divine office, less than a hundred years after Bede's death his *Homilies* did acquire a prominent place in the Night Office in the monasteries of the Carolingian empire. Charlemagne commissioned Paul the Deacon, a monk of Monte Cassino, to assemble a collection of readings for the Night Office of Sundays and major feasts of the year. Charlemagne's letter instructed Paul the Deacon to collect 'certain flowers from the wide-flung fields of the Catholic fathers',[14] and while Paul's two-volume homiliary did include a wide range of authors from both east and west, the writer who supplied the greatest number of readings was Bede. Thirty-four of Bede's fifty *Homilies on the Gospels* are represented, and excerpts from Bede's commentaries, presented as homilies, bring the total number of Bede selections to fifty-seven. Bede's work forms almost one-quarter of the total homiliary, and Cyril Smetana, commenting on these statistics, says that Paul the Deacon 'could not have found more admirable instruction and inspiration for the monks and clerics who attended the night offices [than] Bede's work, [which] was wholesomely orthodox and stylistically correct'.[15]

---

13. See Sister Benedicta Ward's *Preface*, above.
14. Cyril L. Smetana, 'Paul the Deacon's Patristic Anthology' in *The Old English Homily and its Backgrounds*, ed. by Paul E. Szarmach and Bernard F. Huppé (Albany, 1978) 79.
15. Smetana, p. 80. Smetana's calculations are based on the reconstruction of Paul the Deacon's original homiliary. Some variant versions of this homiliary contain an even higher percentage of Bede's work. For example, I have examined two homiliaries from the Austrian abbey of Admont (Admont MSS 65 and 66) which both add more readings from Bede and delete some readings from other writers.

Paul the Deacon's homiliary became, in Smetana's words, 'standard for the western church for eleven hundred years'.[16] Bede's *Homilies on the Gospels* have therefore had an incalculable influence on generations of monks, religious, and clerics who have listened to or read the Matins lessons from Paul the Deacon's homiliary and its descendants. These listeners and readers have in turn transmitted Bede's theological ideas as well as his general approach to biblical explication. The influence of Bede's *Homilies on the Gospels* was not limited to later homilies, sermons, theological treatises, and religious poetry, for the iconography of one of the portals of Chartres cathedral seems to reflect the influence of some of Bede's *Homilies* which are known to have been in liturgical manuscripts preserved at Chartres.[17]

Whatever the specific use for which Bede composed his *Homilies on the Gospels*, he undoubtedly saw his work as a continuation of the patristic tradition of exegetical preaching represented by works like Augustine's *Sermons* and *Tractates on the Gospel of John*, and especially by Gregory the Great's *Homilies on the Gospels*.[18] While Augustine's influence on Bede's *Homilies* is seen in rhetorical patterns of parallelism and balanced construction, and in a fondness for wordplay, it is from Gregory that Bede learned his basic approach, viz., to keep his eye on the biblical story, to begin with the fundamental story-questions of 'Who,' 'When,' 'Where,' and 'What happens,' and to tell us the

---

16. Smetana, p. 75. For changes in the readings of the night office during the Renaissance and later, see Salmon, chs. 4 and 5. Bede did not always fare well in these changes (Salmon, p. 79), which Salmon characterizes as sometimes involving 'reduction and abridgment... to the detriment of liturgical value and of the meaning' (p. 74, cf. pp. 93-94).

17. Adolf Katzenellenbogen, *The Sculptural Program of Chartres Cathedral* (New York, 1959) pp. 8-15 and figures 10 and 13.

18. For a general discussion of Gregory's influence on Bede, see M.L.W. Laistner's classic article 'The Library of the Venerable Bede' in *Bede, His Life, Times and Writings*, ed. by A.H. Thompson (Oxford, 1935), and Paul Meyvaert's 'Bede and Gregory the Great' (Jarrow Lecture, 1964). Laistner (p. 249) speaks of Bede's greatest veneration being for Gregory, and after Gregory came Augustine. Meyvaert (p. 19) says of Gregory and Bede: 'Some kind of spiritual affinity, not easily definable, links them together in a subtle way'.

spiritual meaning of these narrative details. Like Gregory, Bede generally works straight through the gospel reading, verse by verse without feeling compelled to comment upon absolutely every verse. Again like Gregory, rather than like Augustine, Bede sticks with the gospel story, and if he brings in other texts, as he often does, their relation to the reading is usually evident and clear.

There is a striking lack of overlap between Gregory's forty *Homilies on the Gospels* and Bede's fifty *Homilies*. The two collections have only one pericope in common, and this is Luke 2:1-14, where Gregory begins his homily with an apology for not being able to do justice to his text: 'Because by the Lord's bounty I am going to celebrate the eucharist three times today, I cannot speak at length on the gospel lesson'.[19] It is easy to imagine that this statement would have caused Bede to feel justified in treating such an important gospel story at greater length. The lack of overlap between Gregory and Bede suggests that Bede perhaps deliberately chose to compose his *Homilies* only on texts that Gregory had not treated, and to treat them in the spirit of Gregory's *Homilies*, but with adaptations appropriate to a monastic audience. In other words, Bede may have conceived of his own *Homilies on the Gospels* as a sort of complement or even a sequel to Gregory's *Homilies on the Gospels*.

The pericopes used by Bede for his fifty homilies have been said to reflect the usage of Naples, or the Romano-Neapolitan usage,[20] brought to Jarrow in the liturgical notes that had been copied into 'the great Cassiodorian Vulgate Bible which Ceolfrid brought to Jarrow', probably in 678, when he accompanied Benedict Biscop on his third journey to Rome.[21] However, the usage of Naples, as reconstructed in the studies of Morin and Chapman, was sufficiently broad for Bede to work within it and still achieve the aim of supplementing or complementing Gregory's

19. *PL* 76: 1103D.
20. Bolton, p. 166; cf. the introduction to David Hurst's edition of Bede's *Homilies on the Gospels* (*CC* 122, pp. viii-xvi).
21. Dom John Chapman, *Notes on the Early History of the Vulgate Gospels* (Oxford, 1908) 23-25; see pp. 43-44 for Chapman's idea on where these notes ultimately came from.

series of gospel homilies. Most of Gregory's homilies are
on pericopes selected in the Neapolitan liturgical notes,[22]
but many pericopes in those notes were not addressed by
Gregory. Bede perhaps chose forty-nine of these that
seemed most in need of a homily in the spirit of Gregory's
Homilies on the Gospels, and he also added one more homily on a text that Gregory had addressed, viz. Luke's Christmas gospel, because Gregory had himself suggested that
more should be said about that reading.

Although Bede does not generally use direct quotations
from the Fathers in his *Homilies on the Gospels,* this does not
mean that he was not influenced by the ideas of his
predecessors. The abundant source notes in this translation
show the contrary. It is impossible, of course, to indicate
in the source notes the precise nature of Bede's dependence
upon earlier writings. At times Bede simply paraphrases
his source, interpreting the same biblical passage in essen-
tially the same way as did the earlier writer. At other times
Bede's work shows only a very general resemblance to the
source indicated, and some editors would probably not have
included these possible-source notes. The most interesting
cases, however, are those in which Bede clearly draws on
an earlier source, but his predecessor's interpretation is fully
assimilated to Bede's own themes and purposes in a high-
ly original way. Smetana's characterization of Bede's *Homilies* as 'a mosaic of biblical and patristic sources'[23] is surely
an overstatement, and it reflects a negative judgment on
Bede's originality which scholars have uncritically handed
down.[24] It therefore seems appropriate here to offer some
examples of Bede's creativity and originality in his use of
his patristic sources.

---

22. See Chapman ch. 4 for a complete list of the pericopes in the Neapolitan liturgical notes.
23. Smetana, p. 80.
24. Paul Meyvaert's article in *Famulus Christi* (see note 10 above) begins
with a survey of scholarly viewpoints which deprecate Bede's scholar-
ship because of a supposed lack of originality. Meyvaert answers
the charge but he makes no specific reference to Bede's *Homilies on
the Gospels.*

Homily I.18, for the feast of the Purification, offers a particularly striking example of Bede's creative use of patristic sources. Much of this homily is devoted to the spiritual symbolism of 'the two turtle-doves or two young pigeons' offered by the holy family. The pigeon, Bede tells us, represents simplicity, and the turtle-dove indicates chastity. The source notes here point to Augustine's *Fifth Tractate on John's Gospel* for the idea that the pigeon represents simplicity, and to Jerome's *Adversus Jovinianum* for the notion of the turtle-dove as a symbol of chastity in connection with its supposed habit of not seeking another mate if it loses its first one.

It is certain that Bede knew the Augustine and Jerome works in question, since he quotes both of them in commentaries which probably predate his homilies. It is also at least possible that Bede had the indicated passages of his predecessors' work in mind as he wrote his homily. However, the full context of the bird-symbolism passages in both Augustine's and Jerome's work is so different from that of Bede's that it is impossible to accuse Bede here of simply handing on the ideas of the fathers.

First of all, Augustine's *Tractate* concerns a different passage in which a pigeon or a dove happens to appear, viz., the story of Jesus' baptism in the Jordan. More important, the 'simplicity' which the bird represents in Augustine's work is not the quality of soul which Bede calls 'simplicity', but rather simplicity in the sense of the singleness of the baptism inaugurated by Christ as opposed to the notion of the Donatist heretics that baptism could and sometimes should be repeated.

When we look at the Jerome passage, we find a similar situation. Whereas the turtle-dove represents chastity as a general christian virtue in Bede's homily, Jerome uses the idea as a weapon in his controversy with Jovinian over the question of God's evaluation of marriage in relation to the state of consecrated virginity and the question of second marriage for widows. Interestingly, when later in his homily Bede recapitulates the lesson of the two birds, the symbolism is not chastity and simplicity, but 'the sobriety, simplicity and compunction of our heart'. Jerome would probably have regarded this as a fuzzy, liberal watering down of the dove symbol.

Bede's homily also draws a lesson from the sound made by the two birds. Both turtle-dove and pigeon 'bring forth a moaning sound in place of a song', says Bede—these two kinds of birds therefore 'indicate the lamentation of the saints in this world'. Here the source note points to Augustine's *Sixth Tractate on John's Gospel*, where the bird under discussion is again that which descended upon Jesus in his baptism in the Jordan. This time, however, there is no polemical context for Augustine's focus, and there is a real parallel in thought, if not in wording, with Bede's homily. Augustine says that the Holy Spirit, represented by the bird in his gospel story

> teaches us to groan by teaching us that we are pilgrims here, and he teaches us to sigh after our native land, and by that very longing we groan. One for whom things go well in this world, or who thinks that they are going well, so that his joy is in fleshly things and in an abundance of temporal things, and who exults in an empty happiness, has the cry of a raven, for the raven's cry is raucous, not a groaning. However, one who recognizes that he is in the anguish of this mortal life, a pilgrim absent from the Lord, that he does not yet have that eternal blessedness promised to us, but that he has it in hope, and will have it in reality when the Lord comes openly in glory who before came concealed in humility—one who recognizes this does groan, and as long as it is for this that he groans, he does well to groan, for the Spirit has taught him to groan. He has learned to groan from the dove.[25]

Bede may well have been inspired by this passage from Augustine, but it seems also possible that he could have developed the metaphor on his own. To relate the mournful

25. CC 36: 53, 15/27.

sound of an English dove to the eschatological theme of christian discontent in this world and longing for heaven would be a natural metaphorical connection. One thinks in this regard of the way in which the cry of the sea-birds functions in the Old English elegy 'The Seafarer'. In any case, Augustine's context (namely, the baptism of Jesus in the Jordan) has only one bird, a dove, which Augustine contrasts with a raven. Bede's gospel of the Purification, on the other hand, has a pair of turtle-doves or two young pigeons, and Bede develops the symbolism of their groaning call as representing the eschatological hope expressed by the individual Christian in private prayer (represented by the turtle-dove, which according to Bede grieves as it wanders by itself), and the public prayer of the church (represented by the pigeon which utters its groaning call in a flock).

Near the end of his homily for the Feast of the Purification, Bede returns to a different aspect of the question he had raised earlier, namely, why did the law of Leviticus require that these particular kinds of birds be offered? After reviewing the points he had made before, Bede observes that the reason it was ordered that two turtle-doves or two pigeons should be offered, and one of these was offered for sin and the other as a holocaust, was that

> there are two kinds of compunction by which the faithful immolate themselves to the Lord on the altar of the heart, for undoubtedly, as we have received from the sayings of the fathers, the soul experiencing God is first moved to compunction by fear and afterwards by love. For first it stirs itself to tears because when it recalls its bad [deeds and] becomes fearful that it will undergo eternal punishments for them—this is to offer one turtle-dove or a young pigeon for sin. When dread has been worn away by the long anxiety of sadness, a certain security is born concerning the anticipation of pardon, and the intellect is inflamed with the love of heavenly joys. One who previously wept so that he would not be led to punishment

presently starts to weep most bitterly because he is separated from the kingdom—this is to make a holocaust of the other turtle-dove or young pigeon. A holocaust means something that is wholly burned up, and one makes himself a holocaust to the Lord if, having rejected all earthly things, one takes delight in burning with the desire for heavenly blessedness alone, and in seeking only this with lamentation and tears.

Bede's 'from the sayings of the fathers' would seem to indicate some sort of acknowledgment of dependence here, and our source note points to a passage in the *Moralia* of Gregory the Great, a work Bede often quotes in his commentaries. Gregory's comment, however, concerns Leviticus 5:6-8, which refers not to the purification of a woman after childbirth, but to a more general purification ritual which involved the same two birds, and the same specification of 'one for sin and the other for a holocaust'. Gregory says:

We know that young pigeons or turtle-doves have a groan for a song. What is therefore designated by the two young pigeons or the two turtle-doves, unless it be the twofold groaning of our repentance—that when we do not rise up to offer good works, we should bewail ourselves doubly, both because we have not done righteous things and because we have performed wicked things? Hence also it is ordered that one turtle-dove be offered for sin, but the other as a holocaust. Now a holocaust refers to what is entirely burned up. We offer one turtle-dove for sin, therefore, when we give a groan for the sake of our guilt, and we make a holocaust of the other when, for the sake of good things which we have neglected to do, we set ourselves totally on fire and burn with the fire of sorrow'.[26]

26. *CC* 143B: 1629, 57/68.

It is quite likely this passage that Bede has in mind when, in beginning his discussion, he says 'as we have received from the sayings of the fathers'. Nevertheless, even though Bede's approach may be based on what he learned from Gregory, his actual development of the theme is quite different. First, Bede does not here make reference to the birds' sound, since he has already used that theme in a different way. But more importantly, the double sorrow which Gregory describes is repentance for evil things done and good things not done, while for Bede the two birds of the purification rite represent two stages in the psychological process of repentance—fear of punishment and love tinged by the sorrow of separation from the source of all good.

The passages presented here well illustrate Bede's use of sources in his homiletic writings, where he does not use the fathers primarily as authorities to strengthen his own position in matters of interpretation, which is characteristic of his use of patristic sources in his commentaries. Instead, as the above passages from Bede's homily for the feast of the Purification show, Bede often draws on the fathers for motifs to enrich and ornament his own words, quite freely adapting his predecessors' work to suit his own homiletic themes and purposes. By following up the source notes the interested reader may find other examples of Bede's creative adaptation of the work of the fathers.

During the tenth-century Benedictine Reform, Aelfric, abbot of Eynsham and one of the first great prose writers in English, made available in Old English a substantial portion of Bede's *Homilies on the Gospels*.[27] Aelfric's work was probably intended for monks and nuns whose knowledge of Latin was inadequate and also for the instruction of the laity.[28] It has been about a thousand years since Aelfric's work and the time has now come for another englishing

---

27. Cyril Smetana's article 'Aelfric and the Early Medieval Homiliary', *Traditio* 15 (1959) 182-202 lists the sources of each of Aelfric's *Catholic Homilies*, and twenty of Bede's *Homilies on the Gospels* appear in the list. In some cases Bede's influence on Aelfric is of a rather general sort, but in other cases Aelfric simply translates from Bede's homily with few additions.
28. Gatch, pp. 53-55.

of Bede's *Homilies on the Gospels.* In our time the liturgical movement has encouraged a return to the patristic practice of preaching on the gospel reading, and paradoxically there has been a precipitous decline in knowledge of Latin, even among the clergy and religious. The present translation is offered as a contribution to the revival of the patristic tradition of exegetical preaching, a tradition long kept alive in the monasteries by preachers and writers of whom the outstanding representative is the Venerable Bede.

L.T.M.

aBBREVIaTIONS

EDITIONS CITED

CC — *Corpus Christianorum*

CSEL — *Corpus Scriptorum Ecclesiasticorum Latinorum*

Glare — P. G. W. Glare, ed., *Oxford Latin Dictionary*

GCS — *Die Griechischen Christlichen Schriftsteller der ersten Jahrhunderte*

HBS — *Henry Bradshaw Society for Editing Rare Liturgical Texts*

LXX — The Septuagint

Niermeyer — J. F. Niermeyer, *Mediae Latinitatis Lexicon Minus*

PG — *Patrologiae cursus completus*, Series graeca

PL — *Patrologiae cursus completus*, Series latina

RED — *Rerum ecclesiasticarum documenta*

TU   *Texte und Untersuchungen zur Geschichte der altchristlichen Literatur*

Vet. Lat.   The Old Latin translation of the Scriptures

Vulg.   The Vulgate

Scriptural citations have been given according to the enumeration and nomenclature of *The Jerusalem Bible*. Psalm citations are given by Hebrew enumeration with Vulgate enumeration in parentheses.

AUTHORS AND WORKS CITED

Adamnan.   Adamnanus, Priest of Iona (d. 704)
  De loc. sanc.   *On the Holy Places*

Ambr.   Ambrose, Bishop of Milan (340–397)
  Expos. evang. sec. Luc.   *Commentary on the Gospel according to Luke*

Aug.   Augustine, Bishop of Hippo (354–430)
  Ad Gal.   *Commentary on the Epistle to the Galatians*

  Contra Faust.   *Against Faustus*

  Contra Iul.   *Against Julian*

  Contra litt. Pet.   *Answer to Petilian*

  De agone christ.   *The Christian Combat*

  De civ. Dei   *The City of God*

De cons. evang.	*Harmony on the Gospels*
De corrept. et gratia	*On Rebuke and Grace*
De divers. quaest.	*On Eighty-three Different Questions*
De Gen. ad litt.	*Literal Commentary on Genesis*
De Gen. contra Manich.	*Genesis against the Manichaeans*
De nupt. et concup.	*On Marriage and Concupiscence*
De trin.	*On the Trinity*
Ennar. in Ps.	*Commentary on the Psalms*
Ep.	*Letters*
Quaest. ad Simpl.	*Various Questions for Simplicianus*
Retract.	*Retractations*
Serm.	*Sermons* (followed by "Morin" = those additional sermons of Augustine edited by G. Morin in *Miscellanea Agostiniana*)
Serm. dom. in monte	*On our Lord's Sermon on the Mount*
Tract. in Ioh.	*Commentary on the Gospel according to John*

Bede	Bede the Venerable (673–735)
De loc. sanc.	*On the Holy Places*
De tempor.	*On times*
De temp. rat.	*On the System of Time*
Ex. Act. Ap.	*Exposition on the Acts of the Apostles*
HA	*History of the Abbots*
Hom.	*Homilies on the Gospels*
In epist. vii cath.	*Commentary on the Catholic Epistles*
In Luc.	*Commentary on the Gospel according to Luke*
In Marc.	*Commentary on the Gospel according to Mark*
Bened.	Benedict, abbot of Monte Cassino (480–544)
Reg.	*Rule for Monks*
Cyprian	Cyprian, Bishop of Carthage (d. 258)
De unitate	*The Unity of the Catholic Church*
Eusebius/Rufinus	Eusebius, Bishop of Caesarea (264–340)
Hist. eccl.	*Church History* (in the Latin translation of Rufinus of Aquileia [345–410])

Greg.	Gregory the Great, Bishop of Rome (540–604)
Dial.	Dialogues
Hom. de nat.	Homily on Christmas
Hom. in evang.	Homilies on the Gospels
Hom. in Ezech.	Homilies on Ezechiel
Moral.	Morals, Commentary on Job
Gregory of Nyssa	Gregory, Bishop of Nyssa (d. 394)
De vita Moysis	The Life of Moses
Horace	Quintus Horatius Flaccus (BC 65–8)
Ep.	Letters
Isid.	Isidore, Bishop of Seville (c. 560–636)
Etymol.	Etymologies
Jer.	Jerome, monk (340–420)
Adv. Helv.	Against Helvidius
Adv. Iov.	Against Jovinian
De vir. ill.	On Famous Men
Ep.	Letters
Hom. de nat.	Homily on Christmas
In Dan.	Commentary on Daniel
In Ezech.	Commentary on Ezechiel

In Matth.	*Commentary on the Gospel according to Matthew*
Nom.	*Interpretation of Hewbrew Names*
Quaest. Hebr.	*Hebrew Questions*
Sit.	*Book of Places*
Joseph.	Flavius Josephus, Jewish historian (c. 38-c. 100)
Ant. Iud.	*Antiquities of the Jews*
Leo	Leo the Great, Bishop of Rome (d. 461)
Serm.	*Sermons*
Pliny	Pliny the Elder (AD 23–79)
Nat. hist.	*Natural History*
Quoduultdeus	Quodvultdeus, Bishop of Carthage (d. c. 453)
Sermo de symbolo	*Sermon on the Creed*

The Homilies on the Gospels

scriptural homily texts

homily 1.1

Mark 1:4–8   *In Advent*

s you heard in the reading of the holy gospel, dearly
beloved brothers, John, anticipating the coming of our
Lord's preaching, was in the desert baptizing and
preaching a baptism of repentance for the forgiveness of
sins. Here we must look meticulously at the distinction
[involved in] the words which say that 'he was baptizing'
and 'he was preaching a baptism of repentance for the forgiveness of sins'. Now he was baptizing with a baptism of
repentance for the confession and correction of sins, and
he was preaching a future baptism of repentance in Christ
for the forgiveness of sins. Only in this baptism [of Christ]
is the forgiveness of sins granted to us,[1] as is attested by
the Apostle, who said, *One Lord, one faith, one baptism, one
God.*[2] John's baptism is properly called a 'baptism of repentance' because there is no other reason for anyone to want
to be baptized in the font of life except for repenting that
by the offence of the first transgression he is bound by the
death of his soul and his body.

But if we ask why John baptized even though sins could
not be forgiven by his baptism, the reason is clearly that,

1. Greg., *Hom. in evang.* 1, 20, 2 (PL 76: 1160-61)   2. Eph 4:5-6

1

as he held the office of precursor [of Christ], as he was to proclaim in advance that our Lord was to be born and to die, so too was he to baptize. Another reason was so that the Pharisees and scribes, in their envious contentiousness, might not find fault with the Lord's dispensation because he himself was the first to give baptism to human beings.

If they had chosen to inquire about the power by which he baptized, they would have heard at once, *'From where was John's baptism, from heaven or from human beings'?* [3] Since they would not have dared to deny that it was from heaven, they would have been forced to admit that the works of the one whom John preached were also acts of heavenly origin. And even though the baptism of John did not unloose [the bonds of] sins, nevertheless it was not entirely unfruitful for those who received it. Although it was not given for the forgiveness of sins, it was a sign of faith and repentance. All who were initiated by this [baptism of John] were to recall that they should keep themselves from sins, devote themselves to almsgiving, believe in Christ, and as soon as he appeared they were to hasten to his baptism, in which they would be cleansed for the forgiveness of sins.

Now it was in the desert that John gave his own baptism and proclaimed the baptism of Christ. Moreover, he lived his whole life in desert places from the time that he was a boy. This was so that as a first-rate teacher he might add the force of his example to what he was proclaiming in words; and as one who was persuading his hearers to forsake their sins in repentance, he might himself turn away from the vices of sinners, not only by mental punishment, but even by his physical location.

Typologically, however, the desert where John remained separated from the allurements of the world designates the lives of the saints, who, whether they live as solitaries or mingled with the crowds, always reject the desires of the present world with the whole intention of their minds. They take delight in clinging only to God in the secrecy of their heart, and in placing their hope in him. This solitude of

3. Mt 21:25

mind, most dear to God, is what the prophet desired to attain with the help of the grace of the Holy Spirit when he said, *Who will give me wings as of a dove, and I will fly away and rest?*[4] And as soon as he had secured this [solitude] by the Lord's help, he gave thanks, and as though reviling the entanglements of ordinary earthly desires, he continued, *Behold I have withdrawn afar in flight, and I have remained in solitude.*[5]

And, when the people had been liberated from Egypt by the blood of the lamb and had been led through the Red Sea, the Lord first instructed them for forty years in the desert, and so led them into the land of promise. Surely the faithful cannot pass immediately after baptism to the joys of the heavenly fatherland, but first they must be trained by long struggles in the exercise of virtues, and then they will be granted the abiding gift of heavenly blessedness.

Subsequently the fruit of John's preaching is shown when it is said, *And all the region of Judaea and the whole of Jerusalem came out to him, and they were baptized by him in the river Jordan, confessing their sins.* The literal sense is evident, for those who lived closer or were more learned were the first to come flocking to receive the word of salvation. However, since Judaea means 'confession' and Jerusalem means 'vision of peace,'[6] mystically we can understand that those who have learned the confession of right faith, those who have loved the vision of heavenly peace, are the ones designated by the words Judaea and Jerusalem. Just as we must believe that it was especially people of this kind who then went out to John in the desert to receive baptism, so now too it is certain that such people 'go out' from their former way of life when they have heard the word of God, and 'go into' the solitude of the spiritual life after the example of faithful teachers. Undoubtedly they are chastised everyday by the life they lead in their new way of life, just as those others in their daily baptism in the Jordan were purged by their tears of compunction from all the contagion of the vices that led them astray, in accordance with the one who

4. Ps 55:6 (54:7)   5. Ps 55:7 (54:8)
6. Jer., *Nom.* (CC 72: 67, 19; 121, 9/10)

said, *Through each night I will wash my bed and drench my couch with tears.*[7] Hence the river Jordan is properly interpreted as meaninq 'of judgment'.[8] To the extent that the elect more solicitously examine their consciences by scrutinizing them, to that extent they pour forth broader streams of tears from the inmost font of their hearts, and because they apprehend themselves to be less perfect, they wash away the stains of their weakness with the waves of repentance.

There follows: *And John was clothed in camel's hair with a leather girdle around his loins, and he ate locusts and wild honey.* As regards the literal meaning, this shows the poor quality of the garments and means of sustenance proper to one who was a solitary and a herald of repentance. But figuratively speaking, repentance and continence, which he carried out himself and also instructed others in, are represented by camel's hair, out of which sackcloth is made. A leather girdle, which is taken from a living thing that has died, expresses the fact that he had put to death his earthly members and taught the same thing to his hearers. Now it is a fact that self-indulgence[9] is often designated by the loins. Hence for restraining [self-indulgence] and for gaining possession of the glory of chastity the Lord commanded, *'Let your loins be girt and your torches burning'.*[10] Therefore one who has completely subdued the impulse of venereal concupiscence has certainly girded his loins with a leather girdle.[11] By the locusts, which fly briskly up but quickly settle back to earth, and the wild honey, which he was eating as well, are suggested the brevity as well as the sweetness of [John's] preaching, for when he was preaching the people willingly listened to him, and by coming so quickly to the Lord he put an end to his own preaching and baptism.

But if someone desires to interpret John's dress or his diet as a figure of the Lord and Savior, considering this [dress and diet] to be appropriate to the one whom he pointed out by his prophesying and expressed also by his way of life, the intention of this [interpretation] should be willingly

---

7. Ps 6:6 (6:7)   8. Jer., *Nom.* (CC 72: 140, 27)
9. *luxuria*   10. Lk 12:35
11. Greg., *Hom. in evang.* 1, 13, 1 (*PL* 76: 1123-24)

followed. Also it should be understood that on account of
sackcloth, the camel's hair signifies those who take care to
wipe away their sins by repenting, fasting, and weeping.
On account of the death of the living thing from which it
was made, the leather girdle signifies those who *have crucified their flesh with its vices and concupiscences.*[12] And because
it is written, *Therefore as many of you as have been baptized in
Christ have put on Christ,*[13] when such people cling to Christ
with the concentration of zealous love, they are, as it were,
clothed with camel's hair, and they gird their loins with a
leather girdle. On account of their short flight, locusts suggest the Jewish nation's vacillating mind, by which they
were borne up and down between the Lord and idols. The
wild honey signifies the sweetness of the natural wisdom
by which the uncultivated people of foreign countries were
refreshed.[14] And when from both peoples the Lord chose
those whom he would bring by his teaching into the unity
of his body, which is the Church,[15] they were undoubtedly being fed upon locusts and wild honey, because he turned
many into his members, both from the one people, who
sought heavenly things with a wavering intention, and from
the other nation, who knew only the taste of earthly phi-
losophy.

When the place of John's ministry, his dress, and his
nourishment have been described, next is added the design
of his preaching, for there follows, *And he was preaching,
saying, 'One mightier than I is coming after me'.* Mighty is he,
to be sure, who baptizes many for the confession of sins;
mightier is he who baptizes them for the forgiveness of sins.
Mighty is he who is worthy to have the Holy Spirit; mightier is he who is worthy to bestow him. Mighty is he than
whom *none of those born of women is greater;*[16] mightier is he
to whom, as one *made a little less than the angels, all things
were placed under his feet.*[17] Mighty is he who first came to
proclaim the kingdom of heaven; mightier is he who alone
could give it.

---

12. Ga 5:24   13. Ga 3:27
14. Greg., *Moral.* 31, 25, 45 (CC 143B: 1582, 1/17)
15. Col 1:24   16. Lk 7:28   17. Ps 8:5-6 (8:6-7)

'*I am not worthy,*' [John] said, '*to stoop down and undo the strap of his sandals*'. If he professed himself worthy only of the ministry of stooping down and undoing the strap of [Christ's] sandals, it would unquestionably have been an indication of great devotion. Now, however, beyond the virtue of wonderful humility,[18] he bears witness that he could not worthily perform even this ministry.

But if we are attentive to the mystical meaning,[19] this is clearly [a reference to] a decree of the law, for one who did not himself wish to receive a wife due to him by the rule of next of kin, but who wished instead to permit another to receive her, was ordered to give his sandal, undone from his foot, to the one who would receive her, as a sign of his permission in this regard.[20] And because the people rightly believed, as a result of his virtues, that John was the christ, they surely believed that he was the bridegroom of the Church.[21] But in order to show who he was, John himself said, '*He who has the bride is the bridegroom, but the friend of the bridegroom, who stands and listens to him, rejoices with joy on account of the bridegroom's voice*'.[22] And so he did not allow them to believe that he was the bridegroom, lest he lose the bridegroom's friendship, which is [the meaning of] his bearing witness that he was not worthy of undoing [Christ's] sandals. Moses and Joshua, when they were established as leaders of the synagogue, were commanded to undo their sandals.[23] They were to understand that they should believe that the one who gave them these mandates was the bridegroom, that is to say, the Lord of the synagogue, and they themselves ought to be called friends of the bridegroom, and be such, insofar as they were to preside over that same synagogue.

'*I have baptized you with water, but he will baptize you with the Holy Spirit*'. In the evangelist Matthew it is reported that John said, '*I baptize you in water for repentance*'.[24] For this

---

18. vars.: a) 'for the sake of the virtue of wonderful humility'; b) 'by virtue of the aforementioned humility'
19. *mysterium*
20. Dt 25:5-9; Rt 4:7; Greg., *Hom. in evang.* 1, 7, 3 (*PL* 76: 1101)
21. Eph 5:21-32   22. Jn 3:29   23. Ex 3:5; Jos 5:16
24. Mt 3:11

reason, then, was John baptizing with water, that he might, by the mark of his baptism, dissociate from the crowd of the unfaithful and impenitent all those people whom he had been able to persuade to repentance and to belief in Christ. So that they would not believe that this baptism would be sufficient for their salvation, and so that they would hurry instead to the baptism of Christ, he subsequently continued, *'But he will baptize you with the Holy Spirit'*. He indeed baptized with the Holy Spirit who pardoned sins by the favor of the Holy Spirit; and when they had received forgiveness of sins he also bestowed the grace of the same Spirit. Now the giving of charismatic gifts in the Spirit is properly called the 'baptism' of the Spirit, as he himself bore witness. Being about to ascend to heaven, he promised his disciples, saying, *'John, indeed, baptized with water, but you will be baptized with the Holy Spirit not many days hence,'*[25] signifying that on the tenth day after his ascension the Holy Spirit would come upon them in tongues of fire.

The question certainly arises whether the Lord, who baptized all the faithful with the Spirit, also himself baptized some with water. And it ought not to be considered unworthy of his great majesty for him to have shown the ministry of baptizing to some of his disciples, through whom he might extend the gifts of baptism to his other members, since he did not disdain to take on that memorable task of washing his disciples' feet.[26] But whether he then baptized with water himself, or henceforth through his [disciples], nevertheless he alone is the one who baptizes with the Holy Spirit, since he bestowed the Spirit on us and produces virtues in us.

We should take care, my brothers, to preserve his grace in us whole and always unimpaired. We should devote ourselves to good works at all times, but especially now when we desire to celebrate very soon the nativity of our Savior himself. We must be more diligent to keep the customary watch [over ourselves], so that we may be busy with quickly

---

25. Ac 1:5
26. Jn 13:2-11; Aug., *Ep.* 265, 3, 5 (*CSEL* 57: 640, 4/5; 643, 9/14; cf. Bede, *Ex. Act. Ap.* 1, 5 (*CC* 121: 7, 35/40)

wiping away whatever sort of negligence leading us astray
we apprehend within ourselves, and so that we may strive
to more quickly acquire any sort of virtue we ought to have
but that we see is lacking in us. The plants which bear discord, vituperation, wrangling, grumbling, and other vices
must be torn out by their roots. Let us sow within ourselves
*charity, joy, peace, patience, goodness, generosity, faith, gentle-
ness, continence,*[27] and other tokens of the fruit of the Spirit,
so that on that day we may be worthy to approach the altar of the Lord with a clean body and a pure conscience,
and to partake in the most holy sacraments[28] of him who
lives and reigns with the Father in the unity of the Holy
Spirit, God forever and ever. Amen.

27. Ga 5:22-3
28. var.: 'to partake by the sacraments in the most holy mysteries'

homily 1.2

Our Redeemer's precursor unambiguously pronounced testimony concerning him, witnessing to
the eminence of his humanity and at the same time
to the eternity of his divinity. For he cried out, saying what
you of the brotherhood have just now heard when the gospel was read, *'This was he of whom I said to you, ''He who
is to come after me ranks ahead of me because he was before me.'' '*
In saying, *'He who is to come after me,'* [John] suggested the
order of events with respect to the human dispensation, by
which, since [Jesus] was born after him, he would preach,
baptize, perform signs, and suffer death after him. In saying, *'He ranks ahead of me,'* he designated the sublimity of
the same [Jesus'] humanity, by which he would rightly take
precedence over all other creatures. For his stating *'ahead
of me'* does not pertain to the order of time, but to a difference in dignity, with respect to which it was written concerning Joseph when Jacob was blessing his sons, *And he
established Ephraem ahead of Manasses.* [1] There Manasses could
properly say, 'He who comes after me ranks ahead of me,'
that is, 'He who was born after me has surpassed me in

---

1. Gn 48:20

9

the might of his kingdom,' even as John said about the Lord, *'He who is to come after me ranks ahead of me,'* meaning, 'He who is to come to preach after me excels in the preeminence and ruling power of his everlasting priesthood'. He made clear why the one who was to come after him would excel him in dignity when he added, *'because he was before me,'* meaning, 'because he was eternal God before the ages, for this reason, although he was born later than I, even in his assumed humanity the glory of his majesty took precedence over me'.[2]

Now when the evangelist has explained the testimony of the Lord's precursor by which he had borne witness to him, he returns at once to that [statement] of his own assertion with which he began to give testimony to him, for there follows, *And from his fullness we have all received grace for grace.* Now he said earlier that *the word was made flesh and dwelt among us, and we saw his glory, glory as of the only-begotten of the Father, full of grace and truth.*[3] Once he has confirmed that [statement] with the testimony of the precursor too, who said, *'He who is to come after me ranks ahead of me because he was before me,'* then he himself [the evangelist] once again goes on with what he had begun [in verse fourteen], saying, *And from his fullness we have all received grace for grace.*

The Lord was indeed full of the Holy Spirit, full of grace and truth, because as the Apostle says, *In him dwells all the fullness of divinity bodily.*[4] From his fullness we have all received according to the manner of our capacity, because *to each one of us grace was given according to the measure of Christ's granting it.*[5] Now only of the Mediator between God and humankind, the man Jesus Christ,[6] can it truthfully be said, *And upon him will rest the spirit of the Lord, a spirit of wisdom and understanding, a spirit of counsel and strength, a spirit of knowledge and piety, and a spirit of the fear of the Lord will fill him.*[7] In truth, not all the saints receive the fullness of his Spirit, but they receive from his fullness, insofar as he grants it, because *to one through the Spirit is given the*

---

2. Greg., *Hom. in evang.* 1, 7, 3 (PL 76:1101)
3. Jn 1:14   4. Col 2:9   5. Eph 4:7   6. 1 Tm 2:5
7. Is 11:2-3

*utterance of wisdom, and to another the utterance of knowledge
according to the same Spirit, to another faith in the same Spirit,
to another the grace of healings in the one Spirit, to another the
working of miracles, to another prophecy, to another the discern-
ment of spirits, to another varieties of tongues, to another the interpretation of utterances. But all of these are the work of one and
the same Spirit, who distributes to each as he wishes.*[8]

Therefore, because not only some of us, but all of us have
received whatever good we have from the fullness of our
Maker, we must take the greatest care lest one or another
person, if he is unaware [of this], may extol himself about
his own good action or thought. By remaining ungrateful
toward his benefactor, he may lose the good which he has
received, and may deservedly be struck down by the
apostolic rebuke by which he is told, *'For what do you have
that you have not received? But if you have received it, why do
you glory in it as though you have not received it'?*[9] Hence the
Apostle himself elsewhere clearly bears witness that he
could neither know nor do anything if he had not received
it from Christ's fullness, saying, *Not that we are sufficient of
ourselves to think anything as from ourselves, but our sufficiency
is from God.*[10] And in another place he says, *And His grace
has not been fruitless in me, but I have labored more than any
of them, not I, however, but the grace of God in me.*[11] In his hearers he painstakingly inculcated this same thing as something
they must humbly think. Hence there is that [text]: *With
trembling and apprehension work out your salvation. For it is God
who of his own good will works in you both the wishing and the
accomplishment.*[12]

When, however, the evangelist has said that we all have
received from Christ's fullness, he immediately says in addition, *grace for grace.* He is testifying that we have received
a twofold grace, namely one grace in the present and another for the future—in the present, *faith which works through
love,*[13] and for the future, life eternal. Faith which works

8. 1 Co 12:8-11   9. 1 Co 4:7   10. 2 Co 3:5
11. 1 Co 15:10   12. Ph 2:12-13
13. Ga 5:6; Aug., *Tract. in Ioh.* 3, 9; 92, 1 (CC 36: 24, 4-25, 19; 556,
    28/29)

through love is indeed a grace of God, because our believing, our loving, our doing works which we know to be
good—these are not things that we have attained by any
preceding merits of ours but from the one who lavishes them
upon us, and it is he who says, *'You have not chosen me, but
I have chosen you, and I have appointed you that you may go
and bear fruit'.*[14] And that we may attain eternal life on account of faith, love and good works—this is a grace of God,
because in order to keep us from turning aside from the
good path, we always have need of that very leader to
whom it is said, *'Lead me, Lord, in your way, and I will walk
in your truth'.*[15] And also, as if he were saying clearly, 'Unless I have you as my leader when I enter upon the way
of truth which I have begun, by no means am I sufficient
to hold to it'.

So as not to falter in good works we ought always to rely
for support on the help of the one who says, *'For without
me you can do nothing'.*[16] Hence in order to express the fact
that the start of faith and good action is given to us by the
Lord, the psalmist properly says, *My God, his mercy goes before me.*[17] Again, in order to teach that the good things we
do must be accomplished with his assistance, he says, *And
your mercy follows after me all the days of my life.*[18] In order
to show that the prize of eternal life rendered for good works
is bestowed upon us freely, he says, *Who crowns you in compassion and mercy.*[19] He crowns us indeed in mercy and compassion when he repays us with the reward of heavenly
blessedness for the good works which he himself has mercifully granted us to carry out.

And this is what is meant by [the phrase] 'we receive *grace
for grace'*: that for the grace of a good way of life which he
has given (and he himself aids us, watching out lest it be
able to slip away)—for this grace he will give the grace of
a blessed remuneration in which we may sing the praises
of his mercies forever.[20] Accordingly, the Apostle does not
hesitate to call 'a grace' that very partaking in eternal life

---

14. Jn 15:16   15. Ps 86:11 (85:11)   16. Jn 15:5
17. Ps 59:10 (58:11)   18. Ps 23:6 (22:6)   19. Ps 103:4 (102:4)
20. Ps 89:1 (88:2)

which is doubtlessly rendered for preceding merits. Though he had mentioned before that *the wages of sin are death,*[21] he did not want to say, on the other hand, that the wages of justice are eternal life, but he said, *But the grace of God is eternal life in Christ Jesus our Lord.*[22] It is not that it is unjustly given for good merits by a just judge, but the merits themselves for which it is given were first granted freely by a benevolent Savior.

There follows: *For the law was given through Moses; grace and truth came through Jesus Christ.* The law was indeed given through Moses, and there it was determined by a heavenly rule what was to be done and what was to be avoided, but what it commanded was completed only by the grace of Christ. On the one hand, that [law] was capable of pointing out sin, teaching justice, and showing transgressors what they are charged with. On the other hand, the grace of Christ, poured out in the hearts of the faithful through the spirit of charity,[23] brings it about that what the law commanded may be fulfilled. Hence that which was written, *Do not lust,*[24] is the law [given] through Moses because it is commanded, but grace comes through Christ when what is commanded is fulfilled. Truth came through Christ because *the law had a shadow of the good things to come, not the exact image of them.*[25] And, as the Apostle says elsewhere, *Everything happened to them as a figure.*[26] But in place of a shadow Christ displayed the light of truth, and in place of the figure of the law he displayed the exact image of the things which were prefigured when, with the giving of the grace of the Spirit, he made clear to his disciples the meaning so that they could understand the scriptures.[27] The law was given through Moses when the people were commanded to be made clean by the sprinkling of the blood of a lamb.[28] The grace and truth which were prefigured in the law came through Jesus Christ when he himself, having suffered on the cross, *washed us from our sins in his own blood.*[29] The law was given through Moses because when

21. Rm 6:23a   22. Rm 6:23b   23. Rm 5:5
24. Dt 5:21; Rm 7:7   25. Heb 10:1   26. 1 Co 10:11
27. Lk 24:45   28. Ex 12:7   29. Rv 1:5

he educated the people by saving commands, he foretold
that if they observed these things they would enter the land
of promise, and there they would be perpetually victorious,
but if they observed other [laws], they would be laid low
by the enemy. Grace and truth came through Jesus Christ
because, when the gift of his Spirit was given, he granted
also the ability to understand and keep the law spiritually,
and he introduced those who served it into the true blessedness of heavenly life, which is what the land of promise
expressed.

The evangelist makes clear, however, what was the sum
total of the grace and truth which came through Jesus Christ
by adding: *No one has ever seen God. The only-begotten Son,
who is in the lap of the Father, has told about* [1]* [him]. No greater
grace can be given to human beings, and no higher truth
can be recognized by human beings, than that about which
the only-begotten Son of God told his faithful. *'Blessed,'* he
said, *'are the clean of heart for they shall see God'.*[30] And in
supplication to the Father about this he said, *'Now this is
eternal life, that they may recognize you, the one and true God,
and him whom you sent, Jesus Christ'.*[31] This is a partaking
of grace and truth which is undoubtedly most proper to
beatitude, since it cannot happen in the life of this world,
[as] is rightly said, *No one has ever seen God.* That is, while
one is still enclosed in corruptible and mortal flesh one cannot gaze on the uncircumscribed light of divinity. Hence
the Apostle says [even] more openly, *whom no one of humankind has seen or can see.*[32] For 'no one of humankind'
means no one who is still weighed down by the human condition and made unsteady by the human way of life. So
it is that Moses, who saw God in an angel, desired to see
him in his own nature and prayed, *'If I have found grace in
your sight, show me your glory'.* And he heard, *'You cannot
see my face, for no human will see me and live'.*[33]

It should not be supposed that it is contrary to this assertion that elsewhere it is mentioned several times that patriarchs or prophets did see God. The Lord appeared to

30. Mt 5:8   31. Jn 17:3   32. 1 Tm 6:16
33. Ex 33:13, 20

Abraham in the valley of Mambre,[34] and Jacob said, *'I have seen the Lord face to face'.*[35] In the same way Isaiah [says], *In the year when King Uzziah died I saw the Lord sitting on a lofty and elevated chair.*[36] But it must be properly understood that in all visions of this sort holy men contemplated God not through the very form[37] of his nature, but through certain images. Therefore the holy ones saw God through a subordinate creature, for example, fire, an angel, a cloud, or lightning; and so John truthfully attests that *no one has ever seen God,* [and] it was truthfully said to Moses, *'for no human will see me and live,'*[38] for those who are still contained within the weak vessel of the flesh can see him through circumscribed images of things, although they are by no means capable of looking at him through the uncircumscribed radiance of his eternity.[39]

The evangelist subsequently explains by what means one ought to come to the vision of the unchangeable and eternal radiance, saying, *The only-begotten Son who is in the lap of the Father has told us about* [him]. Similar to this is what the Lord himself said, *'No one comes to the Father except through me';*[40] and elsewhere, *'No one knows the Son except the Father, nor does anyone know the Father except the Son and he to whom the Son wishes to reveal* [him]'.[41] Indeed, by the guidance of this very [Son] we are to come to the Father, and by his instruction we are to know the Father and the Son and the Holy Spirit, one God and Lord. He himself was made man for us, and speaking in the condition of man he revealed to us in a bright light what is to be properly understood concerning the unity of the holy Trinity, in what way the faithful are to hasten to contemplation of it, and by what actions they are to come to it. Imbuing us with the sacraments of his incarnation and sanctifying us by the charismatic gifts of the Spirit, he himself aids us so that we may be capable of coming to this. When the last judgment

---

34. Gn 18:1   35. Gn 32:30
36. Is 6:1; Ambr. *Expos. evang. sec. Luc.* (CC 14: 18, 375-19, 399)
37. *species*   38. Ex 33:20
39. Greg., *Moral.* 18, 54, 88 (CC 143A: 951, 16 - 952, 58)
40. Jn 14:6   41. Mt 11:27

has been carried out, he himself in the form of a human being will introduce us in a sublime way to the vision of divine majesty, and he will declare to us in a marvelous way the hidden mysteries of the heavenly kingdom.

The statement *'who is in the lap of the Father'* certainly means 'in the Father's secret thoughts'.[42] For the lap of the Father is not to be thought of in a childish way, in the likeness of the lap-fold which we have in our clothing. Nor is it to be supposed that God, who is not put together in the shape of [our] human members, sits as we do. But because our lap is personal to us, speaking in our customary way scripture says that he was in the lap of the Father,[43] wishing it to be understood that he always remained in the Father's secret thoughts, where human power of vision is not capable of penetrating.

It is not then only that the only-begotten Son will declare God, that he will manifest to human beings, that is, the glory of the holy and indivisible Trinity which is the one God, when, after the universal judgment, he leads all the elect together to the vision of his brightness. He also tells about [him] every day when, for each and every one of the perfect faithful who have just been released from the corruption of the flesh, he begins to fulfill what he promised when he said, *'He who loves me is loved by my Father, and I will love him and manifest myself to him'*.[44] 'I will manifest myself to those who love me,' he says, 'so that the one whom they have recognized as mortal in his nature they may now, in my nature, be able to see as equal to the Father and the Holy Spirit'.[45]

We must believe that this is occurring with respect to the apostles, martyrs, confessors and other men of a more rigorous and more perfect life, [and] one of them, conscious of their strife, did not hesitate to bear witness about himself, *I long to be dissolved and to be with Christ*.[46] Besides there

---

42. *in secreto patris*
43. Aug., *Tract. in Ioh.* 3, 17 (CC 36: 27, 9/14)
44. Jn 14:21
45. Greg., *Moral.* 18, 54, 90 (CC 143A: 953, 101/102)
46. Ph 1:23

are many just people in the Church who, after being freed from the flesh, immediately gain the blessed rest of paradise, waiting in great joy among great choruses of fellow-rejoicers for the time when, having received their bodies, they may come and appear before the face of God. But in truth there are some who were preordained to the lot of the elect on account of their good works, but on account of some evils by which they were polluted, went out from the body after death to be severly chastised, and were seized by the flames of the fire of purgatory. They are either made clean from the stains of their vices in their long ordeal up until judgment day,[47] or, on the other hand, if they are absolved from their penalties by the petitions, almsgiving, fasting, weeping and oblation of the saving sacrificial offering by their faithful friends, they may come earlier to the rest of the blessed. Nevertheless, the only-begotten Son, who is in the lap of the Father, will tell all of these about God, according to the capacity of each, when at the time of resurrection he who gave the law will give blessing, so that, journeying from the virtue of faith and hope to the virtue of contemplation, they may see the God of gods in Zion,[48] that is, in the look-out post of the unchangeable truth.[2*] For his kindnesses and eternal favors be praise and thanksgiving for ages and ages. Amen.

---

47. *examinatio*   48. Ps 84:7 (83:8)

NOTES

1. The verb in the scriptural verse translated 'told about' is *narrauit*. In the long discussion of this verse, which runs nearly to the end of this homily, Bede alternates among *narrare, enarrare,* and *manifestare,* and in quoting Jn 14:6 he uses *reuelare.* In order to maintain Bede's distinction, *narrare* has been translated 'tell about,' *enarrare* 'declare,' *manifestare* 'manifest,' and *reuelare* 'reveal,' even though 'tell about' is admittedly too matter-of-fact for the kind of revelatory action being spoken of in this context. In Homily II.16 Bede seems to make a point of the distinction between *narrare* and *enarrare.*
2. The text as edited has simply 'in Zion, that is, of the unchangeable truth'. The word 'look-out post' is based on *specula,* which is found in three MSS (Two other MSS have *speculo,* that is, 'in the unchangeable mirror of truth'). The reading adopted has the support of Jerome's *Interpretation of Hebrew Names* (CC 72: 108, 25), a source Bede frequently used, where Zion is said to mean *'specula'.*

homily 1.3

Luke 1:26-38   *In Advent*

oday's reading of the holy gospel, dearly beloved brothers, sets forth the elementary stage of our redemption. It tells of an angel sent from heaven by God to a virgin, to proclaim the unheard of nativity in the flesh of the Son of God.[1] Through him we can be renewed once our guilty former self has been cast off, and be counted among God's sons. So that we may be worthy to attain the gifts of the promised salvation,[2] therefore, let us take care to receive with attentive ears the [account of] its source.

The angel Gabriel was sent by God to a city in Galilee named Nazareth, to a virgin who was betrothed to a man named Joseph. A fitting beginning, unquestionably, for human restoration—that an angel should be sent by God to a virgin who was to be consecrated by a divine birth, for the first cause of human perdition was when a serpent was sent by the devil to a woman who was to be deceived by the spirit of pride. Moreover, the devil himself came in the serpent, who once he had deceived our first parents stripped humankind of the glory of immortality. Because death made

---

1. *Gregorian Sacramentary*, ed. H.A. Wilson, *HBS* 49 (London, 1915), p. 11
2. *Sacramentum Veronense*, ed. L.C. Mohlberg, *RED*, ser. maior 1 (Rome, 1956), no. 1268, p. 162

its entrance through a woman, it was fitting that life return through a woman.[3] The one, seduced by the devil through the serpent, brought a man the taste of death; the other, instructed by God through the angel, produced for the world[1]* the author of salvation.[4]

And so the angel Gabriel was sent by God. Rarely do we read that angels appearing to human beings are designated by name, but, whenever this occurs, it is so that they may even by their very name suggest what ministry they have come to carry out. Now Gabriel means 'strength of God,' and rightly he shone forth with such a name, since by his testimony he bore witness to the coming birth of God in the flesh.[5] The prophet said this in the psalm, *The Lord strong and powerful, the Lord powerful in battle*[6]—that battle, undoubtedly, in which he [Christ] came to fight *the powers of the air*[7] and to snatch the world from their tyranny.

To a virgin betrothed to a man whose name was Joseph, of the house of David; and the virgin's name was Mary. What is said of the house of David pertains not only to Joseph, but also to Mary. Now it was a precept of the law that everyone should take a wife from his own tribe and family.[8] The Apostle attested to this when he wrote to Timothy, stating, *Remember, therefore, that Jesus Christ, of the seed of David, has risen from the dead in accordance with my gospel.*[9] For the Lord truly arose from the seed of David because his incorrupt mother took her true origin from David's stock.

As to why he wished to be conceived and born, not of a simple virgin, but of one who was betrothed to a man, several of the fathers have put forward reasonable answers.[10] The best of these is to prevent her from being condemned as guilty of defilement if she were to bear a son when she had no husband. Then too, in the things the care of a home naturally demands, the woman in labor would

---

3. Aug., *De agone christ.* (CSEL 41: 125, 4/5)
4. Irenaeus, *Aduersus haereses* (PG 7: 1175)
5. Greg., *Hom. in evang.* 2, 34, 8-9 (PL 76: 1250-51); Bede, *In Luc.* (CC 120: 30, 426/439)
6. Ps 24:8 (23:8)   7. Eph 2:2   8. Nb 36:7-8
9. 2 Tm 2:8
10. Jer., *In Matth.* 1, 18 (CC 77: 10, 72/76)

be sustained by a husband's care. Therefore blessed Mary had to have a husband who would be both a perfectly sure witness to her integrity, and a completely trustworthy foster-father for our Lord and Savior who was born of her, a husband who would, in accordance with the law, make sacrificial offerings to the temple for him when he was an infant, who would take him, along with his mother, to Egypt when persecution threatened, and bring him back,²* and who would minister to the many other needs consequent upon the weakness of the humanity which he had assumed. It did no great harm if, for a time, some believed that he was [Joseph's] son, since from the apostles' preaching after his ascension it would be plainly evident to all believers that he had been born of a virgin.

Nor should we overlook the fact that the blessed mother of God rendered testimony of her preeminent merits even by her name, for it has the meaning 'star of the sea,'¹¹ and like an extraordinary heavenly body among the storms of this tottering world she shone brightly with the grace of her special privilege.

The angel entered and said to her, 'Hail, full of grace, the Lord is with you. Blessed are you among women'. As unheard of as this greeting was in human custom, so fitting was it to the dignity of blessed Mary. And indeed, truly full of grace was she, upon whom it was conferred by divine favor that, first among women, she should offer God the most glorious gift of her virginity. Hence she who strove to imitate the life of an angel was rightfully worthy to enjoy the experience of seeing and speaking with an angel. Truly full of grace was she to whom it was granted to give birth to Jesus Christ, the very one through whom grace and truth came.¹² And so the Lord was truly with her whom he first raised up from earthly to heavenly desires, in an unheard of love of chastity, and afterwards sanctified, by means of his human nature, with all the fullness of his divinity. Truly blessed among women [was she] who without precedent in the womanly state rejoiced in having the honor of parenthood along with

11. Isid., *Etymol.* 7, 10, 1; Jer., *Nom.* (*CC* 72: 76, 7/8)
12. Jn 1:17

the beauty of virginity, inasmuch as it was fitting that a virgin mother bring forth God the Son.

After this, as in the customary way of human weakness she was upset by the angelic vision and by the unusual greeting, immediately the same angel, by repeating his utterance, exhorted her not to fear. And, what is especially conducive to driving away fear, he called her by her own name, as though she were well-known to him and familiar, and he carefully instructed her as to why he said, 'full of grace':

'*Fear not, Mary,*' he said, '*You have found grace with God. Behold, you will conceive in your womb and give birth to a son, and you will call his name Jesus. He will be great and will be called the Son of the Most High*'. We should carefully note the order of the words here, and the more firmly they are engrafted in our heart, the more evident it will be that the sum total of our redemption consists in them. For they proclaim with perfect clarity that the Lord Jesus, that is, our Savior, was both the true Son of God the Father and the true Son of a mother who was a human being. '*Behold,*' he says, '*you will conceive in your womb and give birth to a son*'— acknowledge that this true human being assumed the true substance of flesh from the flesh of the Virgin! '*He will be great and will be called the Son of the Most High*'—confess too that this same [Son] is true God of true God, coeternal Son forever of the eternal Father!

The use of the future tense in the statement, '*He will be great and will be called the Son of the Most High,*' should not lead anyone to suppose that this is to be understood [in the sense] that Christ was not Lord before his birth from the Virgin. Instead we should understand this statement [to mean] that as a human being born in time he received the same power of divine majesty that he had eternally had as Son of God, so that our Mediator and Redeemer was one person with two natures.

'*And the Lord God will give him the seat of his father David*'. The seat of David refers to the kingdom of the Israelite populace, which in his time David governed with faithful devotion, at the Lord's order, as well as with his help.

Therefore the Lord gave our Redeemer the seat of his father David when he arranged that he become incarnate from David's offspring, so that the people whom David had ruled with temporal sovereignty he might with spiritual grace bring to an eternal kingdom. As the Apostle says, *'He has rescued us from the power of darkness and transferred us into the kingdom of the Son of his charity'*.[13] Thus it was that when he was hastening to Jerusalem to suffer, this same people, prompted by divine impulse, sang his praise rejoicing, *'Blessed is he who comes in the name of the Lord, the King of Israel'!*[14] And according to another evangelist, *'Blessed is the kingdom of our father David which comes'!*[15]

The time had come when, having redeemed the world through his blood, he was to be acknowledged as king not of the house of David alone, but also of the whole Church— moreover, that he was maker and governor of all generations. Hence the angel properly said afterwards, *'And the Lord God will give him the seat of David his father,'* and he immediately added, *'And he will reign in the house of Jacob forever'*. Now the house of Jacob refers to the universal Church, which through its faith in and confession of Christ pertains to the heritage of the patriarchs—either among those who took their physical origin from the stock of the patriarchs, or among those who, though brought forth with respect to the flesh from other countries, were reborn in Christ by the spiritual washing.

In this house will he reign forever, *'and of his kingdom there will be no end'*. In it, indeed, he reigns in the present life when he rules the hearts of the elect, inhabiting them through faith and through his love, and he governs [them] by his continual protection so that the gifts of heavenly reward may be attained. He reigns in the future [life] when he introduces these same [elect], their state of temporal exile ended, into the dwelling of the heavenly fatherland, where, ever prompted by his visible presence, they rejoice to do nothing else than give themselves to his praises.

13. Col 1:13, but 'of his charity'(*caritatis suae*) is a reading unique to Bede
14. Jn 12:13
15. Mk 11:10

But Mary said to the angel, 'How can this be, since I do not know man'? 'How,' she asked, 'can this occur, that I conceive and give birth to a son, since I have determined to live out my life in the chaste state of virginity'? It was not as one incredulous at the angel's words that she demanded to know how these things could be fulfilled; rather she was certain that what she was then hearing from the angel and what she had previously read in the sayings of the prophet necessarily had to be fulfilled, and so she inquired about the way in which it was to be accomplished. The prophet who predicted that this would be did not say how it could be done, reserving that instead for the angel to say.[16]

The angel answered her and said, 'The Holy Spirit will come upon you, and the power of the Most High will overshadow you, and so the holy one to be born will be called the Son of God'. In coming upon the Virgin, the Holy Spirit revealed in her the efficacy of his divine power in two ways: he purified her mind of all stain of vices, to the extent that [her] human weakness had suffered [them], so that she might be worthy of a heavenly child-bearing, and, by his operation alone he created in her womb the holy and venerable body of our Redeemer. That is, without any intervening touch of man he formed that most sacred flesh from the inviolate flesh of the Virgin.

Now [the angel] first plainly said, 'the Holy Spirit,' and then in turn he gave to the same one the name 'the power of the Most High,' according to what the Lord said when he promised the coming of the same Spirit to his disciples, *'And I send upon you the promise of my father; remain in the city until you have been clothed in the power from on high'.*[17] The power of the Most High overshadowed the blessed mother of God because when the Holy Spirit filled her heart, he tempered for her every surge of fleshly concupiscence, he thoroughly cleansed her from temporal desires, and with heavenly gifts he sanctified her mind along with her body.

'And so the holy one to be born,' [the angel] said, *'will be called the Son of God'*—'because you will conceive out of the

16. Ambr., *Expos. evang. sec. Luc.* 2, 15; 2, 18 (CC 14:38, 237/41; 39, 276/80)
17. Lk 24:49

sanctification of the Spirit, what will be produced will be holy. The nativity corresponds to the conception, inasmuch as you who conceive while a virgin, contrary to the ordinary way of the human condition, give birth to the Son of God beyond the common human way'. Indeed, we human beings are all conceived in iniquity[18] and born in moral faults; however, by God's granting it, as many of us are preordained to eternal life as are reborn out of water and the Holy Spirit. In truth, our Redeemer alone, who deigned to become incarnate for us, was thereupon born holy because he was conceived without iniquity.[19] He was born the Son of God since he was conceived of a virgin through the working of the Holy Spirit.

We can indeed understand that saying, *'and the power of the Most High will overshadow you'*, at a more profound level in relation to the sacrament of the Lord's incarnation. For we say that we are 'overshadowed' when in the baking noonday sun we put between ourselves and the sun either an intervening tree or any other sort of shade by which we may render the sun's heat or light more tolerable to ourselves. Thus it is not without reason that our Redeemer is designated by the light or heat of the sun, for he both illuminates us with the knowledge of truth and inflames us with love. Hence he himself says through the prophet, *To you, however, who fear my name the sun of justice shall arise.*[20] It was his rays which the blessed Virgin received when she conceived the Lord. But that same sun, that is, the divinity of our Redeemer, cloaked itself with the covering of human nature as with a shade, and by this means a virgin's womb was able to bear him. Thus the power of the Most High overshadowed her at the time when the divine might of Christ filled her with his presence, and, in order that his substance could be received by her, he veiled himself with our weakness.

'And behold, Elizabeth your cousin has also conceived a son in her old age'. He does not exhort her to faith with examples

18. Ps 51:5 (50:7)
19. Greg., *Moral.* 18, 52, 84 (CC 143A: 948, 25/31)
20. Ml 4:2

as though she were incredulous. Rather to one who already fully believed what she had heard he relates further miracles of the heavenly plan, so that she who was to give birth to the Lord as a virgin might recognize that the precursor of the Lord was also going to be born of an old woman, a long-barren mother.

Nor should we wonder that according to the historical sense Elizabeth is said to be the cousin of Mary, since earlier we are told that the one [Mary] arose from the house of David,[21] and the other [Elizabeth] arose from the daughters of Aaron.[22] Now we read that it was from the tribe of Judah, from which David arose, that Aaron himself received his wife, namely Elizabeth the daughter of Amminadab and sister of Nahshon, who was a leader of the tribe of Judah in the desert when they came out of Egypt.[23] In addition, regarding the later Davidic kings we read that Jehoiada the high-priest had a wife of the kingly tribe, this being Jehosheba the daughter of King Joram.[24] This is the Johoiada whose son Zechariah,[25] a man who was likewise very holy, they stoned between the temple and the altar,[26] as the Lord himself bore witness when he made mention of the blessed martyrs in the gospel.[27] Hence it is proven that both tribes, the priestly and the royal, were always joined to each other by blood relationship. However, it was possible for a joining of this sort to occur in a more recent time too, with the giving of women in marriage from tribe to tribe, so that it is clearly a fact that the blessed mother of God, who descended from the royal tribe, had a blood relationship by birth with the priestly tribe, and this was most aptly fitting to heavenly mysteries.

Now when the Mediator between God and human beings[28] appeared in the world, it was fitting that he had his physical origin from both tribes because, in the humanity which he assumed, he would possess the roles of both priest

---

21. Lk 1:27   22. Lk 1:5   23. Ex 6:23; Nb 1:7; 7:12
24. 2 Ch 22:11; 'Iosabeth' in the Vulgate
25. 'Zacharia' in the Vulgate
26. 2 Ch 24:21-22
27. Mt 23:35; Lk 11:51; Jer., *In Matth.* 23, 35 (CC 77: 220, 306/11)
28. 1 Tm 2:5

and king. On the one hand, the present reading from the holy gospel bears witness concerning his royal power, by which he bestowed an everlasting reign on his elect, for *he will reign in the house of Jacob forever, and of his kingdom there will be no end.* Concerning his dignity as high-priest, on the other hand, in which he deigned to offer the sacrificial offering of his flesh for our redemption, the prophet bears witness as he says, *You are a priest forever in accordance with the order of Melchisedech.*[29]

Let us see, however, how blessed Mary, when she had received so great a grace, continued to be the great stronghold of humility: *Behold the handmaid of the Lord,* she said. *Let it be done to me in accordance with your word.* Indeed she preserved a great constancy of humility, since she named herself the handmaid of her Maker at the time when she was chosen [to be his] mother. She was proclaimed blessed among women by the angelic oracle, [and] was instructed in the hidden mysteries of our redemption, still unknown to other mortals. Nevertheless she did not extol herself in a singular way on account of the singularity of her higher merit, but being mindful instead of her own condition and of God's dignity, she humbly joined herself to the company of Christ's servants and committed herself devotedly to Christ in what was ordered. *'Let it be done to me,'* she said, *'in accordance with your word'*—'Let it be done that the Holy Spirit's coming to me may render me worthy of heavenly mysteries; let it be done that in my womb the Son of God may put on the condition of human substance, and may proceed like a bridegroom from his chamber[30] for the redemption of the world'.

Imitating her voice and mind to the best of our abilities, dearly beloved brothers, let us recall that we are Christ's servants in all of our acts and motions. Let us subject all the members of our body in service to him, and let us direct the whole gaze of our mind to the fulfillment of his will. Thus, since we have received his gifts, let us give thanks by living properly, so that we may deserve to show our-

29. Ps 110:4 (109:4)   30. Ps 19:5 (18:6)

selves worthy of receiving greater [gifts]. Let us unremmit-
tingly pray, along with the blessed mother of God, that it
may be done to us in accordance with his word, that word,
namely, by which he himself explained the reason for his
incarnation when he said, *'For God so loved the world that
he gave his only-begotten Son, so that everyone who believes in
him may not perish but may have eternal life'*.[31] And there is
no doubt that he will very quickly deign to hearken to us
who cry out to him from the depths,[32] since for our sake,
when we did not yet recognize him, he deigned to descend
to this deep valley of tears, Jesus Christ our Lord, who lives
and reigns with the Father in the unity of the Holy Spirit,
for ages and ages. Amen.

31. Jn 3:16   32. Ps 130:1 (129:1)

NOTES

1. The translation cannot here capture Bede's wordplay: *seducta* ('seduced')... *edocta* ('instructed')... *edidit* ('produced').
2. Bede here plays upon etymologically related verbs: *deferret* ('make')... *ferret* ('take')... *referret* ('bring back').

homily I.4

Luke 1:39-55 *In Advent*

The reading of the holy gospel which we have heard proclaims to us the source of our redemption as something we must always venerate, and it commends to us the saving remedies of the humility we are always to imitate. Now because the human race had perished at the touch of the plague of pride, it was proper that the time of salvation should first begin with the putting forward of the medicine of humility by which it might be healed. And because death had entered the world through the rashness of a woman who was led astray, it was fitting that as an indication of the return of life, women should anticipate one another in the services of humility and piety.

The blessed mother of God therefore first showed us the path of humility [leading] to the sublimity of the heavenly fatherland, as much by the example of [her] religious devotion as by that of her venerable chastity. If, indeed, the glory of [her] virginal and inviolate body suggests what sort of life [is lived in] the heavenly city for which we sigh, where *they will neither marry nor be given in marriage, but they are like the angels of God in heaven,*[1] it also indicates the extraor-

---

1. Mk 12:25

dinary virtue of mind by which we ought to reach this [city].
Now we learned in the preceding reading from the holy gospel that, after she was found worthy to be exalted by seeing and hearing the angel, and after she learned that she
was to be honored by a heavenly birth, she by no means
extolled herself for [these] heavenly gifts as though they
[had been given] for her sake. In order that she might be
fit for more and more divine gifts, she placed her steps firmly
in the custody of humility of mind, responding in this way
to the archangel who brought the good news to her, *'Behold the handmaid of the Lord. Let it be done to me according
to your word'.*[2] So in the same way, from today's reading
we have heard that the same humility which she had shown
to the angel she also took care to show to lesser human beings, and what pertains to greater power [she showed] also
to those of less [power].

For who is unaware that a virgin consecrated to God has
a rank preferable to that of a woman who has devoted herself to a husband? Who could doubt that the mother of the
eternal king rightfully should take precedence over the
mother of a soldier? And nevertheless, mindful of that scriptural precept, *The greater you are the more you should behave
humbly in all things,*[3] as soon as the angel who had spoken
to her returned to heaven, she rose and went up to the hill
country, and bearing God in her womb she betook herself
to the dwelling places of the servants of God and sought
conversation [with them].

And it was appropriate that after the vision of the angel
she passed on to the hill country, since having tasted the
delight of the humility of the heavenly citizens, she turned
her steps to the heights of virtue. She entered the house
of Zechariah and greeted Elizabeth, who she knew was going to bear the Lord's servant and precursor. It was not that
she was doubtful concerning the account which she had
received,[4] but [she went] so that she could offer her congratulations concerning the gift which she had learned her
fellow-servant had received. This was not in order to prove

2. Lk 1:38   3. Si 3:20   4. Lk 1:36

the word of the angel by the attestation of a woman. Rather
it was so that as an attentive young virgin she might commit herself to ministry to a woman of advanced age.[5]

*As Elizabeth heard Mary's greeting, the infant in her womb
leapt, and Elizabeth was filled with the Holy Spirit.* When Mary
opened her mouth to greet [her], Elizabeth was immediately filled with the Holy Spirit, and John was filled with
one and the same Spirit. Both of them were fully
informed—[Elizabeth] acknowledged who the person was
who was there greeting her and venerated her as the mother
of her Lord with a due blessing; [John] understood that it
was the Lord himself who was being carried in the Virgin's
womb, and because his tongue was not yet capable [of
speaking], he greeted [him] by a leap that showed his understanding.[6] He told of the office of being his precursor,
which as a youth he was going to fulfill freely and devotedly, and before he was born he told of the coming of the
Lord by the only signs he was capable of giving. Now the
time had arrived when the utterance of the angel would be
fulfilled, in which he had said that *'he* [John] *would be filled
with the Holy Spirit even from his mother's womb'.*[7]

*Elizabeth was filled with the Holy Spirit and she cried out in
a great voice*—properly with a great voice because she recognized the great gifts of God; properly with a great voice because she sensed that he whom she knew to be present
everywhere was also present bodily there. For indeed, by
a 'great' voice is not to be understood so much a loud voice
as a devoted one. For she was not capable of praising the
Lord with the devotion of a moderate voice, since being full
of the Holy Spirit, she was on fire, harboring in her womb
the one than whom no one of those born of woman would
be greater.[8] And she rejoiced that he had come there who,
conceived from the flesh of a virgin mother, would be called,
and would be, the Son of the Most High.

*She cried out and said, 'Blessed are you among women, and
blessed is the fruit of your womb'.* 'Blessed are you among
women'—not only blessed among women, but specially

5. Ambr., *Expos. evang. sec. Luc.* 2, 19-22 (CC 14: 39, 288 - 40, 310)
6. *animo exultante*   7. Lk 1:15   8. Lk 7:28

distinguished among blessed women by a greater blessing. 'Blessed the fruit of your womb'—not that he was blessed in the general way of saints, but, as the Apostle says, *To them belong the patriarchs,* [and] *from them, according to the flesh, is the Christ, who is above all, God blessed for ages.*[9]

Of the origin of this fruit, the psalmist bears witness in a mystical utterance, saying, *For indeed the Lord will give of his generosity, and our earth will give its fruit.*[10] The Lord indeed gave of his generosity in that he arranged to liberate the human race from the crime of its transgression through his only-begotten Son. He gave of his generosity because with the grace of the Holy Spirit he consecrated for his entry the temple of a virginal womb. And our earth gave its fruit because the same virgin who had her body from the earth bore a son who was coequal to God the Father in his divinity, but by the reality of [his] flesh consubstantial with her.[11] Concerning this, Isaiah also, looking toward the time of human redemption, said, *On that day the bud of the Lord will be in magnificence and in glory, and the fruit of the earth will be sublime.*[12] The bud of the Lord was in magnificence and glory when the undying Son of God, appearing temporally in the flesh as a bright light, poured out upon the world the greatness of his heavenly virtues. The fruit of the earth became sublime when the mortal flesh which God received from our nature, already rendered immortal in virtue of the resurrection, was raised up to heaven.

Therefore it was rightly said, *'Blessed are you among women and blessed is the fruit of your womb'.* For incomparably blessed was she who both gained the glory of the divine bud and kept the crown of her integrity.[13] *'Blessed are you among women'*—since through your virginal birth the curse of the first mother was turned away from those born of women. *'Blessed is the fruit of* [your] *womb'*—since through you we have recovered both the seed of incorruption and the fruit of our heavenly inheritance, which we lost in Adam. And truly and singularly blessed is he who did not

---

9. Rm 9:5
10. Ps 85:12 (84:13)
11. Aug., *Serm.* 189 (PL 38: 1005)
12. Is 4:2
13. Aug., *Serm.* 189 (PL 38: 1005)

in our customary way attain the grace of blessing from the Lord after he was born, but in order to save the world, *he came as one blessed in the name of the Lord.* [14]

'And whence does this happen to me, that the mother of my Lord should come to me'? Oh what great humility in the mind of the prophetess! How true the utterance of the Lord in which he said, *Upon whom does my spirit rest if not upon one who is humble and quiet and who trembles at my words?* [15] As soon as [Elizabeth] saw the one who had come to her, she recognized that she was the mother of the Lord, but she discovered in herself no such merit by which she might have become worthy to be visited by such a guest. *'Whence does this happen to me,'* she asked, *'that the mother of my Lord should come to me'?*—because undoubtedly the very Spirit who conferred upon her the gift of prophecy at the same time endowed her with the favor of humility. Filled with the prophetic spirit, she understood that the mother of the Savior had drawn near to her, but being discreet in the spirit of humility, she understood that she herself was less than worthy of [Mary's] coming.

'For, behold, as the voice of your greeting came to my ears, the infant leapt for joy in my womb'. At the same time as she had been filled with the revealing Spirit, Elizabeth understood what that leaping signified about her own infant, that is, that the one who had come was the mother of him whose precursor and proclaimer [her own son] was to be. And what a marvel, how quick was the working of the Holy Spirit! Indeed there is no delay in learning where the Spirit is present as teacher. At one and the same moment, when the voice [of Mary] greeted her, the infant's joy was born. When the bodily voice came to her ears, spiritual power made its entrance into the heart of the hearer, and enkindled not only the mother, but also the child, with the love of the Lord who was coming.

Hence to those who were present and listening, this same mother of the Lord's precursor next took care to plainly bring the good news of those things which she had recog-

---

14. Mt 23:39; Jn 12:13　　　　　　15. Is 66:2 (LXX)

nized in a hidden way, for she went on: '*And blessed is she who has believed, for those things will be accomplished in her which were said to her by the Lord*'. Now Elizabeth too learned through the Spirit the words the angel brought to Mary, because at the moment that she was bringing the good news she believed that these things would, without any doubt, be fulfilled by the working of divine might. And in a marvelous manner the same Spirit, when he filled her, instructed her in the knowledge of present things along with past and future things. She pointed out that she was fully informed concerning present things when, calling blessed Mary the mother of her Lord, she indicated that [Mary] bore in her womb the Redeemer of the human race. Hence too [Elizabeth] avowed that the fruit of [Mary's] womb was singularly blessed. She expressed her reception of an awareness of past things when she divulged the fact that both the words of the angel to Mary, and the consent of Mary who believed, had been made known to her. But she told also how knowledge of future things had not been denied to her when she made clear that those things which had been said to [Mary] would be accomplished by the Lord.

Who, however, my brothers, is competent to say or to judge what grace of the Spirit of God then filled God's mother, when such a light of a heavenly gift gleamed in the mother of the precursor? But we should listen to the words which she said, to see if perhaps we may be capable of distinguishing to some small extent by these [words] what she held within her. Therefore when [Mary] had heard Elizabeth's answer, in which she proclaimed her to be blessed among women, gave her the name of the mother of her Lord, praised her as strong in faith, and expressed the fact that upon [Mary's] entry she, along with her son, had been filled with the Holy Spirit, [then Mary] could no longer remain silent about the gifts which she had attained. Now, when she found the time suitable, she disclosed by the profession of her devotion those things too which had always been in her mind. For, as was proper to her virginal modesty, she for some time covered over with silence the oracle which she had received by divine agency, venerated

the hidden presence of the heavenly mystery concealed in
her inmost thoughts, and reverently awaited what was hidden until the distributor of gifts himself might reveal, at
whatever time he so willed, what sort of special gift he had
bestowed upon her and what sort of secret he had revealed.

But now that she discerned that those same charismatic
gifts with which she had been endowed had been disclosed
to others by the revealing Spirit, she herself then also disclosed the heavenly treasure which she was keeping in her
heart. Therefore she said, *'My soul magnifies the Lord and my
spirit exults in God my Savior,'* and so forth. With these
[words] she first confesses those gifts which had been specially conceded to her, and then she enumerates too those
ordinary kindnesses of God with which he does not stop
consoling the human race forever. Her soul magnifies the
Lord since she commits all the affection of her interior self
to divine praises and subjection, and by her observance of
God's commands she demonstrates that she thinks always
of the might of his majesty. Her spirit exults in God her
Savior since nothing among earthly things is pleasing to her,
no superfluity of perishable things soothes her, nor does
adversity break her down; but she takes delight only in the
memory of her Maker, from whom she hopes for her eternal salvation. These words might be proper and appropriate for all the perfect; nevertheless, it was especially proper
for the blessed mother of God to bring them forward, since
in view of her singular privilege she was rightly on fire with
spiritual love for him in whose bodily conception she was
rejoicing. More so than the rest of the saints, she could rightfully exult with joy in Jesus, that is, in her special Savior,
because she was aware that the very one whom she had
known as the everlasting Author of salvation was, in his
temporal beginning, to be born of her flesh, so that in one
and the same person he would truthfully be both her son
and her Lord.

And in the following words she teaches us how worth-
less she felt of herself, and that she had received by heavenly
grace lavished on her every sort of good merit that she had.
She says, *'For he has considered the humility of his handmaid;*

for behold from this time on all generations will call me blessed'.
She demonstrates that in her own judgment she was indeed
Christ's humble handmaid, but with respect to heavenly
grace she pronounces herself all at once lifted up, and glorified to such a degree that rightly her preeminent blessedness would be marveled at by the voices of all nations.

She also adds, besides, the favors of divine benevolence
which she received in a marvelous way, and with worthy
thanksgiving she offers praises: *'For he who is powerful has
done great things for me, and his name is holy'.* She therefore
attributes nothing to her own merits, but she refers her
whole greatness to him who, showing himself to be powerful and great, is wont to make his faithful ones strong and
great from being small and weak. It is well, however, that
she adds, *'and his name is holy'*, to prompt her listeners—I
should rather say to instruct all those to whom her words
might come—to fly to the invocation of his name, so that
they can also be sharers in eternal sanctity and true salvation, according to that prophetic saying, *And he will be—
everyone who calls upon the name of the Lord—he will be saved.*[16]
For this is the very name concerning which she said above,
'and my spirit exults in God my Savior'.

Hence she adds, more clearly, *'And his mercy* [is] *for generations and generations to those who fear him'.* She names 'generations and generations,' [referring] either to both of the two
peoples, namely the Jews and the gentiles, or alternatively
to all the countries throughout the world which she foresaw would believe in Christ, for, as Peter said, *'God is not
a respecter of persons, but in every nation one who fears him and
works justice is acceptable to him'.*[17]

In agreement with these words of blessed Mary is an utterance of the Lord himself in which he pronounced blessed
not only the mother who was worthy to bring him forth
physically, but also all those who kept his commands. For
when he was teaching the people in a certain place and
working miracles, and everyone was marvelling at his wisdom and virtues, *a certain woman, lifting up her voice from*

16. Jl 2:32; Rm 10:13   17. Ac 10:34-35

*the crowd said to him, 'Blessed is the womb which carried you
and the breasts which nursed you'.*[18] But willingly receiving
this testimony to the truth she had brought forth, he immediately answered, *'Blessed are those who hear the word of
God and abide by it,'* so that the woman herself and every-
body who was listening might trust that they also would
be blessed if they were willing to comply with the divine
mandates. It is as if he were clearly saying, 'She has a singular privilege of blessedness since she, a virgin, was worthy to harbor the incarnate Son of God in her womb, to give
birth to him and to nurture him. Nevertheless those who
conceive his faith and love in a chaste heart, who bear the
recollection of his precepts in a sincere mind, and who busy
themselves nourishing this [recollection] also in the mind
of their neighbors by skillful exhortation, they too will have
a place in the same everlasting life of blessedness.[19]

But because the venerable mother of God taught that his
mercy would come to be present for all those who feared
him throughout the world, it remained for her to also suggest what those who were proud and who despised the
warnings of truth would deserve. *'He has shown,'* she said,
*'might in his arm; he has scattered the proud in the imagination
of their heart'.* 'In his arm' signifies 'under the control of his
own strength'. For he did not stand in need of any outside
help, since, as was written with reference to him, the
[strength] is at hand when he wishes to do something.[20]
This is said in contrast to our working of good, since we
perform [deeds of] virtue not by the potency of our own
freedom to act, but in God.[21] And as it is written in another
place, *'And their arm did not save them, but your right hand
and your arm, and the illumination of your countenance'.*[22] However, *he has scattered the proud in the imagination of their heart*
because *the beginning of every sin is pride.*[23] On this account
the Lord drove the human race far and wide out into the
journeying of this exile, casting them out from the stable

18. Lk 11:27-28
19. Aug., *Serm.* 7 (ed. Morin, *Misc. Agost.* I, 162, 16/28)
20. Ws 12:18   21. Ps 60:12 (59:14)   22. Ps 44:3 (43:4)
23. Si 10:15

dwelling of the heavenly fatherland. But for those who are not afraid to remain in their sins he has reserved the graver punishment of a future scattering.

'*He has put down the mighty from their seat'*. Those he earlier calls 'the proud' he [here] names 'the mighty'. Undoubtedly they are called proud because they extol themselves beyond measure as mighty with regard to their condition—not, however, because they are truly mighty, but because they trust in their own strength and scorn to seek their Maker's assistance. They, however, are truly mighty who know how to say with the Apostle, '*We can do all things in him who strengthens us, the Lord Jesus Christ'*.[24] Concerning such as these it is written, *God does not cast off the mighty since he himself is mighty.*[25] Therefore *he has put down the mighty from their seat, and he has exalted the humble,* since '*everyone who exalts himself will be humbled, and he who humbles himself will be exalted'*.[26] However, this can also be properly understood [to mean] that sometimes those who had been rightly cast down by the Lord because of their [self-] glorification may in turn return to the grace of humility when he has mercy on them. And thus they may rightly be placed higher in glory because of their devoted humility. Accordingly, on account of his pride Saul was put down from the seat of the teaching of the law, but soon, on account of his subjection in humility, he was lifted up to bring the good news of faith in Christ.

'*He has filled the hungry with good things, and he has sent the rich away empty'*. Because they now hunger in a perfect way for eternal goods, and do not stop striving to gain them by the tireless urgency of [their] just works, they will be satisfied when the glory of their Redeemer, which they have desired, appears. But whoever rejoices in giving priority to earthly over heavenly riches will undoubtedly be sent away by the Lord, empty of all blessedness, at the time of the final separation, and so they will be punished along with the devil with the penalty of everlasting misery. We see this fulfilled everyday to no small extent even in this life, namely

24. Ph 4:13   25. Jb 36:5   26. Lk 14:11

both that the humble are filled with the nourishing fare of heavenly goodness and grow rich by the lavishness of heavenly virtues, and that those who are proud, glorying in earthly riches, or those who extol themselves on the wealth of their good works, as if they have these things through their own efforts, become internally empty of the radiance of truth.

To each verse which blessed Mary uttered concerning the state of the proud and the humble, there ought to be joined that which she mentioned before, *'for generations and generations'*. Undoubtedly through all the time of this transitory age the just and merciful Creator is wont to oppose the proud and give grace to the humble.

Hence after her general commemoration of the divine benevolence and justice, she did well to turn the words of her confession to the special divinely-arranged plan of the unheard-of incarnation, by which God deigned to redeem the world, as she said, *'He has taken his child Israel under his protection, being mindful of his mercy'*. Indeed, Israel means *'a man seeing God,'*[27] by which name is designated every society of redeemed human beings. On their account God himself appeared in visible form among human beings, so that they might be capable of seeing God. He took Israel under his protection as a physician does a sick person he is caring for, [or] as a king does the people he defends from the invasion of enemies, whom moreover he returns to liberty when the enemy has been overthrown and allows to reign with him perpetually.

And it is good that she added, *'his child,'* signifying one who is humble and obedient, because it is only through the virtue of humility that one can come into possession of the heritage of redemption. Hence the Lord also said, *'Unless you are converted and become like little children, you shall not enter the kingdom of heaven'*.[28] And she did well to add, *'being mindful of his mercy,'* for the fact that God assumed [the form of] a human being in order to redeem [humankind] was not attributable to the merit of the human condition,

27. Jerome, *Nom.* (CC 72: 75, 21); *Quaest. Heb.* (CC 72: 41, 9/18)
28. Mt 18:3

but to a gift of divine benevolence. For after the fault of transgression, what were we worthy of, except the just anger of our Maker? Hence it remains to be said that all of us who were restored to salvation and eternal life should attribute this not to ourselves, but to the grace of him to whom it was said, *'In your anger you will be mindful of your mercy'.*[29]

'As he said to our fathers, to Abraham and to his seed forever'. When blessed Mary was making [mention of] the memory of the fathers, she properly represented them by naming Abraham in particular, for although many of the fathers and holy ones mystically brought forward testimony of the Lord's incarnation, nevertheless, it was to [Abraham] that the hidden mysteries of this same [Lord's] incarnation and of our redemption were first clearly predicted, and to him it was specifically said, *'And in you all the tribes of the earth will be blessed'.*[30] None of the faithful doubts that this pertains to the Lord and Savior, who in order to give us an everlasting blessing deigned to come to us from the stock of Abraham. However, 'the seed of Abraham' does not refer only to those chosen ones who were brought forth physically from Abraham's lineage, but also to us who, having been gathered together to Christ from the nations, are connected by the fellowship of faith to the fathers, from whom we are far separated by the origin of our fleshly blood-line. We too are the seed and children of Abraham since we are reborn by the sacraments of our Redeemer, who assumed his flesh from the race of Abraham. We are the children of Abraham since we devote all of our resources to striving to see him whose *day* blessed *Abraham exulted that he was to see, and he saw it, and he rejoiced.*[31] And indeed on this basis the Apostle says, *If, however, you are Christ's, therefore you are the seed of Abraham, heirs according to the promise.*[32]

'Forever' is rightly added in conclusion, for undoubtedly the aforementioned promise of a heavenly inheritance will never be closed off by any ending. For all the way to the end of this world there will be no lack of those who, be-

29. Hab 3:2 (Vet. Lat.)   30. Gn 12:3   31. Jn 8:56
32. Ga 3:29

lieving in Christ, become the seed of Abraham, and for this same seed there will remain the everlasting glory of future blessedness.

Hence we, dearly beloved brothers, to whom an eternal prize is promised by the Lord, must exert ourselves in unwearied effort of mind to partake in it. For to obtain a good which we long to have without end, we must strive for it without any intermission until we receive it. Thus, by frequent meditation we should go back over the words of [this] gospel reading, and we should always keep in mind the example of the blessed mother of God, so that being found humble in the sight of God and also submissive with due honor to our neighbors, we may be worthy to be perpetually exalted with her. Let us strive solicitously not to be made unduly proud by the favor of those who praise us, since we see that she kept the constancy of her humility unshaken in the midst of words of true praise. If an immoderate appetite for temporal things delights us, we should call to mind that our judge 'sends the rich away empty'; if a temporal affliction perhaps agitates our minds, we should reflect on the fact that he also 'exalts the humble'. We should never despair of being granted our request for pardon of our failings because *'his mercy is for generations and generations on those who fear him'*. May the more serious fault of being impenitent lead no one astray, along with the bad things he has done, because God opposes the proud, and dissociating them from the heritage of the blessed, he scatters them in various places of punishment in relation to the variety of their sins. If, however, we always recall blessed Mary's acts and sayings, it may happen through the Lord's bounty that we may persevere in the observance of chastity and works of virtue.

Now also a very good and most beneficial custom has developed in holy Church, of her hymn being chanted daily by everyone along with the psalmody of the evening office, so that in this way a very frequent reminder of the Lord's incarnation may enkindle the minds of the faithful to a feeling of devotion, and by reflecting very often on the example of his mother, they may be confirmed in the stability of virtues. And it is pleasingly appropriate that this occurs at vespers, so that our mind, which has been tired out in the course of the day and stretched in different directions by diverse thoughts, may, as we settle into a time of quiet, pull itself together in its reflection. And then, beneficially prompted [by the Magnificat], our mind may, by night-time prayers, and with tears as the occasion offers, make itself clean once more from every sort of superfluous or harmful thing it has become involved in during the day's wanderings.

But, because we have already drawn this sermon out long, let us, having turned to the Lord, implore him for clemency so that we may venerate the memory of blessed Mary with fitting offices, and we may be worthy to come to the celebration of the solemnities of the Lord's nativity with purer souls. He himself aids our desire to do spiritual works and to attain heavenly gifts, he who wished to become incarnate for us, and to give as a model for living among human beings, his only-begotten Son,[1]* Jesus Christ our Lord, with whom he lives and reigns God in the unity of the Holy Spirit throughout all ages. Amen.

NOTE

1. In the final sentence, as Bede leads into the doxology he seems to say that the Lord both became incarnate and gave us his Son as a model. This ambiguity is probably intentional, and it invites comparison with the artistic convention in medieval art of depicting God in the act of creation with a cruciform halo. Also, in Homily I, 25, Bede says that in the story of the woman taken in adultery (Jn 8), Jesus wrote on the ground 'in order to point out that it was he himself who once wrote the ten commandments of the law on stone with his finger, that is, by the action of the Holy Spirit'.

homily 1.5

The evangelist Matthew, in a discourse that was brief indeed but full of truth, described the nativity of our Lord and Savior Jesus Christ, by which the Son of God, eternal before the ages, appeared in time as the Son of man. After [Matthew] has led [us] through the generations of [Christ's] ancestors from Abraham to Joseph, Mary's husband, and showed that they all, by the common order of human creation, were begotten as well as begetting,[1] he then wishes to speak of [Mary] herself. He makes clear what a difference there was between her child-bearing and that of the rest: the rest brought forth by the customary joining of male and female; [Jesus], however, seeing that he was Son of God, was to be born into the world by a virgin. It was entirely fitting that when God wished to become a human being, for the sake of human beings, he be born of none other than a virgin. When it happens that the Virgin bears a child, she bears no other son than one who is God.

When Mary his mother was betrothed to Joseph, before they came together she was found to be with child of the Holy Spirit. The evangelist Luke explains sufficiently in what order [of

1. Mt 1:1-17

events] and in what city the conception took place. Because it is sure that this is well-known to your reverences,[2] something must be said about a few of the things that Matthew wrote, and we should note first that in stating *'before they came together,'* what is suggested by the verb 'come together' is not actual sleeping together, but the period of marriage which customarily preceded the time when she who had previously been betrothed started to be a wife. Therefore *before they came together*, before they celebrated the solemnities of marriage with suitable ceremony, *she was found to be with child of the Holy Spirit*. In the order [of events] recounted they afterwards 'came together' when Joseph, at the angel's command, received his wife, but they did not sleep together, for there follows, *and he did not know her*. She was discovered by no one other than Joseph to be with child. By marital privilege he knew almost everything about his future wife,[3] and so by an inquiring gaze he soon noticed that she was great with child.

There follows: *Joseph, her husband, since he was a just man and did not wish to expose her to scorn, wished to send her away privately*. Joseph saw that his betrothed had conceived, though he knew well that she had not been touched by any man. Since he was just and wished to do everything justly, he chose [what seemed] the best course, that he would neither divulge this to others, nor receive her himself as his wife, but privately changing the proposal of marriage, he would allow her to remain in the position of betrothed woman, as she was. Now he had read in Isaiah that a virgin of the house of David would conceive and give birth to the Lord, and he also knew that Mary took her origin from this house, and so he did not disbelieve that this prophecy had been fulfilled in her. But if he had sent her away privately and not received her as his wife, and if she, as a betrothed woman, were to give birth, there would surely have been few people to call her a virgin rather than a harlot. Hence Joseph all at once changed his intention for a better one, so that to preserve Mary's reputation he would receive her

2. *uestrae sanctitati*
3. Jer., *In Matth.* 1, 18 (CC 77: 10, 81 - 11, 82); *Adv. Helv.* (PL 23: 186)

as his wife, celebrating the marriage feast, but he would keep her perpetually chaste. For the Lord preferred to have some ignorant of the manner of his birth rather than have them attack his mother's reputation.[4]

There follows: *As he was pondering these things, behold, an angel of the Lord appeared to him in his dreams, saying, 'Joseph, son of David, do not fear to receive Mary as your wife, for what is born in her is of the Holy Spirit. She will give birth to a son and you shall call his name Jesus, for he will save his people from their sins'.* Unquestionably by these words the manner of his conception along with the dignity of his birth are taught: she would conceive of the Holy Spirit, and give birth to the Christ. Although the angel did not openly name him Christ, nevertheless in explaining the etymology of the name Jesus he applied to him the terms 'Author of salvation' and 'Savior of the people,' indicating clearly that he was the Christ, so that through these things Joseph might learn what he had not known, and so that he might completely remove from his mind any [thought of] contact with God's mother. Nevertheless, by this divinely-arranged plan of righteous necessity he was ordered to receive her as his wife, but only in name, so that she would not be stoned as an adulteress by the Jews, and so that while fleeing into Egypt she might have the comfort[5] of a masculine person who, with familial care, would be the guardian of her feminine weakness, and the witness of her perpetual virginity. Catholic expositors also put forth other reasons why Joseph was to receive God's mother as his wife, and one who wishes will find these in their writings.

The evangelist also employs the example of a prophetic utterance with reference to the virgin birth, in order that a miracle of such majesty might be the more certainly believed if not only he himself proclaimed this fact, but if he also recalled that it was predicted by the prophet. Now it is usual for this evanglist (that is, Matthew) to also affirm everything that he tells with prophetic testimonies. For he wrote his gospel especially for the sake of those from the

4. Ambr., *Expos. evang. sec. Luc.* 2,1 (CC 14: 30, 15/16)
5. Jer., *In Matth.* 1, 18 (CC 77: 10, 75/76)

Jews who had come to believe, but who, although they were reborn in Christ, were nevertheless not able to be torn away from the ceremonies of the law. On that account he attempted to raise them from the fleshly sense of the law and the prophets to the spiritual sense, which concerns Christ, so that they might attain the sacraments of the Christian faith the more securely insofar as they acknowledged that these were nothing other than those which the prophets had predicted.

Behold a virgin, he says, *shall be with child and give birth to a son, and his name shall be called Emmanuel, which means 'God with us'*. The Savior's name, because of which he is called 'God with us' by the prophet,[6] signifies both natures of his one person. For he who, born before time from the Father, is God himself in the fullness of time, became Emmanuel (that is, 'God with us') in his mother's womb, because he deigned to take the weakness of our nature into the unity of his person when *the Word was made flesh and dwelt among us*.[7] In a wonderful manner he began to be what we are, while not ceasing to be what he had been, assuming our nature in such a way that he himself would not lose what he had been.[8]

Joseph, arising from sleep, did as the angel of the Lord commanded him, and accepted his wife and did not know her. He accepted her as his wife in name for the reasons which we mentioned above, and he did not know her in the marriage act because of the hidden mysteries of which he had learned. But if anyone wishes to oppose this explanation of ours and to contend that the blessed mother of God was never, by the celebration of marriage, taken by Joseph as a wife in name, let him explain this place in the holy gospel better. At the same time let him show that it was allowed among the Jews for anyone to come together with his betrothed in fleshly union, and we willingly defer to his sound understanding—only we may not believe that anything at

6. Is 7:14   7. Jn 1:14
8. Aug., *Serm.* 136, 2 (*PL* 38: 1000); *Serm.* 196, 3 (*PL* 38: 1020); *Serm.* 292, 3 (*PL* 38: 1321); Leo, *Serm.* 21, 2 (*CC* 138: 86, 37–87, 43; *Serm.* 27, 1 (*CC* 138: 132, 18 - 133, 25)

all took place regarding the mother of the Lord for which
public opinion could defame her.

In truth, no one should suppose that the continuation [of
verse 25], *'until she gave birth to her first-born son,'* should
be understood as though after her son was born, [Joseph]
did know her, an opinion that some have perversely held.
For you of the brotherhood ought to be aware that there
have been heretics who, on account of that saying, *'He did
not know her until she gave birth to her son,'* believed that after the Lord was born, Mary was known by Joseph, and
from that [union] arose those whom scripture calls the
brothers of the Lord,[9] and as a support for their error they
take up this [passage], which applies the term 'first-born'
to the Lord. May God turn this blasphemy away from the
faith of us all, and may he grant us to understand with catholic piety that our Savior's parents were always distinguished by inviolate virginity, and that in the customary
way of the scriptures it was not to their children but to their
kindred that the term 'brothers of the Lord' is applied. And
[may he grant us to understand] that the reason why the
evangelist did not take care to say whether [Joseph] knew
her after the Son of God was born, was because he did not
suppose that there would be anyone who would dispute
it. Since it was given to them by a singular grace to have
a son born to them while they remained in the chaste state
of virginity, in no way could they violate the rules of chastity
and pollute the most sacred temple of God with the seed
of their corruption. Also we should note that 'first-born'
are not (in accord with the opinion of the heretics) only those
whom other brothers follow, but, in accord with the authority of the scripture, they are all those who first open the
womb, whether some brothers follow them or none do.[10]

Nevertheless, it can be understood that, for a special reason, the Lord was said to be first-born, according to what
John says in the Apocalypse about him *who is the faithful
witness, the first-born of the dead and the prince of the kings of
the earth.*[11] And the apostle Paul [says], *Now those whom he*

9. e.g., Mt 13:55   10. Jer., *Adv. Helv.* (*PL* 23: 192)
11. Rv 1:5

has foreknown *he has also predestined to become conformed to the image of his Son, that he himself should be the first-born among many brothers.*[12] He is first-born among many brothers because *to as many as received him he gave the power to become sons of God,*[13] of whom he is rightly named the first-born because in dignity he came before all the sons of adoption,[14] even those who in their birth preceded the time of his incarnation.[15] Therefore, they can with the greatest truth bear witness with John, 'He who comes after us was before us'.[16] That is, 'He was born in the world after us, but by the merit of his virtue and kingdom he is rightfully called the first-born of us all'.

Also in his own divine nativity he can appropriately be said to be first-born because, prior to begetting any other creature by making it, the Father begot a Son coeternal with himself; and prior to begetting, by redeeming them, any other sons of adoption for himself by the Word of truth, the eternal Father begot a Word coeternal to himself.[1*] Hence the Word himself, the very Son of God, [his] virtue and wisdom, says, *I came forth from the mouth of the Most High, first-born before every creature.*[17] Mary gave birth to her first-born son, that is, the son of her substance; she gave birth to him who was also born God from God before every creature, and in that humanity in which he was created he rightly 'went before' every creature.

And he [Joseph] *called his name Jesus.* 'Jesus' in Hebrew means 'saving' or 'savior' in Latin.[18] It is clear that the prophets most certainly call upon his name. Hence these things are sung in great desire for a vision of him: *My soul will exult in the Lord and take delight in his salvation.*[19] *My soul pines for your salvation.*[20] *I, however, will glory in the Lord; I will rejoice in God my Jesus.*[21] And especially that [verse]: *God*

---

12. Rm 8:29; several MSS add: 'Indeed he is called the first-born of the dead because although he was incarnate after many brothers, he first of them all rose from the dead and opened to believers the way of heavenly life from death'.
13. Jn 1:12
14. Eph 1:5
15. Isid., *Etymol.* 7, 2, 13
16. Jn 1:15
17. Si 24:5
18. Isid., *Etymol.* 7, 2, 7
19. Ps 35:9 (34:9)
20. Ps 119:81 (118:81)
21. *gaudebo in Deo Iesu meo,* Hab 3:18 (Vet. Lat.)

in your name save me! [22] as if [the prophet] would say: 'You
who are called Savior, make bright the glory of your name
in me by saving'.

Jesus is the name of the Son who was born of a virgin,
and, as the angel explained, [this name] signified that he
would save his people from their sins.[23] He who saves from
sins is doubtlessly the same one who will save from the corruption of mind and body which happen as a result of sins.
'Christ,' is a term of priestly and royal dignity, for from
'chrism,' that is, an anointing with holy oil, in the law priests
and kings were called 'christs,' and they signified him who
appeared in the world as true king and high priest, and was
anointed with the oil of gladness above those who shared
with him.[24] From this anointing, that is, the chrism, he himself [is called] 'Christ,'[25] and those who share this anointing, that is, spiritual grace, are called 'Christians'.[26] In that
he is Savior may he deign to save us from sins. In that he
is high-priest may he deign to reconcile us to God the
Father. In that he is king may he deign to give us the eternal
kingdom of his Father, Jesus Christ our Lord, who with the
Father and the Holy Spirit lives and reigns God for all ages.
Amen.

22. Ps 54:1 (53:3)   23. Mt 1:21
24. Ps 45:7 (44:8); Heb 1:9   25. Isid., *Etymol.* 7, 2, 2-3
26. Aug., *De civ. Dei* 17, 4; 17, 16; 20, 10 (CC 48: 561, 269/70; 580, 25/28;
    720, 26/27)

NOTES

1. This sentence exhibits very well Bede's fondness for etymological wordplay and parallel structure. The translation attempts to preserve the parallel structure and the etymological playing with various forms of the verb *gignor* ('beget'). Note that *primogenitus*, translated 'first-born' is also etymologically related to *gignor*.

homily 1.6

W
e have heard from the gospel reading, dearly beloved brothers, that when the Redeemer of the
world, our Lord and God, Jesus Christ, was
about to be born into the world, an edict went out from
Caesar Augustus, who then held the highest place with
respect to worldly reigns, [and the edict said] that the entire world was to be enrolled. We must not suppose that
this happened by chance, but we must understand that it
was provided through a most certain divinely-arranged plan
of this same Redeemer of ours. And, indeed, just as in his
divinity the Mediator between God and human beings[1] foresaw the mother of whom he willed to be born when he
should so will, so also in his humanity he chose the time
which he wished for his nativity. Moreover, he himself
granted that that [time] should be such as he willed, namely
that in a calm among the storm of wars a singular tranquility of unusual peace should cover the whole world.

For what could be a greater indication of peace in this life
than for the entire world to be enrolled by one man and
to be included in a single coinage. Indeed, he chose a virgin

---

1. 1 Tm 2:5

as mother because it was not fitting for the Son of God to be born in the flesh in any other way than from an inviolate mother. He chose a time of utmost peace as the time when he would be born because this was the reason for his being born in the world, that he might lead the human race back to the gifts of heavenly peace. And, indeed, thus it is written, *He himself is our peace who has made both one,*[2] that is, he who as a benevolent mediator and reconciler has made one house of God of angels and men. Our Lord was born in a time of peace, so that even by the circumstance of the time he might teach that he was the very one of whom the prophecy sent before [him] spoke: *His sovereignty will be multipled, and there will be no end of peace.*[3] Hence in another place the same prophet well said, when he was describing in a mystical utterance the sacraments of [Christ's] incarnation and our redemption, *And in the last days the mountain of the house of the Lord will be established on the top of the mountains, and elevated above the hills, and all nations will flow to it.*[4] And he clearly designated the serenity of the peace which then would be by appending, *And they will convert their swords into plowshares and their spears into sickles. Nation will not lift up sword against nation, nor will they engage in battle any more.*[5] On account of this, he next added by way of encouragement, *House of Jacob come, and let us walk in the light of the Lord.*[6]

The very Author of peace and the Maker of time sent before him a time of peace, and thus when he appeared in the flesh he opened an approach to light and proclaimed the joys of eternal peace first to the house of Jacob (that is, the Israelite people), and then to all the nations which came streaming to him. And we must not pass over the fact that the serenity of that earthly peace, at the time when the heavenly king was born, not only offered testimony to his grace, but it also provided a service, since it bestowed on the preachers of his word the capability of travelling over the world and spreading abroad the grace of the gospel wherever they wished, and this would have occurred to

2. Eph 2:14   3. Is 9:7   4. Is 2:2   5. Is 2:4
6. Is 2:5

much less an extent if the whole world had not been under the rule of one empire.

But this enrollment of the whole world which is recalled as having been done by an earthly king also clearly designates the works of the heavenly king. Undoubtedly the reason he appeared in the world was so that from all the countries throughout the world he might gather the elect into the unity of his faith, just as he himself promised that he would write down their names forever in heaven.[7] Also, the fact that all were going, in response to the edict of Augustus, each to report to his own city, [betokens what] we must do spiritually as a service to our king. Indeed, our city is the holy church, which in part is still journeying away from the Lord on earth, and in part already reigns with the Lord in heaven. And after the end of this age the whole [Church] will reign in a perfected state with him forever. We must all, then, go into this city, and there must be no excuse from such a salutary journey. We must pay the census [tax] which is due to the king who has been born—that is, we must comply with divine commands in the unity of the Church now present, and hasten by the tireless course of good works to our entry into the heavenly fatherland.

In the act of reporting in the census one gave a denarius, which had the weight of ten *nummi*, and which bore the image and the name of Caesar. We also must imitate this spiritually, for we pay a denarius to our king when we busy ourselves with fulfilling the ten commands of his law, and written on this denarius we bear the name of this same king of ours when we remember in all our acts that we are called 'Christians' from 'Christ,' and take care to keep inviolate in us the dignity of his name.

We also ought to represent his image on the same denarius of our good way of life, which is what he himself taught when he said, *Be holy because I the Lord your God am holy.*[8] Now this is the image of God in which we were fashioned in the first human being, namely that by participation in the divine holiness we might be perpetually holy.

7. Is 4:3; Lk 10:20; Greg., *Hom. in evang.* 1, 8, 1 (*PL* 76:1103)
8. Lv 19:2

And indeed thus the psalmist says, *The radiance of your countenance is expressed upon us.*[9] But because a human being lost this radiance of the divine countenance by sinning, it pleased God to assume the condition of a human countenance by being born in the flesh, in order that he might thereby teach us that we ought to be reborn in the Spirit. It pleased him to appear without sin *in the likeness of sinful flesh*[10] so that he might cleanse us thoroughly from every sin, and form again in us the distinctness of his image.

And Joseph went up from Galilee, out of the city of Nazareth into Judaea, to the city of David, which is called Bethlehem, because he was of the house and family of David, to report, along with Mary his betrothed wife, who was pregnant. It was truly by divine influence that it was brought about that everyone proceeded to his own city to report for the census, so that because of this general edict it might happen that the parents of our Savior would go from Nazareth to Bethlehem and thus bring to fulfillment the oracles of the prophets, and that both cities would be distinguished by the hidden mysteries of his incarnation, namely the one would shine forth with the honor of his conception, and the other with the honor of his nativity.

The prophet Isaiah bears witness that our Redeemer had to be conceived in Nazareth when he says, *A rod will come out of the root of Jesse, and a nazareus will ascend from his root.*[11] 'Nazareus' has the meaning of 'flower' or 'clean'.[12] The Son of God made incarnate for us can properly be named by this term, both because he adopted the nature of a human being clean from all vices, and because in him the font and origin of spiritual fruits came forth for all believers, since to them he both pointed out examples, and granted the gifts, of living properly and blessedly. Therefore a branch came out of the root of Jesse, and a *nazareus* ascended from his root, because the inviolate virgin Mary arose from the stock of David, and from her flesh, in the city of Nazareth, the Lord assumed the true reality of flesh without the contamination of the flesh.

9. Ps 4:7   10. Rm 8:3   11. Is 11:1
12. Jer., *Nom.* (CC 72: 137, 24, 27)

It is also indicated in the prophetic oracles that [Christ] was to be born in Bethlehem when it is said, *You, Bethlehem Ephrata, are a little one among the thousands of Judah; from you will come out the one who is to be ruler in Israel.*[13] It is good that he was born in Bethlehem, not only for the sake of [giving] an indication of the royal genealogical tree, since David was from there, but also on account of the name itself, for Bethlehem has the meaning 'house of bread,'[14] and he himself said, *'I am the living bread which descended from heaven'.*[15] Because he descended from heaven to earth in order to grant to us the nourishing fare of heavenly life and to satisfy us with the favor of eternal sweetness, the place where he was born is rightly called 'house of bread'.

There was also another reason in the heavenly disposition why our Lord was not born in the city where he was conceived, but in another, namely so that in this way those who were aware of his nativity, or those who ministered [to him], might more easily avoid the enemies who were lying in wait for him. Indeed, he foresaw that as soon as he was born, Herod would begin to pursue him and seek to kill him, and on this account he willed that the mystery of his nativity would be brought to completion in the city of David. Then his parents would have neither house nor possessions there, but would only draw near [to Bethlehem] as newcomers at the time of his nativity, and would stay there as guests. As soon as [his] nativity was brought to fulfillment, and the heavenly signs which were proper for giving testimony to him had been manifested, [then] they would retire with him to Egypt. And indeed it happened thus not only so that Herod could in no way discover [Jesus] when he was seeking him, but also so that he would have no occasion to trouble [Jesus'] relatives if he had not been able to search out who his parents were.

And we must not pass over in silence the very great condescension of our Maker and Redeemer, who not only willed to become incarnate for us, but also willed to become incarnate at a time when soon after his birth he would be

13. Mi 5:2   14. Greg., *Hom. in evang.* 1, 8, 1 (*PL* 76: 1104)
15. Jn 6:41

inscribed in the report of a census. For he put on flesh so that he might put on us the strength of the Spirit; he descended from heaven to earth so that he might elevate us from earth to heaven; he paid tribute to Caesar so that he might grant us the grace of perpetual freedom. The Son of God in [the form of] a human being did service to a king who was ignorant of [this] divine servitude, so that in this way [Christ] might also bestow upon us a model of humility, suggesting how greatly we ought to serve each other through charity since he himself did not disdain to commit himself to servitude to one who was unaware of true charity. Here also by his example he pointed out in advance what the prince of the apostles was afterwards to teach in words, *Be subject to every human creature for God's sake, whether to the king as sovereign, or to leaders as sent by him.*[16]

It came about, when they were there, that the days for her to give birth were fulfilled, and she gave birth to her first-born son. He calls the Lord 'first-born,' not that we are to believe that the blessed mother of God gave birth to other sons after him, [since] it is true that she was memorable for her unique perpetual chastity with Joseph her husband. But he properly names him 'first-born' because, as John says, *But to as many as received him he gave them the power to become sons of God.*[17] Among these sons he rightfully holds the primacy who before he was born in the flesh was Son of God, born without beginning. However, he descended to earth; he was made a sharer in our nature; he lavished upon us a sharing in his grace, so that, as the Apostle says, *He should be the first-born of many brethren.*[18]

And she wrapped him in swaddling clothes and laid him in a manger because there was no place for him in the inn. And here, dearly beloved brothers, we must look upon the great condescension of our Redeemer; here, from the whole inmost center of the heart, we must each of us say to ourselves with the prophet, *What shall I deliver to the Lord for all the things which he has delivered to me?*[19] For he to whom we truthfully chant, *Great is the Lord and exceedingly praiseworthy, and*

16. 1 P 2:13-14   17. Jn 1:12   18. Rm 8:29
19. Ps 116:12 (115:12)

of his greatness there is no end,[20] was born as a little one for
us so that he might make us from little ones into great ones,
that is, from sinners into just people. He who sits at the
right hand of God the Father in heaven stood in need of
a place in the inn so that he might grant us an abundance
of happy mansions in his Father's house.[21] He who put varied apparel upon every creature (whether the invisible in
heaven or the visible in this world), who in his majesty,
as the prophet says of him, *is wrapped around with radiance
as with a garment,*[22] he is covered with paltry swaddling
clothes in his assumption of our weakness, so that he may
replace for us our original robe—that is, so that having felt
compassion [for us] he may lead us back to the grace of the
immortality which we received in our first parent. He
through whom all things were made arranged to have his
hands and feet, and moreover the whole body which he
put on, wrapped in swaddling bands, so that he might
render our hands ready for good works, so that he might
direct our feet into the way of peace,[23] so that he might
deliver up all the members of our body to divine services.
He whom *heaven and the heavens of the heavens do not hold*[24]
was contained by the narrowness of a small manger so that
he might bestow upon us the amplitude of seats on high.

And it was on account of the preeminent sacrament that,
when he was born, he chose a resting-place for himself in
a manger, where animals are accustomed to come to take
food. For already then he suggested that by the mysteries
of his incarnation he would restore all the faithful upon the
most sacred table of the altar. He indicated that he is wont
to refresh with the grace of inward sweetness all those who
humbly obey him, concerning whom it is well said through
the prophet, *The ox recognizes its owner, and the ass his master's
manger.*[25] By the ox he designates the people of the Jews,
who were accustomed to carry the yoke of the law and to
ruminate upon its words; by the ass he represents the

20. Ps 145:3 (144:3)
21. Ambr., *Expos. evang. sec. Luc.* 2, 41 (CC 14: 49, 583/84)
22. Ps 104:2 (103:2)   23. Lk 1:79   24. 1 K 8:27
25. Is 1:3

people of the nations, who remained always unclean with
the stains of idolatry. From both peoples a great many
turned to the grace of the gospel and recognized the Owner
by whom they were created, and were seeking by means
of his heavenly nourishing fare to grow toward perpetual
salvation. We hear of the first-fruits of these [two] peoples
consecrated to him in the shepherds, who are rightly to be
venerated since, at the angel's announcement, they were
the first to be worthy to see and proclaim him when he was
born; and in the wise men, who, led by the star, came to
his cradle from the east with presents and petitions. Now
the former came to the Lord from the Jews and the latter
from the gentiles. But we will hear more fully about the wise
men on the day of the holy Epiphany, upon which [day]
they came by the Lord's gracious kindness.

In the meantime, let us see what took place concerning
the shepherds, who, since they came to him first, represent the faithful among the earlier people. There follows:
*And there were shepherds in the same region, watching and keep-
ing watch by night over their flock. And, behold, an angel of the
Lord stood near them, and the brightness of God shone around
them.* Suitably enough this was arranged by heavenly Providence, that as the Lord was being born, shepherds would
be watching in the vicinity of the same city, and by watching at night they were shielding their flocks from fear. For
when the great Pastor of the sheep, that is, the nourisher
of the souls of the faithful, was born into the world, it was
suitable that shepherds watching over their flocks should
give testimony of his nativity. For it was he himself who
said, *'My sheep hear my voice, and I recognize them, and they
follow me, and I give them eternal life'.*[26] Now there was already then [an indication] that there would be a time when
chosen shepherds, that is, holy preachers, would be sent
through the whole world, and they would gather believing people into the Lord's sheepfold, namely holy Church.
To the first of these, that is, blessed Peter, when he avowed
that he loved the Lord, the same Lord and prince of shep-

26. Jn 10:27-28

herds, in order to prove that love, commanded him, *'Feed my sheep'.*[27] Surely the only one who loves his Maker perfectly is the one who also commits himself to concern for selfless love of neighbor.

Behold, an angel of the Lord stood by them, and the brightness of God shone around them. What does it mean that, as the angel was appearing to the shepherds, the splendor of divine brightness also enclosed them, something that we have never discovered in the whole course of the Old Testament? Though in countless cases angels appeared to prophets and just people, nowhere do we read of their enclosing the human beings with the brightness of divine light. [Why is this], unless it is because the privilege was properly kept for the dignity of this time? For when the true Light of the world was born in the world, it was unquestionably fitting that the herald of his nativity should also bathe the bodily sight of human beings with the freshness of heavenly light. Now the prophet says concerning his nativity, *A light has arisen in the darkness for those who are righteous in heart.*[28] And as though we were asking what the light was to which he refers, he immediately goes on, *He is a merciful and compassionate and just Lord.*[29] Therefore, when the merciful and just Maker and Redeemer of the human race deigned to illuminate the world by the glory of a wondrous nativity, it was entirely proper that the brightness of a wondrous light should fill that very region in which he was born.

Let us hear what the angel says to the shepherds as he appears [to them] with brightness: *'Do not fear, for behold, I bring you good news of great joy, which will be for all people'*— truly great joy, for [it is] heavenly joy, eternal joy, joy which is not upset by any intervening sorrow, which is granted only to the elect to enjoy. *'Which will be to all people'*—not to all the people of the Jews, nor to all the people of the nations, but to all the people who, either from the Jews or from the nations of the whole world, are brought together in one flock to one confession of Christ. From one and the same partaking of the mysteries of Christ they are called

27. Jn 21:17   28. Ps 112:4a (111:4a)
29. Ps 112:4b (111:4b); with 'Lord' from Ps 111:4 (110:4)

'Christian'. Concerning [this people] the prophet says, *The people who walk in darkness have seen a great light.*[30]

'*A savior who is Christ the Lord has been born to you today in the city of David*'. It is good that [the angel] said, 'has been born today,' and did not say, 'this night,' for with heavenly light he appeared to those who were conducting the watch by night, and brought the good news that day was born, namely the one concerning whom the psalmist foretold saying, *Announce well his salvation day from day.*[31] Indeed the salvation of God, that is, the Lord Jesus, is 'day from day' because he who appeared temporally in the city of David as a human being from a virgin mother was, in truth, himself born before all time, and without spatial limitation,[32] light from light, true God from true God. Because, therefore, the light of life rose for those of us dwelling in the region of the shadow of death,[33] the herald of this rising suitably says, '*A savior has been born to you today,*' so that being always advised by this word we may recollect that the night of ancient blindness is gone past and the day of eternal salvation has drawn nigh, and *let us cast off the works of darkness.*[34] And let us walk as children of light,[35] *for the fruit of the light,* as the same Apostle says, *is in all justice and holiness.*[36]

'*And this will be a sign to you: you will find an infant wrapped in swaddling clothes and placed in a manger*'. It is proper for us who are born in the flesh to always keep in mind this sign of the Savior, so that we may learn to give thanks always for his kindnesses by living well, since he willed to assume the condition of our weakness in such a way that he also did not shun the general state of poverty. And, indeed, an indication of the infirmity he assumed [is] the fact that as an infant he too was wrapped in swaddling clothes, and [an indication] of his poverty [is] the fact that he was found placed not in a bed, but in a manger. Let us there-

30. Is 9:1 (9:2)
31. Ps 96:2 (95:2); 'well' (*bene*) is perhaps an error of eyeskip from *benedicite* in the preceding line of the psalm
32. *non localiter*   33. Is 9:1 (9:2)   34. Rm 13:12
35. Eph 5:8
36. Eph 5:9, with var. *sanctitate* for Vulg. *ueritate*

fore sing forever of the mercies of the Lord,[37] who did not himself refuse to become the companion of our dejection and mortality so that we might live happily forever.

One angel announced the joy of the Lord's nativity: suddenly there was present *a multitude of the heavenly host,* who rendered the service of their devotion to the Lord when he was born; and the one whom they were accustomed always to glorify in heaven, they now celebrated with their customary praise in hymns as he appeared on earth. Here, by their praising, the citizens of heaven also educate us [as to] how we ought to celebrate the joys of this most sacred solemnity, [and] what great praises we ought to say to the Word of God, because on this [feastday] *he was made flesh and dwelt among us,* so that he might raise us up to the vision of his glory and grant us a sharing in *the grace and truth*[38] with which he himself was full.

Therefore they praise God and say, '*Glory to God in the highest, and peace on earth to human beings of good will'.* And it is suitable that [the angels] said 'glory to God' [and] that they proclaimed peace to human beings, for they knew that he whose nativity made them glad was the Mediator between God and human beings, that is, that he was true God and a true human being. They sang 'glory to God in the highest' because they were exulting that the time had already come when, with the casting off of the gods who were made by men, the world would recognize its Maker, who is in heaven. They wanted peace for human beings because they understood that those whom they had previously disdained as rightly cast out, for their sins, from eternal bliss, these they understood would now, because the Lord was redeeming them, be with them in the joys of the heavenly dwelling. They gave a mandate of peace to human beings, whom they desired to have as companions in the heavenly Jerusalem (that is, in the vision of perpetual peace), so that they might also advise these very human beings that they ought to come to their company through the observance of peace.

37. Ps 89:1 (88:2)   38. Jn 1:14

And when [the angels' song] says, *'and on earth peace to human beings,'* it is good that it continues with *'of good will,'* for the Spirits of angelic peace were anxious to have fellowship with those within whose minds they considered there was the purity of good will. They [the angels] were glad that after the dissolution of the flesh those [human beings] would be transported to contemplation of the true peace with them—those [human beings] who, they observed, while they were sojourning in the flesh, brought forth from the root of good will everything which they did or spoke. Now even if perhaps infirmity sometimes, or ignorance, hinders such as these from accomplishing what by their good action they beforehand desire, nevertheless the integrity of the good will which they hold in their heart excuses them in the eyes of the one who examines their inner selves.[39] 'Good will' is to love our Maker from our whole heart, our whole soul, and our whole strength, and our neighbors as ourselves,[40] and to show the vigor of this same love in us by every indication of holy action.

Since we ought to do this at every hour and moment, how much more so when we observe the nativity of our Lord and Savior by [this] annual festivity, or when we recall it by more frequent devotion. Then are we specially taught by angelic exhortation to offer him the votive offerings of good will. Then the citizens of the heavenly fatherland promise to this same good will of ours the company of their peace. Then we are also wont to declare to God the same hymn of the angelic choir. Therefore, dearly beloved brothers, may this solemnity be shared by us—not only may this solemnity be shared by those on earth and those in heaven, but also may all of our way of life be fitting to the company of the heavenly citizens.

Meanwhile, [while we are] on the way, let us meditate on what we desire to have in our fatherland. Let us also be united now, insofar as we are capable, with that most clean life of the blessed Spirits, since we hope then to be associated with the inward purity of [their] mutual love.

---

39. *interni arbitris oculos*   40. Mk 12:30-31

Even in the present, let us eagerly pursue the gifts of divine praising, for which we long to be free of labor in the future. Let us learn to say with the Apostle, *Our way of life is in heaven,*[41] so that we can add with assurance what follows, *from whence also we await the Savior, our Lord Jesus Christ.*[42] Those people await the Savior with joy when he comes to judgment who remember that they have lived their life on earth [directed] toward his heavenly will. Even those of us who are weak and less perfect are given great hope of attaining salvation by our Creator and Savior himself, who, though he appeared weak, for our encouragement soon promised, by the harmonious cry of the heavenly host, [as a reward] for our good will the gifts of his perpetual peace, Jesus Christ, God and our Lord, who lives and reigns with the Father in the unity of the Holy Spirit for all ages. Amen.

41. Ph 3:20a   42. Ph 3:20b

homily 1.7

When the Lord and Savior was born in Bethlehem, as the sacred history of the gospel bears witness, the angel of the Lord appeared with a great light *to shepherds who were watching and keeping watch by night over their flocks in the same region,*[1] and declared to the world that the Sun of justice had arisen,[2] not only by their voice in heavenly utterance, but also by the brightness of a divine light.[3] Nowhere in the whole course of the Old Testament[4] do we find that angels appeared with light, though they frequently appeared to the fathers, but this privilege was properly kept for this day, when *a light arose in the darkness for the righteous, the merciful and compassionate Lord.*[5] But lest the authority of a single angel should seem small, after one [angel] taught the mystery of the new birth, at once there was present a multitude of the heavenly host, who sang, 'Glory to God,' even as they proclaimed peace to human beings, clearly demonstrating that through this nativity human beings were to be directed toward the peace of one faith, hope and love, and to the glory of divine praise.

1. Lk 2:8   2. Ml 4:2   3. Lk 2:9
4. *ueteris instrumenti*   5. Ps 112:4 (111:4)

Mystically, however, these shepherds represent teachers of flocks, and also directors of the souls of the faithful. The night in which they kept watch over their flocks indicates the dangers of temptations, from which all those who watch perfectly do not stop guarding themselves and their subjects. And it is good that when our Lord was born, shepherds were watching over their flocks, for indeed the one born was he who said, *'I am the good shepherd; a good shepherd gives his life for his sheep'.*[6] But the time was drawing near when the same supremely good Shepherd would, by shepherds sent into the world, recall to the always-green pastures of heavenly life his sheep who were wandering, scattered far and wide. Of these [sheep] he commanded the supreme shepherd, *'If you love me, feed my lambs'.*[7] Making this clear he said, *'Strengthen your brothers'.*[8]

And when the angels had withdrawn from them into heaven, it happened that the shepherds were speaking to one another, [saying], 'Let us go over to Bethlehem and see this Word which has come to be, which the Lord has made and shown to us'. And they came hurrying and found Mary and Joseph, and the infant lying in a manger. The shepherds hastened with happy joy to see what they had heard about, and because they sought [it] with a burning love, they were worthy to find immediately the Savior whom they sought.[9] By their words as well as their deeds, they showed the shepherds of spiritual flocks and, moreover, all of the faithful, with what diligence of mind they too ought to be seeking Christ. *'Let us go over,'* they said, *'to Bethlehem and see this Word which has come to be'.*

Let us also, therefore, dearly beloved brothers, go over in thought to Bethlehem, the city of David, and let us also recall [it] with love; let us celebrate [Christ's] incarnation with fitting honors. Having cast aside fleshly concupiscence, let us go over with the whole desire of our mind to the heavenly Bethlehem, that is, the house of living bread, not made by hands[10] but eternal in heaven, and let us lovingly

---

6. Jn 10:11   7. Jn 21:16-17   8. Lk 22:32
9. Greg., *Hom. in evang.* 2, 25, 2 (*PL* 76: 1190); Jer., *Hom. de nat.* (ed. Morin, *Anecd. Mared.* III, 2, 395, 14/15)
10. 2 Co 5:1

recall that the word which was made flesh[11] has ascended in the flesh to where he sits at the right hand of God the Father. Let us follow him to that place with the whole urgency of our virtues, and with solicitous reproof of heart and body let us take care that we may deserve to see reigning in his Father's chair the one they saw crying in a manger.

'And let us see,' they said, *'this Word which has come to be'.* What a right and pure confession of holy faith! *In the beginning was the Word, and the Word was with God, and the Word was God.*[12] The Word born of the Father was not made[1*] because God is not a creature. In this divine nativity he could not be seen by human beings, but that he might be seen *the Word was made flesh and dwelt among us.*[13] Therefore they said, *'Let us see this Word which has come to be* — for before it came to be we were unable to see this [Word]'. [They said,] *'which the Lord has made and shown to us* — what the Lord made to become flesh and thereby displayed to us in visible [form]'.

And they came hurrying and found Mary and Joseph, and the infant lying in a manger. The shepherds came hurrying and found God born as a human being, and at the same time they found those who were ministering to his nativity. We also should hurry, my brothers, not by the steps of our feet, but by progress in good works, to see this same glorified humanity with these same ministers who were rewarded for their service by a worthy prize. Let us hurry to see him shining in divine majesty, which is the Father's and his own. Let us hurry, I say, for such blessedness is not to be sought with idleness and sluggishness, but Christ's footsteps must be followed briskly. He also desires to help our progress by giving us his hand, and he is delighted to hear from us, *'Draw us; we will run after you in the odor of your ointments'.*[14] Let us follow more quickly with the steps of virtues so that we may be worthy to overtake [him]. Let no one be slow to be turned to the Lord; let no one delay from day to day. [Let us] entreat him through all and before all that he may

---

11. Jn 1:14   12. Jn 1:1
13. Jn 1:14; Jer., *Hom. de nat.* (ed. Morin, *Anecd. Mared.* III, 2, 395, 10/12)
14. Sg 1:3

direct our steps according to his word, and that no injustice may have dominion over us.[15]

Once they saw they acknowledged the word that had been said to them about this child. And let us in the meantime hurry, dearly beloved brothers, to perceive with pious faith and to embrace with full love those things which have been said to us about our Savior, [who is] true God and true human being, so that we may be capable of comprehending these things in the future vision which is perfect recognition. For indeed this is the only true life of the blessed, not only of human beings, but of angels as well, to continually behold the face of their Creator, which the psalmist ardently desired [to behold], who said, *My soul has thirsted for the living God; when shall I come and appear before the face of God?*[16] He expressed the fact that his desire could be satisfied by the vision of [God] alone, and not by any superfluity of earthly things, when he said, *I will be satisfied when your glory is manifested.*[17] But since it is not the indifferent and the idle, but those who sweat in working at virtues, who are worthy of divine contemplation, before this he carefully mentioned, *I, however, will appear with justice in your sight.*[18] When the shepherds had seen, therefore, they recognized the word that had been said to them about Christ because the vision of God is a recognition of him, and this is the only blessed life of a human being, as he himself says and bears witness who, when commending us to the Father, said, among other things, *'This, however, is eternal life, that they may recognize you the one true God, and him whom you sent, Jesus Christ'.*[19]

And all who heard marveled at those things which were said to them by the shepherds. The shepherds did not hide in silence the hidden mysteries which they had come to know by divine influence, but they told whomever they could. Spiritual pastors in the Church are appointed especially for this, that they may proclaim the mysteries of the Word of God, and that they may show to their listeners that the marvels which they have learned in the scriptures are to

15. Ps 119:133 (118:133)   16. Ps 42:2 (41:3)   17. Ps 17:15b (16:15b)
18. Ps 17:15a (16:15a)   19. Jn 17:3

be marveled at. It is not only bishops, presbyters, deacons, and even those who govern monasteries, who are to be understood to be pastors, but also all the faithful, who keep watch over the little ones of their house, are properly called 'pastors,' insofar as they preside with solicitous watchfulness over their own house. And the office of pastor should [be acknowledged] in anyone of you who presides over even just one or two brothers by daily guidance, since he is ordered to feed them with a banquet of the word insofar as he is able. Moreover, every single one of you, brothers, who is believed to live as a private person holds the office of pastor, and feeds a spiritual flock, and keeps watch by night over it, if, gathering a multitude of good acts and pure thoughts to himself, he tries to govern them with just control, to nourish them with the heavenly pastures of the scriptures, and by vigilant shrewdness to keep [them safe] against the snares of evil spirits.

But Mary preserved all these words, pondering them in her heart. Abiding by the rules of virginal modesty, Mary wished to divulge to no one the secret things which she knew about Christ, but she reverently waited for the time and place when he would wish to divulge them. However, though her mouth was silent, in her careful, watchful heart she weighed these secret things. And this is what [the evangelist] says, *pondering in her heart*—indeed, she weighed those acts which she saw in relation to those things which she had read were to be done. Now she saw that she herself, who had arisen from the stock of Jesse, had conceived God's Son of the Holy Spirit. She had read in the prophet, *A shoot will sprout from the root of Jesse, and a nazareus will ascend from his root, and the Spirit of the Lord shall rest upon him.* [20] She had read, *And you, Bethlehem Ephrata, are a little one among the thousands of Judah; out of you will come forth for me the one who is ruler in Israel, and his coming forth is from the beginning, from the days of eternity.* [21] She saw that she had given birth in Bethlehem to the Ruler of Israel, who was born eternal from the Father, God before the ages. She saw

20. Is 11:1-2   21. Mi 5:2

that she had conceived as a virgin, and given birth to a son, and called his name Jesus. She had read in the prophets, *Behold, a virgin will conceive and give birth to a son, and his name will be called Emmanuel.*[22] She had read, *An ox recognizes its owner and an ass its master's manger.*[23] She saw the Lord lying in a manger, where an ox and an ass used to come to be nourished. She remembered that it had been said to her by the angel, *'The Holy Spirit will come upon you, and the Power of the Most High will overshadow you, and so the holy one who will be born from you will be called the Son of God'.*[24] She had read that the manner of his nativity could be recognized only by the revelation of an angel, in accordance with Isaiah's saying, *Who will tell of his generation?*[25] She had read, *And you, tower of the flock, misty daughter of Zion, to you shall [it] come, the former power shall come, the kingdom of the daughter of Jerusalem.*[26] She heard that angelic powers, who are daughters of the city on high, had appeared to shepherds in a place which was in former times called 'tower of the flock' from the gathering of cattle—and this is one mile to the east of Bethlehem, and there, even now, the three tombs of these shepherds are pointed out in a church.[27] She then knew that the Lord had come in the flesh, whose power is one and eternal with the Father, and he would give to his daughter the Church the kingdom of the heavenly Jerusalem. Mary was comparing these things which she had read were to occur with those which she recognized as already having occurred.[28] Nevertheless, she did not bring these things forth from her mouth, but kept them closed up in her heart.

And the shepherds went back glorifying and praising God for everything they had heard and seen, just as it was said to them. Let us also learn, dearly beloved brothers, how to be turned from contemplation of the Lord's divinely-arranged plan, by which he deigned to come benevolently to our aid, to

---

22. Is 7:14; Ambr., *Expos. evang. sec. Luc.* 2, 15 (CC 14:38, 237/39)
23. Is 1:3   24. Lk 1:35   25. Is 53:8   26. Mi 4:8
27. Bede, *De loc. sanc.* 7, 3 (CC 175: 265, 20/22); Adamnan., *De loc. sanc.* 2, 6, 1-2 (CC 175: 208, 4/12)
28. Jer., *Hom. de nat.* (ed. Morin, *Anecd. Mared.* III, 2, 396, 2-3)

giving thanks always for his kindnesses. For if they, who as yet only knew about his nativity, went back glorifying and praising God in everything which they had seen and heard, we who know about the whole progress of his incarnation in succession, and who are imbued with his sacraments, are all the more obliged to proclaim his glory and praise in everything, not only in words, but also in deeds, and never to forget that the reason why God was born as a human being was so that he might restore us through our being born anew to the image and likeness of his divinity.[29]

The reason he was baptized with water was so that he might make the flowing of all waters fruitful for the cleansing of our wicked deeds. The reason he was tempted in the desert was so that by being victorious over the tempter he might bestow upon us too knowledge and power to make us victorious. The reason he died was so that he might destroy the sovereignty of death. The reason he rose and ascended into heaven was so that he might present to us a hope and an example of rising from the dead and reigning perpetually in heaven. Having 'gone back' to gaze upon his most benevolent divinely-arranged plan, let us for the sake of each of these [actions] glorify and praise God himself, and our Lord Jesus Christ, who lives and reigns with the Father in the unity of the Holy Spirit for all ages. Amen.

29. Jn 3:3

NOTE

1. Bede's discussion is built around wordplay which is not fully apparent in translation. In the scriptural text (Lk 2:15), the shepherds say 'Let us go over to Bethlehem and see this Word which has come to be' *(hoc uerbum quod factum est)*. Bede then plays this off against the opening of John's gospel, up to Jn 1:14: 'And the Word became flesh' *(uerbum caro factum est)*. Also, in the present case he asserts that the Word born of the Father 'is not made' *(non factum est)*.

homily 1.8

ow that we have acknowledged the birth in time of
the Mediator of God and human beings,[1] the man
Jesus Christ, which occurred today, [which has been]
put before us by the words of the holy evangelists Matthew
and Luke, we can also examine the words of the blessed
evangelist John concerning the eternity of the Word, that
is, concerning the eternity of his divinity, in which he remained always equal to the Father. As a privilege of his singular chastity [John the evangelist] deserved to grasp the
hidden mysteries of [Christ's] divinity at a more profound
level and at the same time to disclose these to others. For
it was not mentioned without reason that at supper he
leaned upon the breast of the Lord Jesus,[2] but through this
we are taught typologically that he drank the draught of
heavenly wisdom from the most holy font of [Jesus's] breast
in a more outstanding way than the other [evangelists].[3]
Hence, in the symbolic representation of the four animals,
[John] is rightly matched with the flying eagle. The eagle,
indeed, is wont to fly higher than all other birds, and to
direct its sight toward the rays of the sun more piercingly

1. 1 Tm 2:5   2. Jn 13:25; 21:20
3. Aug., *Tract. in Ioh.* 36, 1 (CC 36: 323, 16/21)

than all other living things.[4] The other evangelists, as though
they were walking with the Lord on the earth, explained
sufficiently his temporal generation, along with his temporal
deeds, [but] they said little concerning his divinity; [John],
however, as though he were flying to heaven with the Lord,
expounded very few things concerning [Christ's] temporal
acts, [but] by flying more sublimely in mind and watching
more sharply, he recognized the eternal power of [Christ's]
divinity, through which all things come into being, and he
handed this on in writing for us to learn. The other evangelists describe Christ born in time; John bears witness that
this same [Christ] was in the beginning, saying, *In the beginning was the Word.* The others record his sudden appearance among human beings; John declares that he was
always with God, saying, *and the Word was with God.* The
others confirm that he is a true human being; John confirms
that he is true God, saying, *and the Word was God.* The others
[show] that [Christ] was a human being keeping company
for a time with human beings; John shows that he was God
abiding with God in the beginning, saying, *He was in the
beginning with God.* The others testify to the wonders which
[Christ] did as as human being; John teaches that God the
Father made every creature, visible and invisible, through
him, saying, *All things were made through him, and without
him nothing was made.*

And to a remarkable extent blessed John, at the beginning of his gospel, properly imbues [us with] the faith of
believers concerning the divinity of the Savior, and he
powerfully wins out over heretics' lack of faith. Now there
were heretics who said, 'If Christ was born, there was a
time when he did not exist'. [John] refutes them with his
first utterance when he says: *In the beginning was the Word.*
He does not say, 'In the beginning the Word began to be,'
[because he wrote] in order to point out that [Christ's] coming into being was not from time, but that he existed at the
emergence of time,[5] and so that through this [wording] he
might point out that he was born of the Father without any

4. Greg., *Moral.* 31, 47, 94 (CC 143B: 1615, 28 - 1616, 55)
5. var.: 'before the emergence of time'

temporal beginning, according to what he himself said in [the Book of] Proverbs, *The Lord possessed me at the start of his ways, before he made anything from the beginning. From eternity I was appointed.*[6]

In the same way there were heretics who, denying that the holy Trinity is three persons, said, 'The same God is Father when he wills, Son when he wills, Holy Spirit when he wills; nevertheless, he himself is one'. Destroying this error, [John] adds, *And the Word was with God.*[7] For if the one was with the other, unquestionably the Father and the Son are two, and not one as if he himself were now Father, now Son, and now also Holy Spirit, and the nature of the divine substance were mutable. The apostle James says most clearly, *With whom* [God] *there is no transmutation nor shadow of alteration.*[8]

In the same way there were some authors of a wrong-headed dogma who, professing that Christ was only a human being, did not believe that he was God as well. [The evangelist] consequently silences them when he says, *And the Word was God.*

There were others who supposed that [Christ] was God, but made from the time of the incarnation, not eternal and born from the Father before the ages. Hence certain persons of this sort are recorded to have said, 'I do not envy Christ's being made God, for I also, if I will it, can become as he is'.[9] The evangelist refutes their detestable notion when he says, *He was in the beginning with God.* That is, this Word, which is God, did not begin from time, but in the beginning he was God with God.

In the same way there were haters of the truth who did not deny that Christ already existed before his birth from the Virgin, but they nevertheless did not believe that he was God, born of the Father. [Instead they believed] that he was made by the Father, and therefore was less than the Father

---

6. Pr 8:22-23 (Vulg.)
7. Aug., *Serm.* 71, 3, 5 (*PL* 38: 448); *Serm.* 183, 5, 7 (*PL* 38: 990); *Serm.* 3 (ed. Morin, *Misc. Agost.* I, 476, 3 - 477, 8); Bede, *Hom.* II. 24 (*CC* 122: 362, 154/70)
8. Jm 1:17
9. Greg., *Moral.* 18, 52, 85 (*CC* 143A: 948, 34)

because he was a creature. The gospel discourse also condemns them when it says, *All things were made through him, and without him nothing was made.* For if no creature was made without him, it is unquestionably evident that the one through whom every creature was made is not himself a creature.

And lest someone, hearing of a creature made by the Lord, might believe that his will was mutable, as though he suddenly willed to make a creature which he had never before from eternity made, the evangelist clearly teaches that a creature is made in time, but what would be created and when was a decision always in the eternal wisdom of the Creator.

And this is what he says, *That which was made, in him was life.*[1*] That is, whatever was made in time, whether alive or lacking life, appeared in the spiritual judgment of the one who made it[10] as though it had always lived and is alive. It is not that what he created was coeternal with the Creator, but that the judgment of his will is coeternal with him. In [his judgment] from eternity, he possessed and possesses what he would create and when he would create [it], and the way in which he would govern what was created so that it would abide; he would lead each thing to the end for which he had created it.

And the life was the light of human beings. By this sentence we are clearly taught that life-giving judgment,[11] through which all things are arranged and ruled, does not enlighten every creature, but only a rational one, so that it may be able to have consciousness. Human beings, who are made in the image of God, can attain wisdom; beasts cannot.[12] But whatever *human being* is *bestial does not attain those things which are of the Spirit of God.*[13] Hence, when he had said, *And the life was the light of human beings,* it is good that he added [something] about those who, when they become far detached from the honor of the human condition, are compared to ignorant beasts of burden and have become like them,[14] and are properly deprived of the light of truth.

---

10. *spiritali factoris ratione*
11. *ipsa uitalis ratio*
12. Aug., *Tract. in Ioh.* 1, 18 (CC 36: 10, 1/7)
13. 1 Co 2:14
14. Ps 49:12 (48:13)

And the light gives light in the darkness, and the darkness did not comprehend it. The light of human beings is indeed Christ, who illuminates by the presence of his knowledge all the hearts of human beings which are worthy to be enlightened. The stupid and iniquitous are 'darkness'. The light of eternal wisdom clearly recognizes their blind inmost hearts to be of such a sort. They can by no means grasp with their intelligence the rays of this light — just as any blind person can be flooded by the brilliance of the sun, although he himself does not behold the sun, with whose radiance he is bathed. Nevertheless, heavenly benevolence does not entirely despise such ones, but employs for them the cure of salvation, by which they may be able to come to see the light. The very Light invisible, the very Wisdom of God, put on flesh in which he could be seen. Appearing in the condition of a human being and speaking to human beings, he gradually brought hearts purified by faith to the recognition of his divine image.

There was sent before him a man of great merit, by whose testimony all would be prepared to hear the very Wisdom of God as soon as he appeared, and to see the very Sun of justice[15] now covered over by the cloud of [his] body, that is, to see and hear the human being who would be God, *full of grace and truth.*[16] *There was a man sent from God, whose name was John. He came as a witness to bear witness concerning the light, so that all might believe through him.* It does not say, 'That all might believe in him,' *for cursed is a human being who trusts in a human being and makes flesh his arm.*[17] No, it says *that all might believe through him*, that is, that through his testimony they might believe in the light which they were not yet able to see, namely, the Lord Jesus Christ, who bore witness about himself, *'I am the light of the world. One who follows me does not walk in darkness but has the light of life'.*[18]

There follows, *He was not himself the light, but* [came] *to bear witness concerning the light. He* [the Word] *was the true light which enlightens every human being who comes into the world.* Holy human beings are also properly called 'light'.

15. Ml 4:2   16. Jn 1:14   17. Jr 17:5   18. Jn 8:12

The Lord says to them, *'You are the light of the world,'*[19] and the apostle Paul says, *At one time you were darkness; now, however, you are light in the Lord.*[20]

But there is a great difference between a light which is enlightened and light which enlightens; between those who receive a share of the true light so that they may give light, and the perpetual Light itself, which is sufficient to not only give light in itself, but also illuminates by its presence whoever comes into contact with it.[21] Not only for the lesser ones of the elect, but even for John himself (than whom no one of those born of women rose greater),[22] no claim is made to comparison with the true light, so that it may be pointed out that he was not the Christ as was supposed. For, as is written, *He was a lamp burning and giving light,*[23] burning by faith, and giving light in word and action by love. In truth, to communicate the gift of light to hearts is proper only to him concerning whom it is said, *He was the true light which enlightens every human being who comes into the world*—namely, every one who is enlightened either by natural disposition, or certainly by divine wisdom. For just as no one can exist of himself, so also no one can be wise of himself, but by being illuminated by him concerning whom it is written, *All wisdom is from the Lord God.*[24]

Subsequently, the evangelist describes [Christ's] two natures, namely both the divine, in which he always and everywhere remains complete, and the human, by means of which he appeared to be contained by place when he was born in time: *He was in the world, and the world was made through him, and the world did not recognize him. He came to his own, and his own did not accept him.* Indeed, he was in the world and the world was made through him because he was God, because he was complete everywhere, because by the presence of his majesty he ruled without labor, and without burden he held together what he had made.

And the world did not recognize him because *the light gives light in the darkness and the darkness did not comprehend*

19. Mt 5:14   20. Eph 5:8
21. Aug., *Tract. in Ioh.* 2, 6-8 (CC 36: 14, 4 - 16, 23)
22. Mt 11:11; Lk 7:28   23. Jn 5:35   24. Si 1:1

it. Now [the evangelist] says 'the world' in this place [to mean] human beings deceived by love of the world, and by being attached to a creature turned back from acknowledging the majesty of their Creator. *He came to his own* because when he was born he appeared through his humanity in the world which he had made through his divinity. *He came to his own* because he deigned to become incarnate in the nation of Judaea, which he had united to himself beyond other countries by a special grace.

He was in the world, and he came into the world. He was in the world through his divinity; he came into the world through his incarnation. Indeed, to come or to go away is [a function] of humanity; to remain and to exist is one of divinity. Because, therefore, when he was in the world through his divinity, the world did not recognize him, he deigned to come into the world through his humanity so that perhaps thus the world might acknowledge him.

But let us see what follows: *He came to his own, and his own did not accept him.* The one whom they had not recognized as creating and ruling in all the power of his deity, this same one they were unwilling to receive gleaming with miracles in the infirmity of the flesh. And, what is more serious, *his own did not accept him,* the human beings whom he himself created. The Jews whom he had chosen as his own people, among whom he had revealed the hidden mystery of knowledge of himself, whom he had glorified by the wondrous acts of [their] ancestors, to whom he had conferred the teaching of his law, from whom he had promised to take his flesh, and among whom he showed himself incarnate as he had promised—these people for the most part refused to accept him when he came. Not everyone refused; otherwise, no one would have been saved, and his incarnation would have been in vain.

Now, however, many from both peoples have accepted him by believing. The evangelist subsequently suggests something about them, saying, *However, to as many as accepted him he gave the capacity to become sons of God, to those who believe in his name.* Let us consider, dearly beloved brothers, how great is the grace of our Redeemer and how

great is the abundance of his sweetness.[25] He and no other
was born of the Father, and he did not choose to remain
the only one; he descended to the earth where he might
acquire brothers for himself, to whom he could give the
kingdom of his Father.[26] He was born God from God, and
he did not wish to remain only the Son of God; he deigned
to become also Son of man, not losing what he had been,
but taking up what he had not been, so that by this he might
transform human beings into sons of God, and might make
them co-heirs of his glory, and they might by grace begin
to possess what he himself had always possessed by nature.[27]

Let us consider what great power there is in faith, in consequence of which the capacity is given to human beings
to become sons of God. It is well written, *he who is just lives
by faith.*[28] He who is just lives by faith, not that which is
only brought forward in the confession of the lips, but that
which works through love.[29] *Faith, if it does not have works, is
dead in itself.*[30] No one should despise himself; no one should
despair of his salvation. Let each and every one of us make
haste so that we who have been far away may be worthy
to come near in the blood of Christ.[31] Let us look at that
saying, *to as many as accepted him he gave the capacity to become sons of God. To as many,* [the evangelist] says, *as accepted
him—for God is not a respecter of persons, but in every nation
one who fears him and works justice is acceptable to him.*[32]

Following after [this], the evangelist indicates in what way
believers can become sons of God, and how great a difference there is between this generation and the fleshly kind:
Who were not born of blood, he says, *nor of the will of the flesh,
nor of the will of man, but of God.* Indeed, the carnal generation of each of us takes its origin from blood, that is, from
the nature[33] of male and female, and by marital intercourse.
But in truth [our] Spiritual [generation] is provided for by

25. Ps 31:19 (30:20)
26. Aug., *Tract. in Ioh.* 2, 13 (CC 36: 17, 3/12)
27. Bede, *Hom.* I.5 (CC 122: 34, 89/91)
28. Ga 3:11   29. Ga 5:6   30. Jm 2:17
31. Eph 2:13   32. Ac 10:35-36   33. var.: 'seed'

the grace of the Holy Spirit. Distinguishing it from the fleshly, the Lord said, *'Unless someone be born again of water and the Spirit, he cannot enter into the kingdom of God. That which is born of flesh is flesh; that which is born of the Spirit is Spirit'.*[34] But lest anyone doubt that a human being can become a son of God and co-heir with Christ, the evangelist gives an example, that the Son of God himself deigned to become a human being and to dwell among human beings, so that by existing as a sharer of human weakness he might grant to human beings to be sharers in his divine power.[35]

And the Word became flesh and dwelt among us. That is to say: 'and the Son of God became a human being and kept company with human beings'. Now Scripture's practice is to designate the whole human being by the term 'soul' at one time, and by the term 'flesh' at another,[36] 'soul,' for example, as when it is written that Jacob descended into Egypt among seventy souls;[37] 'flesh' as when it is written, *'And all flesh shall see the salvation of God'.*[38] Souls cannot descend into Egypt without bodies, nor can flesh see anything without a soul: the whole man is expressed in the former place by 'soul,' and in the latter by 'flesh'. Thus in this place where it is said, *and the word became flesh*, we should understand nothing other than [we would] if it were said, 'and God became man,' evidently by putting on flesh and soul, so that just as each of us, as one [being], is composed of flesh and soul, so from the time of the incarnation Christ, as one [being], was composed of divinity, flesh, and soul. Existing as true God from eternity to eternity as he had been, he assumed, in time, true humanity, which he had not possessed, in the unity of his person.

There follows: *And we saw his glory, glory as of the only-begotten of the Father, full of grace and truth.* The glory of Christ, which before the incarnation human beings had not been able to see, they did see after the incarnation, as they beheld his humanity shining out from miracles and under-

---

34. Jn 3:5-6
35. Leo, *Serm.* 25 (CC 138: 123, 129/30)
36. Greg., *Hom. in euang.* 2, 25, 4 (PL 76: 1192)
37. Gn 46:27; Dt 10:22   38. Lk 3:6

stood that his divinity was hidden within—especially those who were worthy to contemplate his brightness when he was transfigured on the holy mountain before his passion, *as from out of the magnificent glory a voice came down to him* [speaking] *in this way: 'This is my beloved Son in whom I am well pleased'*[39]; and those who, after the passion looked at the glory of his resurrection and ascension, and were wondrously restored by the gift of his Spirit. By all of these things they clearly recognized that glory of this kind was not appropriate to any of the saints, but only to that human being who, in his divinity, was the only-begotten of the Father.

This follows: *Full of grace and truth.* Filled with grace was that same human being, Christ Jesus, to whom, by a singular favor beyond other mortals, it was given that immediately from the time when he was going to be conceived in the womb of the Virgin and to become a human being, he was also true God. Hence also, the same glorious ever-virgin Mary is rightly believed and confessed to be mother not only of the human being Christ, but also of God. He was also filled with truth, that very divinity of the Word, which had deigned to assume the singularly chosen human being with whom he would be one person, Christ, not altering anything of his divine substance in making his human nature (as heretics wish), but remaining with the Father, completely what he had been, gaining from the seed of David the nature of a true human being, which he had not possessed.

Hence, dearly beloved brothers, we who today recall in yearly devotion the human nativity of our Redeemer, must always embrace his divine nature as well as his human nature with a love that is not yearly, but continual—his divine nature, through which we were created when we did not exist, and his human nature, through which we were recreated when we were lost. Certainly our Maker's divine power was adequate to recreate us without [his] assuming humanity; the human weakness of this Redeemer of ours,

39. 2 P 1:17

however, was unable to recreate us without divinity assuming it and inhabiting it and working through it. And so *the Word became flesh,* that is, God became a human being and dwelt among us, so that by keeping company with us in the form of a human being akin to us, he would be able to unite with us; by speaking to us he would be able to instruct us and present to us a way of living; by dying he would be able to struggle for us against the enemy; by rising he would be able to destroy our death—and so that through a divinity coeternal with the Father's, he might raise us to divine things by bringing us back to life interiorly, he might grant us forgiveness of sins and at the same time the gifts of the Holy Spirit, and after the perfection of good works he might not only lead us to see the glory of his glorified humanity, but also show us the unchangeable essence of his divine majesty, in which he lives and reigns with the Father in the unity of the Holy Spirit throughout all ages. Amen.

NOTE

1. Bede's division of the Johannine text, following Augustine, assumes
   a different punctuation from that which is familiar in modern trans-
   lations. The phrase *'quod factum est'* is normally attached to the preceding clause in verse 3: 'Without him was made nothing *that has been
   made'*. Bede, however, takes this phrase as beginning the sentence
   of verse 4: *'That which was made,* in him was life'. For Augustine's
   explicit defense of this punctuation, which Bede takes for granted,
   see *Tract. in Ioh.* 1.16 (CC 36: 9, 1 - 10, 25).

homily 1.9

John 21:19-24   *Feast of St John the Evangelist*

Each of the words of the lesson from the holy gospel which has been read to us ought to be pondered, my brothers, with very great concentration, since it is so full of the sweetness of heavenly grace. For the most blessed evangelist and apostle John sets down for us the privilege of the preeminent love by which he deserved to be more amply honored by the Lord than the other apostles. He sets down the testimony of the gospel description which, since it rests on divine truth, none of the faithful is permitted to deny. He sets down the tranquil release from his flesh which he attained in a special way when the Lord visited him.

But so that we may be capable of fully considering the beginning of this reading, I would like to reflect briefly on what comes before it. After the resurrection the Lord appeared to seven disciples, among whom were Peter and John. They had been laboring all night without success in fishing, and as [Christ] stood on the shore he filled their net with a huge multitude of fish, and soon, when they had come out [of the boat] onto the land, he invited them to a meal. While they were eating their meal, three times he asked Peter whether he loved him, and three times he confessed his love (because three times [Peter] had denied him),

and three times [Christ] committed to him the feeding of
his sheep. And [Christ] told him that for the sake of the
same sheep, that is, in pastoral care of faithful souls, he
would come to the martyrdom of the cross, saying, *'Amen,
amen, I say to you, when you were young you girded yourself
and walked where you wished. However, when you are old you
will extend your hands, and another will gird you and lead you
where you do not wish'.*[1] Now in [referring to] the extension
of his hands [Christ] indicated that [Peter] would be
crowned by martyrdom through the death of a cross; in
[referring to] being girded by another, that he would be
overcome by a persecutor; in [saying that] he was going to
be led where he did not wish, that he would suffer the torments of suffering against his will in his human weakness.
But lest perhaps the suffering on a cross predicted by the
Lord might seem to Peter hard to bear, [Christ] took care
to assuage this right away with his own example, so that
he might bear the agony of martyrdom more easily when
he remembered that he had received a sentence of death
like that of his Redeemer.[1]*

After [Christ] had signified to [Peter] by what death he
was to glorify God, he straightaway continued with what
we heard in the first part of this reading. *And He said to him,
'Follow me'.* It is as if he were clearly saying, 'Since previously I did not fear to take on the torment of the cross for
your redemption, why do you dread to suffer the cross for
the confession of my name, you who will be glorified by
a more glorious palm of martyrdom when you follow the
path of your master to merit it'?

At this point the evangelist does not go on to say what
the Lord and the disciples did after these things were said,
but nevertheless some idea is given from what he adds:
*When he turned, Peter saw the disciple whom Jesus loved follow-
ing.* Now apparently when [Christ] said to Peter, *'Follow me'*
(that is, 'Imitate me by suffering the cross'), he rose from
the place of the feast and then began to go away. Peter followed him, desiring to fulfill what he had heard (namely,

1. Jn 21:18

'*Follow me'*) by the movement of his feet. And the disciple whom Jesus loved also followed. He did not suppose that he was to be prevented from the following of Christ, since he knew that he had been included by Christ in no less a grace of love. And so it is not hard to believe that both disciples followed the footsteps of the Lord with their bodily steps because they did not yet understand what he signified when he commanded Peter to follow him.

I know that it is known to you of the brotherhood who 'the disciple whom Jesus loved' is, namely John himself, whose heavenly birthday we celebrate today—the one who wrote this gospel, and so preferred to designate his person by the indication of things appertaining [to himself] rather than by his own name. Jesus did not love him alone in a singular way to the exclusion of the others, but he loved [John] beyond those whom he loved, in a more intimate way as one whom the special prerogative of chastity had made worthy of fuller love. Indeed, he proved that he loved them all when before his passion he said to them, '*As the Father has loved me, I have also loved you. Remain in my love'.*[2] But beyond the others he loved the one who, being a virgin when chosen by him, remained forever a virgin. Now stories handed down say that [Christ] called [John] from his marriage ceremony when he wished to marry, and on that account he granted the more desirable sweetness of his own love to one whom he had withdrawn from fleshly pleasures.[3] Accordingly, when [Christ] was about to die on the cross, he commended his mother to [John],[4] so that virgin might watch over virgin, and when he himself ascended to heaven after his death and resurrection, a son would not be lacking to his mother, whose chaste life would be protected by his chaste services.

The blessed John also puts down another indication of his identity when he adds [to verse 20], '*the one who at*

---

2. Jn 15:9
3. *Praefatio uel argumentum Iohannis* (Wordsworth & White, *Nouum Testamentum Latine, Euangelia*, 485-89); cf. R.A. Lipsius, *Die apokryphen Apostelgeschichten und Apostellegenden*, I, 408-33
4. Jn 19:26-7

*supper leaned upon his breast and said, 'Lord, who is it who will
betray you'?* Earlier places in this gospel show more fully how
this happened, namely that at the supper which the Savior held as the last [supper] with his disciples before his passion, where he washed their feet and handed over to them
the mysteries of his body and blood to be celebrated, the
disciple whom he loved leaned upon his breast. And when
[Jesus] said to them, *'Amen, amen, I say to you that one of you
will betray me,'*[5] that disciple, when Peter made signs that
he should ask, said to [Jesus] in response, *'Lord, who is it'*?
And the Lord said, *'It is the one to whom I shall hold out the
bread which has been dipped'.*[6]

This disciple's leaning upon the master's breast was not
only a sign of present love, but also of future mystery. Already at that time it was prefigured that the gospel which
this same disciple was going to write would include the hidden mysteries of divine majesty more copiously and pro-
foundly than the rest of the pages of sacred scripture. For
because in Jesus' breast *are hidden all the treasures of wisdom
and knowledge,*[7] it was fitting that the one who leaned upon
his breast was the one to whom he had granted a larger
gift of unique wisdom and knowledge than to the rest. Indeed, we know that the rest of the evangelists spoke more
about our Savior's miracles and less about his divinity. John,
however, wrote very little about [Christ's] human acts, and
instead applied himself to explaining the hidden mysteries
of his divine nature, unmistakably suggesting [by this] what
great matters of heavenly teaching he had imbibed from Jesus' breast, and which he was pouring forth for us.[8]

There follows, *Peter, therefore, seeing him, said to Jesus, 'Lord,
what of this man'?* Because blessed Peter had heard that he
himself was going to glorify God through the suffering of
the cross, he wished to know about his brother and fellow-
disciple as well, by what death he was going to pass over
from death to eternal life.

---

5. Jn 13:21   6. Jn 13:25-26   7. Col 2:3
8. Aug., *De cons. evang.* (*CSEL* 43, 7, 13/16); *Tract. in Ioh.* 36, 1 (CC 36:
   323, 5/17)

Jesus said to him, 'I wish him to remain thus until I come. What is that to you? You follow me'. He said, 'I do not wish that he be brought to perfection through the suffering of martyrdom, but that without [undergoing] violence from a persecutor he wait for the last day, when I will come myself and receive him into the mansion of eternal blessedness. And what is that to you? Only remember that you are to follow in my footsteps by going to the gibbet of the cross'.

The brothers of that time took this response of the Lord to mean that John was never to die. John himself took care to advise that it should not be so understood, for when he mentioned that this utterance had gone out among the brothers, that that disciple was not to die,[9] he meticulously inserted the statement, *And Jesus did not say to him, 'He is not to die,'* but, *'I wish him to remain thus until I come. What is that to you'?* It was not to be supposed, therefore, that that disciple was not going to die in the flesh, for the Lord did not predict concerning him that this would be, and the psalmist says, *Who is the man who lives and will not see death?*[10] Rather it was to be understood thus—that while the rest of Christ's disciples were brought to perfection through suffering, he would wait in the peace of the Church for the coming of his heavenly calling. And what the Lord said was this, *'I wish him to remain thus until I come'* — not that he would not first undergo for the Lord's sake many labors and distresses from evil people, but that he would conclude his final old age in peace, after the churches of Christ had been founded far and wide throughout Asia, where he ruled.

Now in the Acts of the Apostles it is found that he was scourged with the rest of the apostles when *they went forth rejoicing from the presence of the council, since they were accounted worthy to suffer indignity for Jesus' name.*[11] And it is told in church history how he was put by the emperor Domitian into a tub of boiling oil, from which, since divine grace shielded him, he came out untouched, just as he had been

9. Jn 21:23   10. Ps 89:48 (88:49)   11. Ac 5:41

a stranger to the corruption of fleshly concupiscence. And not much after, on account of his unconquerable constancy in bringing the good news, he was banished in exile by the same prince to the island of Patmos,[12] where although he was deprived of human comfort, he nevertheless merited to be relieved by the frequent consolation of the divine vision and spoken message. Accordingly, in that very place he composed with his own hand the Apocalypse, which the Lord revealed to him concerning the present and future state of the Church.[13]

Hence it is sure that the promise of his remaining thus until the Lord would come did not point to the former [meaning, namely] that he would be victorious in the world without laboring in a struggle, but rather to the latter, [namely] that he would pass over from the world without the pain of suffering. For as we find in the writings of the fathers, when he had reached a ripe old age he knew that the day of his passing away was drawing near; his disciples were called together and, after advising them with exhortations and the celebration of mass, he said his last goodbyes to them. Then he descended into the place dug for his grave, and when the prayers had been performed, he was taken to his fathers, being found as free of the pain of death as he was a stranger to the corruption of the flesh. And so was brought to fulfillment that true statement of the Savior, that he wished [John] to remain thus until he himself should come.

However, mystically speaking we can take these things which were predicted by the Lord to Peter and John, and which [later] took place, as designating the two ways of life in the Church which are carried out in the present, namely the active and the contemplative. Of these, the active is the way of living common to [all] the people of God. Very few ascend to the contemplative, and these more sublime ones

---

12. Jer., *Adv. Iov.* 1, 26 (*PL* 23: 247); *In Matth.* 20, 23 (*CC* 77: 178, 1074/1079)

13. Jer., *De vir. ill.* 9 (*TU* 14: 13, 25/27); Eusebius/Rufinus, *Hist. Eccl.* (*GCS* 9: 231, 14/16); cf. P. Corssen, *Monarchianische Prologe zu den Vier Evangelien* (*TU* 15: 78-82)

[do so] after [achieving] perfection in good deeds. The active life is Christ's zealous servant devoting himself to righteous labors: first to keeping himself unspotted by this world,[14] keeping his mind, hand, tongue, and the other members of his body from every stain of tempting fault,[15] and to perpetually subjugating himself to divine servitude; and then also to coming to the aid of his neighbor in need, according to his ability, by ministering with food to the hungry, drink to the thirsty, clothing to those who feel the cold, by receiving the needy and the wandering into his house, by visiting the sick and burying the dead,[16] by snatching a destitute [person] from the hand of one stronger than he, and a poor and needy man from those laying hold of him;[17] and also by showing the way of truth to the erring,[18] by delivering himself up for others in services of brotherly love, and by struggling, moreover, for justice even to the point of death.

The contemplative life, however, is [lived] when one who has been taught by the long practice of good actions, instructed by the sweetness of prolonged prayer, and habituated by the frequent sting of tears, learns to be free of all affairs of the world and to direct the eye of his mind toward love alone; and he begins, even in the present life, to gain a foretaste of the joy of the perpetual blessedness which he is to attain in the future, by ardently desiring it, and even sometimes, insofar as is permitted to mortals, by contemplating it sublimely in mental ecstasy. This life of divine contemplation especially takes in those who, after long [practice in] the rudiments of monastic virtue, spend their lives cut off from human beings, knowing that they will have a mind which is freer for meditating on heavenly things inasmuch as it has been separated from earthly tumults.

Now the active life is proposed as something to be entered upon not only by monks in community, but, as we have said, also by all the people of God in general. And

---

14. Jm 1:27
15. 2 Co 7:1
16. Mt 25:35-36; Is 58:7; Si 7:32-35
17. Ps 35:10 (34:10)
18. Jm 5:19-20

although it is a fact that both apostles (namely, both Peter and John) held a high place among human beings for their outstanding grace, and each was perfected in both [types of] life, nevertheless, one life is designated by Peter and the other by John. For that which the Lord said to Peter, *'You will extend your hands, and another will gird you and lead you where you do not wish,'* represented the perfection of the active way of life, which is normally proven by the fire of temptations. Hence elsewhere he says more clearly about this, *'Blessed are you who suffer persecution on account of justice'.*[19] To [his words to Peter] he properly adds, *'Follow me,'* because undoubtedly, according to the words of the same Peter, *Christ has suffered for us, leaving us an example that we may follow in his footsteps.*[20]

[Christ's] saying about John, *'I wish him to remain thus until I come,'* suggests the state of contemplative virtue, which is not to be ended through death, as the active life is, but after death is to be more perfectly completed with the coming of the Lord.[21] Now active labor, when it comes to an end with death, will receive an eternal reward after death. For who gives bread to the hungry in that life where no one hungers? Who gives water to the thirsty where no one thirsts? Who buries the dead where it is *the land of the living*[22]? Who carries out the rest of the works of mercy where no one is found to be in need of mercy? And so no laborious action will be there, but only the everlasting fruit of past action. Contemplative happiness, however, which commences here, will there be made perfect without end when the presence of the heavenly citizens and of the Lord himself will be seen, not through a mirror and in a dark manner as now, but face to face.[23] Hence about this [life], Jesus properly said under the image of the disciple whom he loved and whom he made to lean upon his breast, *'I wish him to remain thus until I come'.* It is as if he were clearly saying, 'I do not want the taste of contemplative delight, which I especially love in my saints, who are hoping in the

---

19. Mt 5:10   20. 1 P 2:21
21. Aug., *Tract. in Ioh.* 124, 5 (CC 36: 685, 75 - 686, 116)
22. Ps 27:13 (26:13)   23. 1 Co 13:12

protection of my wings, inebriated by the abundance of my house, and who have been made to drink from the torrent of my refreshment[24] — I do not want this to be ended by the act of dying, as [happens after] laborious action, but [I wish it] to be more sublimely perfected after death, when I will appear and lead them into the sight of my majesty'.

There follows: *This is the disciple who gives testimony concerning these things and who has written these things, and we know that his testimony is true.* At this point, blessed John clearly designates his person from his office, though he avoids designating himself by name. However, we should not pass over looking at his saying, *he who gives testimony concerning these things and who has written these things.* He gave testimony to the word of God by preaching, he gave it by writing, he gave it in turn by teaching the things which he had written, [and] he gives it also at this point by disseminating the gospel, which he wrote to the churches to be read. From the time of the Lord's passion, resurrection and ascension into heaven, up until the last years of the ruler Domitian, during about sixty-five years, he had preached the word without any supporting base in writing.

But when he was sent into exile by Domitian, who was the second persecutor of the Christians after Nero, there were heretics forcing their way into the Church, like wolves into a sheepfold devoid of a shepherd—Marcion, Cherinthus, Ebius, and other antichrists, who denied that Christ had existed before Mary, and who soiled the simplicity of the gospel faith with their perverse teachings. But when, after the killing of Domitian, he returned to Ephesus with the permission of the pious ruler Nerva, he was compelled by almost all of the bishops then in Asia and by delegations from many churches to compose a discourse at a more profound level concerning Christ's coeternal divinity with the Father,[25] because it seemed to them that in the writings of the [other] three evangelists, namely Matthew, Mark and Luke, they had sufficient testimony concerning [Christ's] humanity and the things which he had done as a human

---

24. Ps 36:7-8 (35:8-9)
25. Jer., *De vir. ill.* 9 (TU 14: 12, 31 - 13, 32)

being. He responded that he would not do so unless, with the proclamation of a fast, everyone were together to entreat the Lord that he might be able to write worthy things. And when this had been carried out, instructed by revelation and intoxicated by the grace of the Holy Spirit, he drove out all the darkness of the heretics by a suddenly-disclosed light of truth, affirming, *In the beginning was the Word, and the Word was with God, and the Word was God.*[26] And making the whole course of his discourse similar to its start, he taught with the clearest of assertions that just as our Lord Jesus Christ truly became, in time, a true human being from a human being, so also as true God he was truly born, in eternity, from God the Father, [and] he truly always existed with the Father and the Holy Spirit. However, with the clearest of assertions, [John] disclosed all the hidden mysteries of divine truth and true divinity, to an extent that was permitted to no other mortals. And this privilege was properly kept for a virgin, so that he might put forth for consideration the mysteries of the incorruptible Word, having not only an incorrupt heart, but also an incorrupt body. So that no one might call into question the truth of his sayings, he himself took care to show it, for when he had said, *This is the disciple who gives testimony concerning these things, and who has written these things,* he immediately attached this statement, *And we know that his testimony is true.* Therefore, because we also, with the rest of the faithful, know that his testimony is true, let us in all things, by understanding with right faith what he taught, and carrying it out with right working, take care to come to the undying gifts which he promised through our Lord Jesus Christ, who lives and reigns with the Father in the unity of the Holy Spirit throughout all ages. Amen.

26. Jn 1:1; Jer., *In Matth.* Pref. (CC 77: 2, 42 - 3, 55)

NOTE

1. From this point on, excerpts from this homily were printed among the sermons of St. Augustine in *Noua Patrum Bibliotheca*, ed. A. Mai (I, 378-9, 381, 1, 2, and 5).

homily 1.10

The sacred reading of the gospel which has been read out to us is about the precious death of the innocent martyrs of Christ, dearly beloved brothers. Nevertheless, in this [death] is represented the precious death[1] of all Christ's martyrs. The fact that little children were killed signifies that through the merit of humility one comes to the glory of martyrdom, and that unless one has turned and become as a little child,[2] one will not be able to give one's life for Christ. The fact that they were killed *in Bethlehem and in all its regions* shows that not only in Judaea, where the Church originally began, but in all the regions of that same Church, wherever throughout the world it was spread, persecution by those who lack faith would rage, and the patience of the holy would be crowned. Those killed at two years old indicate those who are perfect in teaching and working, but those under [two years] denote the simple or the ordinary people, who nevertheless have a faith which is not feigned,[3] and who are likewise strong in constancy. The fact that they were killed, but Christ, who was being sought, escaped alive, suggests that bodies[4] can be deprived

1. Ps 116:15 (115:15)   2. Mt 18:3   3. 1 Tm 1:5
4. var.: 'the bodies of the martyrs'

96

of life by the godless, but that Christ, for whom the whole persecution raged, could in no way be taken from them, either from the living or from those who had been killed, but that they were called to witness truthfully that *if we live, we live to the Lord; if we die, we die to the Lord. For whether we live or die, we are the Lord's.*[5]

According to the oracle of Jeremiah, *A voice was heard in Rama,* that is, 'on high,'[6] *of lamentation and great wailing.*[7] This clearly denotes that holy Church's mourning, by which she grieves for the violent death of her members, does not, as our enemies foolishly claim, pass away into a void, but it ascends right to the throne of the heavenly Judge; and like the protomartyr Abel's blood,[8] so also that of the other martyrs cries out from the earth to the Lord, in accordance with that [saying] of the wise man, *He will not scorn the petition of the orphan, nor the widow if she pours forth an expression of grief. Do not the widow's tears descend on her cheek, and her cry upon the one who causes them? For from her cheek they ascend up to heaven and the Lord who hears does not take delight in them.*[9]

The fact that Rachel is said to have bewailed her children, and not wished to be consoled *because they are not* signifies that the Church bewails the removal of the saints from this world, but she does not wish to be consoled in such a way that those who have been victorious over the world by death should return once again to bear with her the strife of the world, for surely they should no longer be called back into the world from whose hardships they have once escaped to Christ for their crowning. Now figuratively speaking, Rachel, which means 'sheep' or 'seeing God,'[10] stands for the Church, who with her whole attention keeps watch so that she may deserve to see God. And she is that hundredth sheep whom the good shepherd goes out to seek on earth, having left behind the ninety-nine sheep of the angelic

---

5. Rm 14:8
7. Jr 31:15
9. Si 35:17-19

6. Jer., *Nom.* (CC 72: 138, 2)
8. Gn 4:10
10. Jer., *Nom.* (CC 72: 70, 25/26)

virtues in heaven; and when he finds her, he puts her on his shoulders and carries her back to the flock.[11]

However, according to the literal sense, the question arises how it may be said that Rachel bewailed her children, since the tribe of Judah, which contained Bethlehem, sprang not from Rachel, but from her sister Leah. The answer is easily come by in this case, because the children were slaughtered not only in Bethlehem, but also in all its regions. The tribe of Benjamin, which sprang from Rachel, was neighbor to the tribe of Judah. Hence we should rightly believe that the area where this most cruel slaughter occurred also included no small number of children of the stock of Benjamin, and Rachel bewailed these descendants with her voice raised on high.[12]

It can also be understood in another way: Rachel was buried close to Bethlehem, just as the inscription of her tomb, which remains until today to the west of the city beyond the road which leads to Hebron, bears witness;[13] wherefore, in the manner of prophetic speech she is properly said to have done those things which were done in that place, since the place itself was distinguished by her body and her name.

The fact that the Lord himself was taken by his parents into Egypt, so that he would not be killed by Herod, signifies that the elect will very often have to flee from their places, or even be condemned to exile, because of the outrageous behavior of the wicked. Here also an example is given to the faithful that they should not hesitate to turn away from the ferocity of persecutors by fleeing when there is a chance to do so, since they will remember that their Lord and God did this. He himself, who would command them, *'When you are persecuted in one city, flee to another,'*[14] first did what he commanded by fleeing as a human being

---

11. Lk 15:4-5; Ambr., *Expos. evang. sec. Luc.* 7, 209-10 (CC 14: 287, 2316/27)
12. Jer., *In Matth.* 2, 17-18 (CC 77: 15, 177/85)
13. Gn 35:19-20; Bede, *De loc. sanc.* 7, 4 (CC 175: 265, 25/27); Adamnan., *De loc. sanc.* 2, 7, 1-3 (CC 175: 208, 1 - 209, 10)
14. Mt 10:23

from a human being, in the land where a little while before the star from heaven had pointed him out to the magi.[15]

Not long after the children had been killed in place of the Lord, Herod met his death, and Joseph, upon an angel's advice, returned the Lord with his mother to the land of Israel. This signifies that all persecutions which were to be brought against the Church would be avenged by the death of the persecutors themselves, and when these persecutors had been given their just deserts, peace would be restored to the Church, and the saints who had been in hiding would return to their places.

We can also take Herod's hatred, by which he wished that Jesus would perish, as concerning especially the persecutions which happened in Judaea in the time of the apostles, when, as envy increased in strength, almost all the preachers of the word were expelled from the province, and those who were going to preach among the nations were scattered far and wide. It happened in this way so that the gentile world, which was prefigured by Egypt, even though it had before been darkened by sins, might attain the light of the word. For this is [the meaning of] the boy Jesus and his mother being conveyed by Joseph to Egypt, namely that the faith of the Lord's incarnation and the fellowship of the Church was committed to the nations by holy teachers.

Figuratively speaking, their being in Egypt up to [the time of] Herod's meeting his death indicates that the faith of Christ would remain among the nations until their full number would come into [the Church],[16] and thus all of Israel would be saved. Herod's meeting his death suggests the end of the malicious intention with which Judaea at that time raged against the Church. The killing of little children designates the death of those humble in spirit whom the Jews deprived of life when they had disposed of Christ. The fact that when Herod was dead, Jesus returned to the land of Israel denotes the end of the world, when with the preaching of Enoch and Elijah, the Jews will have received faith in the truth and the flame of their present-day envy

15. Some MSS add: 'to be adored as God'
16. Rm 11:25-26

will have been put to rest. And it is good that when he leaves
Judaea, it is said that he fled this place in the night,[17] but
when he comes back no mention is made of flight, nor of
night, for undoubtedly those whom he left were once persecutors, on account of the darkness of their sins, [while] those
whom he sees again were finally seeking him on account
of the light of faith.

Although [Jesus] was condemned by Herod, it was for
fear of Archelaus his son that Joseph dreaded to go to
Judaea, where he had his capital, [and] as an angel warned
him, he withdrew to Nazareth in Galilee. This designates
the last times of the Church of the present age, when, in
place of the universal blindness which is now [characteristic]
of that nation, in virtue of which they do not stop persecuting Christians to the extent that they are able, a fiercer persecution by the antichrist will arise among certain ones, and,
although quite a few will have been converted from their
lack of faith by the preaching of Enoch and Elijah, the rest
will go on battling with all their might against the faith at
the instigation of the antichrist. Therefore the part of Judaea
where Archelaus was reigning shows us the unbelieving
followers of the antichrist.

Nazareth in Galilee, where the Lord was taken, designates
that part of the same nation which would then, in time, wel-
come the faith of Christ. Hence it is good that Galilee means
'an emigration completed,'[18] and Nazareth means 'a flower'
or its 'vegetation,'[19] for undoubtedly the more ardent the
desire with which holy Church emigrates from the things
which she sees on earth to heavenly things which are to
be earned, the more she will overflow with the flower and
branch of spiritual virtues.

Hence it is fitting that we venerate the first fruits of the
martyrs by today's feast, dearly beloved brothers, and let
us think attentively about the eternal feast of the martyrs,
which is in heaven, and by following in their footsteps insofar as we can, let us also take care to become ourselves

17. Jer., *In Matth.* 2, 13 (CC 77: 14, 158/61)
18. Jer., *Nom.* (CC 72: 140, 25)
19. Jer., *Nom.* (CC 72: 137, 24/25)

participants in this heavenly feast, for, as the Apostle bears witness, if we have been companions of his passion, we will at the same time be companions of his consolation.[20] Nor should we mourn their death[21] as much as we should rejoice about their attaining the palm of righteousness.[22] Rachel must groan over each of them when, through torments, they are driven away from this life—that is, the Church which begot [them] escorts them with mourning and tears, but when they have been driven out, the heavenly Jerusalem, who is the mother of us all,[23] soon receives them into another life by ministers of gladness who are ready at hand, and introduces them into the joy of the Lord to be crowned as his forever.

Hence, says John, they were standing before the throne *in the sight of the Lamb, dressed in white robes, and palms were in their hands.*[24] For they now stand before God's throne, crowned, who once lay, worn down by pain, before the thrones of earthly judges. They stand in the sight of the Lamb, and for no cause can they be separated from contemplating his glory there, since here they could not be separated from his love through punishments. They shine in white robes, and have palms in their hands, who possess the rewards for their works; while they get back their bodies, glorified through resurrection, which for the Lord's sake they suffered to be scorched by flames, torn to pieces by beasts, worn out by scourges, broken by falls from high places, scraped by hoofs, and completely destroyed by every kind of punishment.

And they were crying out, he says, *with a loud voice, saying, 'Salvation from our God, who sits upon the throne, and from the Lamb'.*[25] With a loud voice they sing of salvation from God, since they recall with great giving of thanks that they have triumphed, not by their own virtue but by his help, in the struggle with the tribulations assailing them.

Again, he says of them, describing their past struggles and their everlasting crowns, *'These are they who have come*

---

20. 2 Co 1:7   21. var.: 'their unjust death'
22. var.: 'their just attaining of the palm'
23. Ga 4:26   24. Rv 7:9   25. Rv 7:10

*out of the great tribulation, and have washed their robes and made
them white in the blood of the Lamb'*.[26] Martyrs wash their robes
in the blood of the Lamb, while as for their members, which
seem to the eyes of the ignorant[27] [to be] defiled by the squalor
of their pains, they instead have made [these members]
clean of all contagion by their blood which is poured forth
for Christ. In addition, they have rendered [their members]
worthy of the blessed light of immortality, which is [the
meaning of] their having made their washed robes white
in the blood of the lamb. *'Therefore they are,'* he says, *'before
the throne of God and serve him day and night in his temple'*.[28]
To be continually present at the praises of God is not a
laborious servitude, but a servitude which is pleasant and
desirable. ' Day and night,' indeed, do not exclusively signify the vicissitude of time, but typologically [they signify]
its perpetuity. *For there will be no night there,*[29] but one day
in the courts of Christ will be better than thousands,[30] when
Rachel will not bewail her children, but *'God will wipe away
every tear from their eyes,'*[31] and give them the voice of gladness and of eternal salvation in their tabernacles,[32] he who
lives and reigns with the Father in the unity of the Holy
Spirit for ages and ages. Amen.

26. Rv 7:14   27. Ws 3:2   28. Rv 7:15
29. Rv 21:25   30. Ps 84:10 (83:11) 31. Rv 7:17; 21:4
32. Ps 118:15 (117:15)

homily 1.11

The evangelist seizes in a few words the holy and venerable subject of the present feast, but he leaves it laden
with no small power of heavenly mystery. The angels
proclaimed the joys of the Lord's nativity with praises worthy of its glory; the shepherds celebrated [the occasion] by
visiting devoutly; all who then heard marvelled at it, and
we also have very recently taken time to [celebrate] it to the
best of our abilities with fitting solemnities of masses and
hymns, as the Lord has granted us to do.

After his explanation of the Lord's nativity, [the evan-
gelist] added this statement: *And after eight days were over,
so that the boy might be circumcised, his name was called Jesus,
which is what he was called by the angel before he was conceived
in the womb.* These are the joys of today's feast which are
to be venerated; this is the solemnity of a sacred day; these
are the most sacred gifts of divine benevolence which the
Apostle commends to the hearts of the faithful when he
says, *When the fullness of time came, God sent his Son, born
of a woman, born under the law, so that he might redeem those
who were under the law, that we might receive the adoption of
sons.*[1]

1. Ga 4:4-5

By a great divinely-arranged plan, God the Father in his
benevolence deigned to send not an angel or an archangel,
but his only-begotten Son, for the redemption of the human race. Because we were unable to see him in the splendor of his divinity, he provided[2] by a great exercise of his
love that he should bring him forth *born of a woman*, that
is, conceived of the substance of her maternal flesh, without male participation, a true human being in his appearance to human beings.[3] Although in his divine power and
substance he would remain in all respects what he was, he
would put on the true weakness of a mortal nature, which
he did not [before] have. And in order to set forth for us
the necessity of the virtue of obedience by a preeminent example, God sent his Son into the world *born under the law*,
not that he should be under any obligation to the law, for
One is our master,[4] one is lawgiver and judge, but so that
he might by his compassion help those under the law who
were unable to carry the burdens of the law, and so that,
when they had been snatched from the servile condition
which was theirs under the law, he might lead them by his
bounty to the *adoption of sons*, which is by grace.

He therefore received in the flesh the circumcision decreed
by the law, although he appeared in the flesh absolutely
without any blemish of pollution. And he who came in the
likeness of sinful flesh[5] — not in sinful flesh — did not turn
away from the remedy by which sinful flesh was ordinarily
made clean; just as not because of necessity, but for the sake
of example, he also submitted to the water of baptism, by
which he wished the people of the new [law of] grace to
be washed from the stain of sins.[6] For you of the brotherhood ought to be aware that, under the law, circumcision
offered the same help of a health-giving treatment against
the wound of original sin that now, in the time of revealed
grace, baptism is wont to do, except that they [who were

2. *prouidit*, a well-attested MS. variant for *praeuidit*, 'foresaw'
3. Aug., *Ad Gal.* 30 (*PL* 35: 2126); *Tract. in Ioh.* 4, 10 (*CC* 36: 36, 14/21)
4. Mt 23:8
5. Rm 8:3
6. Aug., *Contra Litt. Pet.* 2, 36, 87; 72, 162 (*PL* 43: 290; 309); *Tract. in Ioh.* 4, 13 (*CC* 36: 37, 1/7)

under the law] could not yet enter the gate of the heavenly kingdom, until by his coming he who gave the law would give his blessing, that the God of gods might be seen in Zion;[7] and so, consoled in the bosom of Abraham by a blessed rest after death, they awaited with blissful hope their entry into heavenly peace. For the one who now cries out in a terrible but saving way through his evangelist, *'Unless a man shall be reborn of water and the Spirit, he cannot enter the kingdom of God,'*[8] is the one who previously cried out through his law, *A male, the flesh of whose foreskin is uncircumcised, that soul shall vanish from his people because he has made my pact null and void.*[9] That is, because Adam by his transgression went against the pact of life given to human beings in paradise, and in him all sinned,[10] [a person] will vanish from the society of the saints if he is not aided by a saving remedy.[11] Both purifications, namely that of circumcision under the law and that of baptism under the gospel, were provided as graces for taking away the first transgression.

And so that the favors of heavenly condescension might not be lacking to any period of this transitory world, those who [lived] from the inception of the world up to the time of the giving of circumcision, and those from other countries who [lived] after the giving of circumcision, also pleased God, either by the offering of sacrificial offerings, or alternatively by the virtue of faith alone, since they committed their souls and those of their own to the Creator, [and so] took care to free [themselves] from the bonds of the original guilt. For *without faith it is impossible to please God.*[12] And, as it is written in another place, *The just man lives by faith.*[13]

When the Son of God came in the flesh, since he took from Adam only the nature of flesh and no contagion of sin, and because he was conceived and born of a virgin by the power of the Holy Spirit, he stood in no need of the

---

7. Ps 84:7 (83:8)   8. Jn 3:5   9. Gn 17:14
10. Rm 5:14,12
11. Aug., *De Civ. Dei* 16, 27 (CC 48: 531, 1 - 532, 35); *Contra Iul.* 2, 6, 18; 6, 7, 18-21 (*PL* 44: 686; 833-35); *De Nupt. et Concup.* 2, 11, 24 (*CSEL* 42: 276, 3 - 277, 19); *Serm.* 2 (ed. Morin, *Misc. Agost.* I, 694, 5/12)
12. Heb 11:6   13. Rm 1:17

favor of the grace of rebirth. [But] he deigned to submit to
both kinds of purification, being circumcized by his parents
eight days after his birth, and being baptized by John at
thirty years of age. Moreover, the Lord of the temple also
did not turn away from a third duty, that of being offered
himself as a saving sacrificial victim for his own sake[14] —
with the Lord's assistance you dear ones will hear of this,
and at the same time celebrate the mystery,thirty-three days
from now. The Lord did not scorn to adopt all kinds of
purification, I say, those of the law and of the gospel, though
he did not stand in need of any, in order to teach that the
decrees of the law were most salutary, though it was then
in his time about to be brought to perfection, and in order
to show that with the coming of the gospel remedies, all
the faithful were likewise to submit to them.

On the day of his circumcision he received a name, that
he might be called Jesus. He did this in imitation of a former
observance which, as I believe, was based upon the fact that
the patriarch Abraham, who first received the sacrament
of circumcision in testimony of his great faith and of the
divine promise to him, upon the same day as that of his
own circumcision and that of his [male relatives], merited
to be blessed together with his wife, by the amplification
of his name. He who until then had been Abram (that is,
'lofty father') would henceforth be called Abraham (that is,
'father of many nations'),[15] *'for I have established you as father*
of many nations'.[16] It is evident that this most trustworthy
promise has now been fulfilled so widely throughout the
world that even we ourselves, who have been called from
the nations to the practice of his faith, may rejoice in spiritually having him as our father, even as the Apostle says to
us, *If you are Christ's, therefore you are the seed of Abraham,*
heirs according to the promise.[17] [God] said, *'And you shall not*
call your wife Sarai but Sara,'[18] that is, 'You shall not call her
"my ruler," but "ruler," '[19] teaching clearly that since

---

14. Lk 2:22; Lv 12:2-4
15. Aug., *De Civ. Dei* 16, 28 (CC 48: 532, 1 - 533, 17); Jer., *Nom.* (CC 72:
61, 28/29)
16. Gn 17:5   17. Ga 3:29   18. Gn 17:15
19. Jer., *Nom.* (CC 72: 71, 22; 150, 25)

she had become a companion and sharer of such great faith, he should call her [by a name which expressed what] he understood her to be—not exclusively the ruler of his own house, but ruler absolutely, that is, the parent of all rightly-believing women. Hence when blessed Peter was urging believing women from the nations to the virtues of humility, chastity and modesty, he remembered our mother Sara with due praise, saying, *Just as Sara was obedient to Abraham, calling him lord, you are her daughters when you do rightly and do not fear any disturbance.*[20]

We have taken care to prompt your love, brothers, with these things so that each of you will also remember that since you have received the faith of Christ, you also have deserved to share, with the patriarchs, possession of a lofty name. Those who have received in Christ the purification of saving baptism derived from the name of Christ should rejoice in having changed their proper name, and they should exert themselves to keep this [name] up to a secure and inviolate end, rejoicing that they have fulfilled in themselves that oracle of Isaiah, *And he will call his servants by another name,*[21] that is, the Christian name, by which now all servants of Christ take delight in being distinguished. *'For there is no other name under heaven given to human beings in which we must be saved'.*[22] Hence the prophet subsequently continued *In which he that is blessed upon earth will be blessed in the Lord. Amen.*[23] And in another place, speaking about the same thing to the Church, which is to be increased also from the nations, he said, *The nations will see your just one, and all the kings your renowned one, and you will be called a new name which the mouth of the Lord will name.*[24]

The reason why the child who was born to us, the son who was given to us,[25] received the name Jesus (that is, 'Savior') does not need explanation in order to be understood by us, but [we need] eager and vigilant zeal so that we too may be saved by sharing in his name. Indeed, we read how [the name of Jesus] is interpreted by the angel: *'He will save his people from their sins'.*[26] And without a doubt

20. 1 P 3:6   21. Is 65:15   22. Ac 4:12   23. Is 65:16
24. Is 62:2   25. Is 9:6   26. Mt 1:21

we believe and hope that the one who saves [us] from sins is not failing to save [us] also from the corruptions which happen because of sins, and from death itself, as the psalmist testifies when he says, *Who becomes well-disposed to all your iniquities, who heals all your illnesses.*[27] Indeed, with the pardoning of all of our iniquities, all our illnesses will be completely healed when, with the appearance of the glory of the resurrection, our last enemy, death, will be destroyed.

And our true and complete circumcision is this—when on judgment day, having put off all corruptions of soul as well as body, as soon as the judgment is brought to completion we enter the court of the heavenly kingdom to see our Creator's face forever. Typologically speaking, this is [represented by] the circumcised children being brought with praises to the temple of the Lord at Jerusalem as an acceptable sacrifical offering. A person is purged by true circumcision and enters the temple of the Lord with offerings when, having been purified from every blemish of mortality by the glory of [the Lord's] resurrection, he passes with the fruit of his good works to the undying joys of the heavenly city, saying, *You have burst my bonds. I will sacrifice to you the sacrificial offering of praise; I will give my votive offerings to the Lord in the courts of the house of the Lord, in the sight of all his people, in your midst, Jerusalem.*[28]

The eighth day, when circumcision is celebrated, indicates that greatly-desired time of entrance into heaven.[29] There are six ages of this world, divided by well-known points of time, in which it is necessary to devote oneself to labors for God, and to work toward the time for securing undying rest. The seventh is the age of rest, not in this life but in another, lasting until the time of the resurrection of souls.[30] The eighth age is that blessed day of resurrection

27. Ps 103:3 (102:3)   28. Ps 116:16-19 (115:16-19)
29. Aug., *Contra Faust.* 16, 29 (*CSEL* 25: 474, 11 - 475, 26)
30. Aug., *De Civ. Dei* 22, 30 (*CC* 48: 865, 124 - 866, 148); *Ep.* 55, 9, 17 (*CSEL* 34: ii, 188); *Ep.* 199, 51 (*CSEL* 57: 289); *De Gen. Contra Manich.* 1, 23, 35-39 (*PL* 34: 190-93); *Serm.* 259, 2 (*PL* 38: 1197-98); *De Trin.* 4, 7 (*CC* 50: 169, 9 - 170, 23); Bede *De Temp. Rat.* 10 (ed. Jones, CC 123B: 310, 1 -312, 57); *De Tempor.* 16 (ed. Jones, CC 123C: 600, 1 - 601, 22)

itself, without any temporal end, when, as the true glory of every sort of circumcision shines forth, *the body which is corrupted will no longer weigh down the soul,* nor *will the earthly habitation press down the mind which is thinking of many things,*[31] but the then-incorruptible body will gladden the soul, and the heavenly habitation will raise up the whole human being, who is clinging to the vision of his Maker.[32]In that psalm which we called to memory above, the prophet subsequently explains the blessedness of this eternal day, rousing his own soul, and all the feelings of his interior man,[1*] to bless the Lord, and to recollect all his rewards,[33] as he says, *Who redeems your life from dissolution, who satisfies your desire with good things, who crowns you in compassion and mercy. Your youth will be renewed like the eagle's.*[34]

And so, dearly beloved brothers, since we desire to attain the rewards of this most beautiful renewal, [which is] as it were the highest [form of] circumcision, we must take care that in the meantime we submit to the remedies of the simple[35] circumcision and renewal which happens in the daily practice of the virtues. Let us *put off the old man of our former way of life, which is being corrupted in accordance with his desires for error.* Let us *be renewed in the spirit of* our *mind and put on the new man, who, after God's image, is created in justice and the holiness of truth.*[36] And when we hear of circumcision in one member of our body, we should not believe that it is sufficient to set us right, but as the same Apostle advises elsewhere, *Let us cleanse ourselves of every blemish and contamination of flesh and spirit, perfecting* [our] *sanctification in the fear of God.*[37] Let us reread the Acts of the Apostles and see the most blessed protomartyr Stephen as he thunders forth in a terrible way to the Jews who were persecuting him along with his Lord, *'You stiff-necked* [people], *uncircumcised in hearts and ears, you are always resisting the Holy Spirit'.*[38]

---

31. Ws 9:15
32. Ambr., *Expos. evang. sec. Luc.* 2, 55 (CC 14: 55, 753/54); Aug., *Serm.* 169, 2-3 (*PL* 38: 916); *Serm.* 3 (ed. Morin, 335, 10)
33. Ps 103:1-2 (102:1-2)
34. Ps 103:4-5 (102:4-5)
35. *primitiuae*
36. Eph 4:22-24
37. 2 Co 7:1
38. Ac 7:51

If those who resist the warnings of the Holy Spirit are uncircumcised in their hearts and ears, surely there is a circumcision of hearts and ears. And if there is a circumcision of hearts and ears, there is also [a circumcision] of all of the senses of the exterior and the interior man.[39] A person's sight is uncircumcised if he *looks at a woman to lust after her,*[40] or if he has *haughty eyes.*[41] Those to whom it is said with the voice of truth, *'He who is of God hears the words of God; therefore you do not hear, because you are not of God,'*[42] are uncircumcised in their ears.[2*] Uncircumcised in tongue and hands [are those] *whose mouth has spoken vanity and their right hand is the right hand of iniquity,*[43] those who speak peace with their neighbor, but evil things are in their hearts,[44] and their right hand is filled with bribes.[45] Uncircumcised in taste are those whom the prophet accuses, saying, *Woe to you who are heroes at drinking wine and valiant men in mixing strong drink.*[46] Uncircumcised in smell and touch are those who are steeped in ointment and various odors, who pursue the embraces of a harlot, sprinkling their bed with myrrh, aloes and cinnamon.[47] Uncircumcised in their steps are those about whom the psalmist records, *Dismay and unhappiness in their ways, and they have not recognized the way of peace.*[48] But those who keep their heart under every [form of] custody, who turn away their eyes so that they do not see vanity,[49] who hedge their ears with thorns so that they do not hear a depraved tongue,[50] who taste and see how delightful the Lord is and how blessed the man who hopes in him,[51] who guard their ways so that they do not transgress with their tongue,[52] who speak no iniquity with their lips and whose tongue will not plan falsehood as long as breath survives in them and the Spirit of God is in their nostrils,[53] who lift their hands to God's mandates which they love,[54] who keep from their feet every evil way so that they guard the word of

---

39. Jer., *In Ezech.* 13, 44, 6-8 (CC 75: 649, 1292 - 651, 1340)
40. Mt 5:28   41. Pr 6:17   42. Jn 8:47
43. Ps 144:8 (143:8)   44. Ps 28:3 (27:3)   45. Ps 26:10 (25:10)
46. Is 5:22   47. Pr 7:17   48. Ps 13:3 (LXX)
49. Ps 119:37 (118:37)   50. Si 28:28   51. Ps 34:8 (33:9)
52. Ps 39:1 (38:2)   53. Jb 27:3-4   54. Ps 119:48 (118:48)

God[55]— all these show that they have senses which are circumcised with the rock of spiritual asceticism. We read that circumcision was done with knives made of rock,[56] *and the rock was Christ.*[57] And by [Christ's] faith, hope and charity the hearts of the good are purified not only in baptism, but furthermore in every devout action. This daily circumcision of ours (that is, the continual cleansing of our heart) does not cease from always celebrating the sacrament of the eighth day, for after the example of the Lord's resurrection, which occurred on the eighth day, that is, after the seventh [day] of the sabbath, it is customary that we sanctify ourselves *so that as Christ has risen again from the dead through the glory of the Father, so we also may walk in newness of life,*[58] by the assistance of our Lord Jesus Christ, who with the Father and the Holy Spirit lives and reigns, God for all ages. Amen.

---

55. Ps 119:101 (118:101)
56. Jos 5:2; Aug., *Serm.* 169, 2, 3 (*PL* 38: 916)
57. 1 Co 10:4
58. Rm 6:4

NOTES

1. 'All the feelings of his interior man' = *omnes interioris sui hominis affectus.* 'Feelings' is admittedly a weak translation for *affectus.* Bede clearly refers here to Ps 103:1 (102:1), where paired with 'soul' is the phrase 'all that is within me' (*omnia quae intra me sunt* in Jerome's translation of the Septuagint, the version Bede quotes immediately below.) There seems to be no English word meaning 'all emotional and mental states taken together,' which is presumably what Bede intends by *affectus.*
2. The translator has chosen a different punctuation from that of the Latin edition, in which *incircumcisi sunt auribus* is related to the following series of psalm quotations instead of to the preceding quotation from John's gospel.

homily 1.12

The reading from the holy gospel which we have just now heard, brothers, gives us a noble example of perfect humility, both in the Lord and in his servant. In the Lord because, although the Lord was God, he not only deigned to be baptized by a servant who was a human being, but even came to him to be baptized.[1] And [there is a noble example of humility] in the servant because, although he was aware that he was the intended precursor and baptizer of his Savior, nevertheless, being mindful of his own weakness, he humbly excused himself from the office imposed upon him, saying, *'I ought to be baptized by you, and do you come to me'*? But because *everyone who humbles himself will be exalted*,[2] and the Lord appeared from God the Father in the humble form of a human being for the sake of instructing human beings, it soon appeared how greatly he stood out above human beings, and even above the angels and every created thing, when *a voice came down to him from out of his magnificent glory* [speaking] *in this way: 'This is my beloved Son in whom I am well pleased'*.[3] And the most faith-

---

1. For this entire homily cf. Aug., *Serm.* 292, 3, 3-4 (*PL* 38: 1321-23) and *Tract. in Ioh.* 4, 12 - 6, 19 (*CC* 36: 37, 10 - 64, 31)
2. Lk 14:11   3. 2 P 1:17

ful and humble servant, John, who wanted to be baptized
by the Lord rather than to baptize the Lord, merited both
to baptize the Lord himself, and, with the eyes of his mind
open, to see, beyond other mortals, the Spirit descending
upon [Christ].

But since we have only briefly sampled these things, in
order to explain it all more fully at this point, let us look
at the opening of this sacred reading: *Then Jesus came to John
at the Jordan, to be baptized by him.* The Son of God came to
be baptized by a human being, not because of an anxious
necessity to be cleansed of any sin of his own, since *he did
no sin, nor was any treachery found in his mouth,*[4] but because
of his holy plan to be cleansed of the whole contagion of
our sin, since *in many things we have all offended,*[5] and *if we
say that we have no sin, we deceive ourselves, and the truth is
not in us.*[6] He came to be baptized in water, though he was
the maker of water, so that to us, who were conceived in
iniquity and brought to life in moral faults,[7] he might suggest the mystery of the second nativity, celebrated through
water and the Spirit, that we are to try to reach. He deigned
to be washed in the waters of the Jordan although he was
clean of all stains, so that he might sanctify the flowing of
water for the washing away of the stains of all of our wicked deeds.[8]

But since we recognize in the gospel reading the Lord's
most humble divinely-arranged plan, let us also look with
eager attention at the most humble obedience of the servant. There follows: *John forbade him, saying, 'I ought to be
baptized by you, and do you come to me'?* [John] was very much
afraid because [Christ] had come to him to be baptized,
though there was in him no fault to be wiped clean by baptism, and moreover, through the grace of his Spirit [Christ]
would take all sin from the world's believers. Hence John's
saying here, *'I ought to be baptized by you,'* is properly understood [in the light of] what we are told by John the evangelist that [the Baptist] said when [Jesus] came to him:

---

4. 1 P 2:22   5. Jm 3:2   6. 1 Jn 1:8   7. Ps 51:5 (50:7)
8. Ambr., *Expos. evang. sec. Luc.* 3, 21-22 (CC 14: 67, 1124/27); Jer., *Ep.*
   108, 12 (CSEL 55: 321, 21/23); *In Matth.* 3, 13 (CC 77: 19, 281/83)

'Behold the lamb of God, behold him who takes away the sins of
the world'.[9] For we all have to be baptized by him who came
into the world for this reason, to take away the sins of the
world.

John himself needed to be baptized by [Christ], that is,
to be cleansed of the contagion of original sin, since although
he was not inferior to any other person of those born of
women,[1*] nevertheless, as one born of a woman he did not
lack the blemish of sin; so along with others born of women
he had need of being cleansed by him who, although he
was God, appeared in the flesh born of a virgin. It is written: 'What is man that he should be immaculate, and he that is
born of a woman that he should appear clean'?[10] In view of this,
therefore, since [John] was a human being, although a holy
one, he was nevertheless born of a woman and therefore
not exempt from the stain of sin, and he rightfully feared
to baptize God, whom he knew to have been born of a virgin and furthermore to have no stain of sin. But because
true humility is that companion which obedience does not
desert, he humbly fulfilled that office of which at first he
had been afraid.[11]

Now there follows: *Jesus answered and said to him, 'Let it
be* [so] *now, for thus it is fitting for us to fulfill all justice'. Then
he permitted him.* That is, only then did he permit him, then
did he consent, then did he allow himself to be baptized
by him, when he had recognized that in such an order was
all justice to be fulfilled. 'Let me now,' he says, 'let me now
be baptized by you in water as I have ordered, and afterwards you will be baptized by me in the Spirit, as you are
asking.[12] So it is fitting that we give an example of *all justice*, [which is] to be fulfilled, namely, so that the faithful
may learn that no human being can be perfectly just apart
from the waters of baptism, and that the ceremony of life-
giving regeneration is necessary for all, no matter how

9. Jn 1:29   10. Jb 15:14
11. var.: 'because of what he had heard and what had been done, he
    soon obediently fulfilled that office of which he had at first been afraid
    in his humility'
12. Jer., *In Matth.* 3, 15 (CC 77: 19, 284/85)

innocently and justly they may live, when they recognize
that although I was conceived and born by the working of
the Holy Spirit, I was subject to a second birth, or rather
that I consecrated the bath [of baptism] for them. None of
the more important people should scorn to be baptized in
the forgiveness of sins by my humble ones, when they
remember that the Lord, who was wont to forgive sins as
he baptized in the Holy Spirit, lowered his head to be baptized in water at the hands of his servant'.

There follows: *And when [Jesus] had been baptized, he immediately came up from the water. And behold, the heavens were
opened to him, and he saw the Spirit of God descending like a
dove, coming upon him.* And this pertains to the fulfillment
of all justice — that when the Lord was baptized, the
heavens were opened to him, and the Spirit descended
upon him. By this was our faith to be strengthened, [that]
through the mystery of sacred baptism an entrance into the
heavenly fatherland was opened for us, and the grace of
the Holy Spirit was administered to us. Can it be proper
[for us] to believe that heavenly secrets were then accessible to the Lord for the first time, since right faith has it that
he remained in the bosom of the Father, and kept his seat
in heaven not less at the time when he lived among human beings than he did before and afterwards? Or did he
attain the gifts of the Holy Spirit after his thirtieth year of
age when he was baptized, although he had always been,
from his very conception, full of the Holy Spirit?

It is for us, dearly beloved brothers, for us that these mysteries were celebrated. For by the most sacred bathing of
his body the Lord dedicated for us the bath of baptism, and
he also pointed out to us that, after the reception of baptism, the right of entry into heaven is accessible to us, and
the Holy Spirit is given to us. And there is a very fitting
difference [in the fact] that the first Adam, deceived by an
unclean spirit through a serpent, lost the joys of the heavenly kingdom, [while] the second Adam, glorified by the Holy
Spirit through a dove, opened the entrance to this kingdom.
The second Adam on this day points out that through the
water of the bath of rebirth the flickering flame by which

the cherub guardian blocked the entry into paradise when the first Adam was expelled would be extinguished.[13] Where the one went out with his wife, having been conquered by his enemy, there the other might return with his spouse (namely the Church of the saints), as a conqueror over his enemy. Further, *the Father of the age to come, the Prince of peace,*[14] might grant to those redeemed from sin the better gift of immortal life, which the father of this present age, the prince of discord, lost after he was sold, together with his descendents, into the slavery of sin. Even though that most blessed life which Adam lost was sublime in its incomparable light and peace, clear of every cloud of stinging cares, and glorified by the frequent vision and spoken message of God and angels on earth, nevertheless it took place on this earth, although those who sought earthly fruits were supplied with nourishment without any labor. What Christ bestowed in the height of heaven is everlasting life, renewed not by the frequent but by the constant light of divine contemplation. The first blessed life of man was immortal in such a way that man could not die in it if he kept himself on guard against the seduction of sin; the second blessed life, in truth, will be immortal in such a way that man will not be able to die in it, nor be tempted by any seduction of sin assailing him.[15]

It is good, however, that the reconciling Spirit appeared as a dove, which is a very simple bird, so that he might show through this animal's form the simplicity of his own nature as well, for *the Holy Spirit of discipline will flee the deceitful,*[16] and so that he might teach that the one upon whom he descended would be gentle and mild to the world, a herald and minister of heavenly mercy. And at the same time all those who are to be renewed by his grace are advised to enter, being simple and clean of heart, according to what was written: *Perceive the Lord in goodness and seek him in simplicity of heart. For wisdom will not go into a malevolent soul*

---

13. Gn 3:24   14. Is 9:6
15. Aug., *De Civ. Dei* 22, 30 (CC 48: 864, 65/68); *De corrept. et gratia* 12, 33 (PL 44, 936); *De Gen. ad Litt.* 6, 25 (CSEL 28: 197, 6/24)
16. Ws 1:5

nor dwell in a body subject to sins.[17] Hence it is that Simon, who did not cease to remain *in the gall of bitterness and in the bonds of iniquity,* was able to have neither part nor lot[18] in this Spirit. For he was full of that spirit which appeared to mankind as a serpent, so that he himself was infected with the pestilence of malice and snares, and he diligently taught hearts.[19]

But as the Spirit descends upon the Lord, let us see what follows: *And behold a voice from heaven said, 'This is my beloved Son in whom I am well-pleased'.* The Son of God is baptized in a human being; the Spirit of God descends in the dove; God the Father is present in the voice — the mystery of the holy and indivisible Trinity is declared in the baptism.[20] And it is right that he who was to command the stewards of his sacraments to teach all nations, and to baptize them in the name of the Father and the Son and the Holy Spirit,[21] would first himself reveal that the whole Trinity was personally present in his [own] baptism. What the Father's voice said, *'This is my beloved Son in whom I am well-pleased,* it said in relation to earthly man, in whom, when he was sinning, God his maker suggested that he was in some way displeased, when he said, 'I repent that I have made man on earth'.[22] Of course, no repentance belongs in God, but we speak in our customary way, we who tend to be pricked with compunction when we see our works turned contrary to what we had wished.[23] He said that he repented that he had made man when he beheld him falling away by sinning from the righteousness for which he made him. In his only-begotten Son he was singularly well-pleased, because he recognized that this human nature[24] which he had put on remained exempt from sin.

---

17. Ws 1:1, 4   18. Ac 8:23, 21
19. var.: 'and taught [them] what sort of hearts he loved'
20. Jer., *In Matth.* 3, 16 (*CC* 77: 19, 297/99)
21. Mt 28:19   22. Gn 6:6-7
23. Aug., *De divers. quaest.* 83, 52 (*CC* 44A: 83, 1 - 84, 32); *Enarr. in Ps.* 105, 35; 109, 17; 131, 18 (*CC* 40: 1566, 5/13; 1617, 37/46; 1920, 4/15); *Quaest. ad Simpl.* 2, 4 (*CC* 44: 79, 130 - 80, 139)
24. *hominem*

And in this word of the Father, just as in the other mysteries of the Lord's baptism, all fulfillment of justice is declared. For as the Spirit descends upon him, human beings are told that the Son is coeternal and consubstantial with the Father: in this way human beings are to learn that through the grace of baptism they can, by the reception of the Holy Spirit, be changed from sons of the devil into sons of God. So the Apostle teaches the faithful, speaking thus, *You have received the spirit of adoption as sons whereby we cry out, 'Abba, Father'.*[25] And John the evangelist says, *But to as many as accepted him he gave them power to become sons of God.*[26]

Now that we have recorded these things concerning the baptism of our Savior, as he himself has granted [us to do], dearly beloved brothers, let us turn to ourselves, and because we have heard about the humility and obedience of the Baptist, together with that of the one who was baptized, let us also take care to keep through humble obedience the baptism which we have received, *making ourselves clean from all contamination of flesh and spirit, making perfect [our] sanctification in the fear of God,*[27] humbly subjecting ourselves to and serving his mysteries. Let us persuade those who have not yet been initiated in these [mysteries]; and let as many of us as have been advanced to priestly rank humbly fulfill the office imposed upon us of dispensing his sacraments. Let us all eagerly strive that we may not block for ourselves with allurements the gate of the heavenly fatherland which was opened up for us humans by divine mysteries. For it is not without reason that by the evangelist Luke it is recorded that after his baptism the Lord prayed, and thus as the heavens were opened there came the Spirit and voice of the Father,[28] since, as the three evangelists agree, soon after he had been baptized he performed a fast of forty days by himself,[29] and he taught and informed us by his example that, after we have received forgiveness of sins in baptism, we should devote ourselves to vigils, fasts, prayers and other spiritually fruitful things, lest when we are sluggish

25. Rm 8:15   26. Jn 1:12   27. 2 Co 7:1
28. Lk 3:21-22   29. Mt 4:2; Mk 1:13; Lk 4:2

and less solicitous, the unclean spirit which had been expelled from our heart by baptism may return, and finding us fruitless in spiritual riches, may weigh us down with a sevenfold pestilence, and our last state may be worse than the first.[30]

Let us attentively beware that we do not frequently light with the kindling of our vices the fire which blocks us in our voyage of life. Now whatever sort of flaming sword it is that guards the doorway of paradise has been extinguished for each of the faithful in the font of baptism, and it has been put away so that they may return. For the unfaithful, however, it remains always immovable, and also for those falsely called faithful though they have not been chosen, since they have no fear of entangling themselves in sins after baptism, it is as though the same fire has been rekindled after it has been extinguished, so that they may not merit to enter into the kingdom that they try to obtain with a deceitful and duplicitous heart — with the fraudulent tooth of a serpent rather than the simple eye of a dove, which the Lord shows that he loves very much in his Church when he says in the song of love, *Behold, you are beautiful, my friend, behold you are beautiful. Your eyes are those of doves.*[31]

Since the image of a dove is placed before us by God so that we may learn the simplicity favored [by him], let us look diligently at its nature, so that from each one of its examples of innocence we may take the principles of a more correct life. [The dove] is a stranger to malice[32]— may all bitterness, anger and indignation be taken away from us, together with all malice. It injures nothing with its mouth or talons, nor does it nourish itself or its young on tiny mice or grubs, which almost all smaller birds [do] — let us see that our teeth are not *weapons and arrows,*[33] lest gnawing and consuming one another we be consumed by one another. Let us keep our hands from plundering — *he who has now been stealing, let him steal no more; let him labor by working*

---

30. Mt 12:43-45; Lk 11:24-26   31. Sg 1:15 (1:14)
32. var.: 'the malice of gall'
33. Ps 57:4 (56:5); some mss. continue the quotation: *'and our tongue a sharp sword'*

with his hands, which is a good thing, so that he may have some-
thing he can bestow upon one who is suffering need.[34] It is also
reported that the dove often supplies nourishment to
strangers as though they were her own young; she feeds
them with the fruits and seeds of the earth — let us listen
to the Apostle: *It is good not to eat flesh and not to drink wine.*[35]
And the apostle Peter says, *Supplement your faith with vir-*
tue, and virtue with knowledge, and knowledge with abstinence,
and abstinence with patience, and patience with piety, and piety
with love of the brothers.[36] For a song [the dove] has a sound
of grief — let us be pitiful and let us mourn and wail[37] in
the presence of the Lord who made us.[38] May our *laughter*
be turned into mourning and [our] *joy into sadness,*[39] for *blessed*
are those who mourn: they shall be consoled.[40] [A dove] is inclined to sit above water so that it may avoid being seized
by a hawk coming, since it has seen its shadow beforehand
in the water — let us also be clean, and take care to sit attentively at the cleansing streams of the scriptures, and,
thoroughly instructed by the mirrors [of the scriptures], may
we be capable of distinguishing and guarding ourselves
against the snares of the ancient enemy.[41]

The Church, the spouse of Christ, loves such as these;
she sings in praise of her lover, '*His eyes* [are] *like doves, which*
were washed with milk, and sit by full-flowing streams'.[42] [The
dove] is accustomed to make its nest *in the clefts of a rock,*
in the cavity of a stone wall[43]— the rock is Christ,[44] whose
hands were pierced by nails and whose side was pierced
by a lance on the cross. From these there immediately went
out blood and water[45]— namely the mystery of our sanctification and cleansing. [The dove's] stone wall is the united
virtue of the saints; the cavity in it is the lap of fraternal
love,[2*] in which, like doves making their nest, they make
a place among themselves for more tender souls among the
faithful, when they receive them to be nourished in the perfection of faith, hope and love. Therefore we who are still

---

34. Eph 4:28
35. Rm 14:21
36. 2 P 1:5-7
37. Jm 4:9a
38. Ps 95:6 (94:6)
39. Jm 4:9b
40. Mt 5:5
41. var.: 'the wicked enemy'
42. Sg 5:12
43. Sg 2:14
44. 1 Co 10:4
45. Jn 19:34

very small in faith should humbly be subject to these helps
of the stronger, [and] take care to be always sanctified by
these sacraments of the Lord's passion. Now the Lord seeks
such a way of life in us all; he desires to see the life of each
one of us attentive to such practices; he gives thanks that
we recite and proclaim his praises with the voice of such
as these. *'Arise,'* he says, *'my friend, my fair one, and come.
My dove, in the clefts of a rock, in the cavity of a stone wall, show
me your face, let your voice sound in my ears'.*[46]
   Let it suffice that we have recorded these seven examples of virtue concerning the nature of the dove. And perhaps this is rightly done because the grace of the Holy Spirit,
who descended as a dove, is sevenfold. But of all the things
that human resourcefulness can ascertain by interpreting
[the dove's] nature according to its moral significance, one
thing which sacred history tells about its acts stands out
mystically speaking. When the Lord cleansed wicked deeds
at the origin of the world with the waters of the flood, as
a figure of the baptism to come, Noah wanted to know how
things stood on the face of the earth when the inundation[47]
had come to an end, and he sent forth a raven, which
scorned to return to the ark,[48] signifying those who, although they have been cleansed by the waters of baptism,
nevertheless neglect putting off the very black dress of their
old selves by living more faultlessly; and lest they deserve
to be renewed by the anointing of the Holy Spirit, they at
once fall away from the inmost unity of catholic peace and
rest by following exterior things, that is, the desires of the
world. After [the raven] he sent a dove, and it came to him
in the evening, carrying in its mouth an olive branch with
green leaves.[49]
   You are paying attention, I believe, brothers, and with
your intellect you anticipate me as I speak — the olive branch
with green leaves is the grace of the Holy Spirit, rich in the
words of life,[50] the fullness of which rests upon Christ, [as]
the psalm says, *God, your God, has anointed you with the oil*

46. Sg 2:13-14   47. *inundatione*; var.: 'cleansing' (*mundatione*)
48. Gn 8:6-7   49. Gn 8:8-11
50. Ambr., *Expos. evang. sec. Luc.* 2, 92 (CC 14: 73, 1301 - 74, 1307)

of gladness above your fellows.[51] Concerning this gift given to Christ's fellows, John speaks: *You have the anointing from the holy one, and you know all things.*[52] And by a most beautiful conjunction, the figure is in agreement with the fulfillment[53]— a corporeal dove brought the olive branch to the ark which was washed by the waters of the flood; the Holy Spirit descended in the form of a corporeal dove upon the Lord when he was baptized in the waters of the Jordan. Not only the human beings who were in the ark with Noah, but also the living things which the ark contained, and also the very wood from which the ark was made, prefigure us members of Christ and of the Church after our reception of the washing of the waters of regeneration. Through the anointing of the sacred chrism may we be signed with the grace of the Holy Spirit, and may he deign to keep it inviolate in us who himself gave it [to us], Jesus Christ our Lord who with the almighty Father in the unity of the same Holy Spirit lives and reigns for all ages. Amen.

51. Ps 45:7 (44:8)   52. 1 Jn 2:20   53. *umbra ueritati concinit*

NOTES

1. Not inferior to any other person of those born of women' (*nullo inter natos mulierum minor*), a curiously awkward and negative way of paraphrasing Mt 11:11 (Lk 7:28), this must be regarded as Bede's original wording, since it is the harder reading. Some MSS., however, apparently corrected it to the more straightforward *nullus inter natos mulierum major* ('no one was greater of those born of women'.)

2. 'The lap of fraternal love' (*sinus fraternae dilectionis*)—Bede here plays upon a double meaning. *Sinus* has a physical meaning of 'the cavity or fold produced by the looping of a garment' (Glare 1771, sense 1), and this relates to the cavity in which a dove builds its nest, but figuratively *sinus* can mean the breast in the sense of a place of shelter and security, (Glare, sense 3) which is, of course, appropriate to fraternal love.

homily 1.13

Matthew 19:27-29   *Feast of St Benedict Biscop*

Since Peter heard from the Lord that a rich man may enter the kingdom of heaven [only] with difficulty,[1] and since he was aware that he and his fellow disciples had entirely rejected the deceiving pleasures of the world, he wished to know what greater reward they and other despisers of the world ought to expect for their greater virtue of mind. And in answer to the Lord he said, *'Behold we have left all things and followed you. What, therefore, will be ours'?* Here we must carefully observe that he gloried not merely in their having left all things, but also in their following the Lord. For it is unquestionably foolish to follow Plato, Diogenes and certain other philosophers in trampling underfoot the riches of this life, and not to do this in order to secure eternal life, but [merely] to grasp after the empty praise of mortal men; it is foolish to take on additional hardships in the present without hope of future rest and peace.

That man is perfect who goes away, sells everything he has, gives to the poor, and comes to follow Christ.[2] In heaven he will have a treasure that will not come to an end.[3] Hence it is good that Jesus says this in response to Peter's

---

1. Mt 19:23   2. Mt 19:21; Lk 18:22   3. Lk 12:33

inquiry, *'Amen, I say to you that you who have followed me, in the regeneration when the Son of man sits on the throne of his majesty, you also will sit on twelve thrones, judging the twelve tribes of Israel'*. Indeed, he taught those laboring for the sake of his name in this life to hope for a reward in another life — that is, 'in the regeneration,' namely when by rising again we will be regenerated to immortal life, just as we were brought forth in the manner of mortals to perishable life. And a further just reward for those who have here neglected the glory of human eminence for Christ's sake will be that there they will be singularly glorified by Christ, sitting as judges with him of the human way of life, for they could not be torn away for any reason from following in his footsteps.[4]

No one should suppose that only the twelve apostles (since Matthias was chosen on account of Judas' transgression[5]) are to judge at that time, just as it is not only the twelve tribes of Israel who are to be judged. Otherwise, is the tribe of Levi, which is the thirteenth tribe, to be left unjudged? And is Paul, who is the thirteenth apostle (since Matthias was chosen on account of Judas' transgression),[1*] to be deprived of his heritage of judging, since he himself said, *Are you not aware that we will judge angels? How much the more worldly things?*[6] We must be aware that all of those who after the example of the apostles have left all their things and followed Christ will come as judges with him, just as also every race of mortal men will be judged. Since it is often the custom in the scriptures for totality to be designated by the number twelve, the great number of all who will judge is indicated by the twelve seats of the apostles, and the great number of those who are to be judged is indicated by the twelve tribes of Israel.[7]

Hence we should note that there are two classes of elect in the judgment to come,[8] one [made up] of those who will

---

4. Several MSS add: 'following him they will come to the summit of judicial power'
5. Ac 1:25-26   6. 1 Co 6:3
7. Aug., *Ennar. in Ps.* 86, 4 (CC 39: 1201, 11 - 1202, 26)
8. Jer., *Adv. Iov.* 2, 22 (PL 23: 316)

judge with the Lord (concerning them he records in this place [that] they left all things and followed him), and another [made up] of those to be judged by the Lord — these did not leave all things in the same way, but nevertheless from the things which they possessed they took care to give daily alms to the poor. Hence at the judgment they will hear, *'Come, blessed of my Father; come into possession of the kingdom prepared for you from the establishment of the world. For I was hungry and you gave me to eat; I was thirsty and you gave me to drink,'* and so forth.[9] The Lord was mindful of [this second class of elect] in that [passage] which precedes the present reading, where he said to a certain ruler[2*] who was inquiring of him what sort of good work he had to do to have everlasting life: *'If you wish to enter into life, keep the commandments. Commit no murder or theft; do not speak false testimony; honor your father and mother, and love your neighbor as yourself'.*[10] Therefore, one who keeps the Lord's commandments enters into eternal life. One, however, who not only keeps the commandments, but who also follows the counsel which the Lord gave about despising the riches and luxuries of the world, will not only attain life, but he will also be judge, with the Lord, of the lives of others. And thus it will come about that at the judgment there will be, as we have said, two classes of the good.

But we ascertain from what the Lord tells us that there will also be there [at the last judgment] two classes of condemned. One is [made up] of those who, after having been initiated into the mysteries of the Christian faith, scorn to carry out the works of faith. To them he will proclaim at the judgment, *'Withdraw from me, you accursed, into the eternal fire which has been prepared for the devil and his angels. For I was hungry and you did not give me to eat,'*[11] and so forth. The other [class of condemned] is [made up] of those who either never adopted the faith and mysteries of Christ, or, having adopted it, threw it off through apostasy. Concerning them he says, *'He who does not believe is already judged, because he does not believe in the name of the only-begotten Son*

9. Mt 25:34-35   10. Mt 19:16-19   11. Mt 25:41-42

of God'.[12] For those who did not choose to worship Christ, even nominally, will not deserve to hear his words by which they are convicted; instead they will come to judgment only for this — so that they may be sent into eternal damnation with those who are judged as sinners.

But now that we have briefly recorded these things with due fear and trepidation, let us turn instead to hearing the most joyful promises of our Lord and Savior, and let us see what a great grace of benevolence is pledged to his followers: not only the rewards of eternal life, but also extraordinary favors in the present. *'And everyone,'* he says, *'who has left house or brothers or sisters or father or mother or wife or children or lands for my name's sake will receive a hundredfold, and will come into possession of eternal life'.* One who renounces earthly affection or possessions for the sake of Christ's discipleship, to the extent that he has made progress in his love, will find more comrades who will rejoice to receive him with inner affection and to support him with their material goods. By their professions of the same [Christ], they will delight in accepting in their homes and lands one who has been made a poor man for Christ's sake, and even more than wife, parent, brother, or son in the flesh, they will take delight in restoring warmth to him by the greater devotion of charity. Now the hundredfold of which he speaks does not show the number of those loving in Christ and serving the faithful for Christ's sake, but the entirety and perfection with which they serve each other through charity.

We too have often had an example of this in our own case, dearly beloved brothers, when going somewhere on account of necessary matters, we found that all monastic dwelling-places were open to us as if they were our own, [and] we beheld everyone dedicated with most sincere devotion to our service. And especially in [the case of] our father Benedict of blessed memory, whose revered death day we today recall with due solemnity,* we see the whole gist of this reading most perfectly fulfilled. For having left everything behind, he followed Christ when, after he had rejected

12. Jn 3:18

those things which he had acquired while he was the king's thane[13] (or which he was capable of acquiring, since he was of noble birth), he was quick to go on pilgrimage to Rome, the gateway of the blessed apostles, so that because the faith among the English people was still unrefined, and the founding of churches was going forward, he might take up a perfect form of living at the place preferably, where, through the chief apostles of Christ, the whole Church had its special center. There he was educated in Christ; he was tonsured in that region; there he was imbued with monastic practices, and he would have spent the whole of his life [there], if the apostolic authority of the lord Pope had not forbidden it: he commanded him to return to his fatherland in order to guide Archbishop Theodore of blessed memory to Britain.[14]

Not long afterwards, secular rulers, having recognized the zeal of his virtues, were concerned to give him a place to construct a monastery, a place not taken away from some lesser persons, but granted from their own personal property.[15] He soon established [this place] which he had received most perfectly, according to regular discipline, interiorly and exteriorly. He did not establish decrees for us for the sake of what he could himself gain, but he set forth the well-proven statutes of earlier monasteries, which he had learned of abroad, to be observed by himself and his [monks].

And it should not seem tedious to any of you, brothers, if we speak of things which are well-known, but instead you should judge it delightful that we speak the truth when we tell of the spiritual deeds of our father, to whom the Lord by a manifest miracle fulfilled what he promised to his faithful ones, that *'everyone who has left home or brothers or sisters or father or mother or wife or children or lands for my name's sake will receive a hundredfold in this time, and in the world to come eternal life'.*[16] He left his relatives when he departed from his fatherland; he received a hundredfold, for not only

13. *in ministerio regali;* (cf. *HA*, ch.1)
14. *HA*, ch.3.   15. *HA*, ch.4.
16. Bede here conflates Mt 19:29 with Mk 10:30.

was he held in deserved veneration by everyone in this land,
on account of the diligence of his virtues, but even in Gaul,
and in Italy, in Rome too, and in the islands of the sea, he
was loved by everyone who was able to know him, to such
an extent that the apostolic Pope himself, in order to further the progress of this monastery (which he rejoiced that
[Benedict Biscop] had recently founded), put at its disposition John, abbot and archchanter of the Roman Church, as
you dear ones well remember, so that he might be brought
from Rome to Britain, and through him this monastery
might receive the manner of singing and performing rituals according to the canonical rite of the holy Roman and
apostolic Church. The homes and lands which [Benedict]
had possessed he left for the sake of Christ, from whom
he hoped to receive the land of an ever-verdant paradise,
and a home not made by hands but eternal in heaven.[17] He
left wife and children — not, to be sure, that he had taken
a wife, and had children born of her, but out of love of
chastity he scorned taking a wife from whom he could have
children, preferring to belong to that hundred and forty-
four thousand of the elect who sing before the throne of
the Lamb a new song which no one except they can sing.[18]
*These are they who were not defiled with women and who follow
the lamb wherever he goes.*[19] And he received a hundredfold
when, not only in his own region, but also in regions beyond the sea, many desired to receive him into their homes
and to refresh him with the fruits of their fields; when so
many matrons and men devoted to God served him, on account of the excellence of his steadfast soul, with an earnestness of love no less than that which they had for their
own marriage-partners or parents. He received homes and
lands a hundredfold when he secured these places where
he would build his monasteries. He gave up having a wife
for Christ's sake, and in this he received a hundredfold,
because undoubtedly then the value of charity between the
chaste would be a hundredfold greater on account of the
fruit of the Spirit, than that between the lascivious, on

17. 2 Co 5:1   18. Rv 14:1, 3   19. Rv 14:4

account of the desire of the flesh, had once been. The children which he had disdained to have in a fleshly way he deserved to receive a hundredfold as spiritual children. The number one hundred, indeed, as has often been said, figuratively speaking, denotes perfection. Now we are his children, since as a pious provider he brought us into this monastic house. We are his children since he has made us to be gathered spiritually into one family of holy profession, though in terms of the flesh we were brought forth of different parents. We are his children if by imitating [him] we hold to the path of his virtues, if we are not turned aside by sluggishness from the narrow path of the rule which he taught.

Now, brothers, we who were able to know him remember to say frequently in the hearing of those of you whom heavenly benevolence has gathered into the fellowship of our fraternity after his death, that as long as he survived in the body he excelled in laboring always for the sake of the glory of God's holy Church, and especially for the peace, honor, and tranquility of this monastery. As often as he crossed the sea, he never returned, as is the custom with some people, empty-handed and without profit, but one time he brought an abundance of holy books, and another time he brought a venerable present of relics of the blessed martyrs of Christ. Another time he had architects come for the construction of the church; another time it was glaziers to cover its windows with ornament; and another time he brought with him masters to sing and perform the rituals in the church throughout the whole year. Another time he carried back a letter of privilege sent from the lord Pope, by which our freedom from every outside interference was maintained. Another time he transported pictures of the holy histories which were put up, not only for the ornamentation of the church, but also for the instruction of those who looked at them, namely so that those who could not read might learn of the works of our Lord and Savior through gazing on images of these [works].[20]

20. *HA*, ch. 6

In these, and matters of this sort, he strove to labor in so many ways in order that no necessity of our laboring would remain. He went away to so many places across the sea so that we would be plentifully supplied with all sorts of nourishment of saving knowledge, and we would be able to remain at rest within the cloister of the monastery to serve Christ with a liberty secure. Even when he was attacked and painfully afflicted by infirmity of the body, while giving due thanks to God, he took delight in speaking again and again, always about the keeping of the monastic rules that he had learned and taught, always about the ecclesiastical observances which he had seen throughout all cities and especially [the ones] of Rome, always about the holy places which he remembered having visited as a young man. Thus made proficient by long practice of the virtues, and withered besides by the martyrdom of the infirmity of old-age, he passed over to eternal life after a hundredfold favor of grace in this present time.

Hence, dearly-beloved brothers, it is necessary that as good children worthy of such a parent we should take care to observe his example and commands in all things, and that no allurements of the soul or of the flesh should call us back from following in the footsteps of such a teacher. Then, since we also have left behind fleshly affection and earthly goods, and have turned away from taking a wife and begetting children in a fleshly way, out of love for an angelic way of life, we may, as our spiritual virtues become greater, rightly deserve both to receive a hundredfold in the present time for the society of holy people, and to come into possession of eternal life in the world to come, through the surpassing grace of our Redeemer, who lives and reigns with the Father in the unity of the Holy Spirit, God through all ages. Amen.

NOTES

1. The clause 'since Matthew was chosen on account of Judas' transgression' presumably occurs in both this sentence and the preceding sentence as a result of scribal error.
2. 'Ruler' = *principe*. Actually, Matthew simply calls him 'one' (*unus*) [Mt 19:16], and 'a young man' (*adulescens*) [Mt 19:20]. In the parallel passage in Luke, however, he is identified as 'a certain ruler' (*quidam princeps*) [Lk 18:18].
3. In several manuscripts the remainder of this homily is devoted to Benedict of Nursia rather than Benedict Biscop.

homily 1.14

When he was invited to a marriage, our Lord and Savior not only deigned to come, but even to work miracles there to gladden the guests. Figural meanings regarding heavenly sacraments aside, even according to the literal sense this confirms the faith of right believers. Besides, it suggests how damnable is the lack of faith of Tatian, Marcion, and the rest who disparage marriage. For if there were fault in an immaculate marriage bed and in a marriage celebrated with due chastity, the Lord would by no means have wished to come to this [marriage], and by no means would he have wished to consecrate it with the first of his miracles. But since conjugal chastity is good, the continence of a widow is better, and the perfection of a virgin is best, to demonstrate his approval of the choice of all these ranks while yet determining the merit of each, he deigned to be born from the inviolate womb of the virgin Mary; soon after being born he was blessed by the prophetic voice of the widow Anna;[1] then as a young man he was invited by those celebrating a marriage, and he honored them by the presence of his power.

1. Lk 2:36-38

But there is a more profound gladness in the heavenly figural meanings. The Son of God, who was to work miracles on earth, came to a marriage to teach that he himself was the one the psalmist foretold under the image of the sun: *And he, like a bridegroom coming forth from his nuptial chamber, has exalted like a giant to run the way. His coming out is from the highest heaven and his course is to its height.*[2]

In a certain place he said concerning himself and his faithful ones, 'Can the friends of the bridegroom mourn as long as the bridegroom is with them? The days will come when the bridegroom will be taken away from them, and then they will fast'.[3] From the time that the incarnation of our Savior was first promised to the patriarchs, it was always awaited by many of the saints with tears and mourning until he came. Similarly, from that time when, after his resurrection, he ascended to heaven, all the hope of the saints hangs upon his return. Only at the time when he kept company with human beings were they unable to weep and mourn, for they then had with them, even bodily, the one whom they loved spiritually. Therefore the bridegroom is Christ, the bride is the Church, and *the friends of the bridegroom,*[4] or *of the marriage*[5] are each and every one of his faithful. The time of the marriage is that time when, through the mystery of the incarnation, he joined holy Church to himself. Thus it was not by chance, but for the sake of a certain mystical meaning, that he came to a marriage celebrated on earth in the customary fleshly way, since he descended from heaven to earth in order to connect the Church to himself in spiritual love. His nuptial chamber was the womb of his incorrupt mother, where God was conjoined with human nature, and from there he came forth like a bridegroom to join the Church to himself. The first marriage-place was in Judaea, where the Son of God deigned to become a human being and to consecrate the Church by a sharing in his body,[6] confirming it in faith by the pledge of his Spirit. But

---

2. Ps 19:5-6 (18:6-7); Aug., *Tract. in Ioh.* 8, 4 (*CC* 36: 83, 1 - 84, 25)
3. Mt 9:15   4. Mt 9:15; Lk 5:34   5. Mk 2:19
6. Some MSS add: 'and his blood'

the same joyful marriage vows reached to the ends of the earth when the gentiles were called to faith.

And it is not devoid of mystical meaning that the marriage is reported to have taken place on the third day after those things which the preceding discourse of the gospel described. [This] indicates that the Lord came to link the Church to himself during the third age. Indeed, the first age shone brightly in the world with the examples of the patriarchs before the law, the second with the writings of the prophets under the law, the third with the proclamation of the evangelists in the time of grace, as if by the light of the third day. In this [third age] our Lord and Savior appeared, born in the flesh for the redemption of the human race.[7]

But we are also told that this marriage was performed in Cana of Galilee (that is, in the 'zeal' of 'emigration').[8] Typologically speaking, this denotes that especially worthy of Christ's grace are those who are aflame with the zeal of pious devotion, and who know how to emulate the greater charismatic gifts,[9] and to emigrate from vices to virtues by doing good works, and from earthly to eternal things by hoping and loving.

While the Lord was reclining at the marriage, the wine ran short, so that, when in a marvelous fashion he made better wine, the glory of God lying hidden in a human being might be manifested, and the faith of those who believed in him might increase. If we seek the mystical meaning in this, when the Lord appeared in the flesh the undiluted sweetness of legal meaning had gradually begun to 'run short' of its former virtue because of its fleshly interpretation by the Pharisees. [Christ] soon turned those mandates which seemed fleshly to spiritual teaching, and he changed the whole exterior appearance of the letter of the law to the gospel virtue of heavenly grace — which is [the meaning of] his having made wine from water.

---

7. Aug., *Ep.* 55, 3, 5 (*CSEL* 34, ii, 174, 23); *Serm.* 110, 1 (*PL* 38: 638); Greg., *Hom. in evang.* (*PL* 76: 1228)
8. *in zelo transmigrationis;* Isid., *Etymol.* 7, 9, 18; Jer., *Nom.* (*CC* 72: 131, 2)
9. 1 Co 12:31

But first let us strive to search out [10] the meaning of what Jesus' mother said to him when the wine ran short, *'They have no wine,'* [and of what] he answered, *'What is that to me and you, woman? My hour has not yet come'.* He would not dishonor his mother, since he orders us to honor our father and mother; and he would not deny that she was his mother, since he did not disdain to adopt flesh from her virginal flesh, as the Apostle also bears witness when he says, *Who was made to him of David's seed according to the flesh.* [11] How [could he be] of David's seed according to the flesh, if [he were not] from the body of Mary according to the flesh, since she descended from the seed of David? But when he was to work a miracle he said, *'What is that to me and you, woman'?* and by this he signified that he had received no beginning of the divinity by which the miracle would be executed from his mother in time, but had always possessed eternity from his Father. *'What is that,'* he says, *'to me and you? My hour has not yet come'* — 'There is nothing in common between the divinity which I have always possessed from the Father, and your flesh, from which I adopted flesh. My hour has not yet come when, by dying, I may demonstrate the weakness of the humanity taken from you; first must I disclose the power of [my] eternal deity by exercising [my] powers'. [12] The hour came, however, to show what was in common between him and his mother when, as he was about to die on the cross, he took care to commend her, a virgin, to the virgin disciple. [13] When he was enduring the weakness of the flesh, he dutifully acknowledged his mother, from whom he had received it, and commended her to the disciple whom he especially loved; when he was about to do divine things he pretended not to acknowledge her, because he recognized that she was not the source of his divine nativity. [*]

There were six stone hydrias placed there in accordance with the Jews' [rites of] *purification, each holding two or three measures.* Vessels prepared as receptacles for water are called hydrias, for in Greek water is called *ydor.* Water represents

10. var: 'let us see'   11. Rm 1:3   12. *uirtutes operando*
13. Jn 19:26-27; Aug., *Tract. in Ioh.* 8, 8-9 (CC 36: 86, 3 - 88, 56)

knowledge of sacred scripture, which both cleanses its hearers from the stain of sins, and gives [them] drink from the
font of divine cognition. The six vessels in which it was contained are the devout hearts of the holy, whose perfection
of life and faith was set before the human race as an example of believing and living properly through the six ages
of this transitory world, up to the time of the Lord's preaching.[14]

And it is good that the vessels were of stone, for the inmost hearts of the just are strong, inasmuch as they have
been made firm by the faith and love of that stone which
Daniel saw cut off from the mountain without hands, becoming a great mountain, and filling all the earth,[15] concerning which Zachariah too speaks, *In one stone there are
seven eyes*[16]— that is, the entirety of spiritual knowledge
dwells in Christ. The apostle Peter also recalls this, saying,
*Approaching him, a living stone...you also are built up as liv-
ing stones.*[17]

It is good that the hydrias were placed there in accordance
with the Jews' [rites of] purification, for it was only to the
Jewish people that *the law was given through Moses;*[18] on the
other hand, the *grace and truth* of the gospel *came through
Jesus Christ,* no less to the nations than to the Jews.

The gospel says, *each [hydria] holding two or three measures,*
for the authors and interpreters of holy scripture along with
the prophets speak sometimes only of the Father and the
Son — as in this case: *You have made all things in wisdom,*[19]
for the power and wisdom of God is Christ.[20] At another
time they also mention the Holy Spirit — according to [this
line] of the psalm: *By the word of the Lord the heavens were
made firm, and all the power of them by the Spirit of his mouth.*[21]
By the Word of the Lord and the Spirit understand the
whole Trinity, which is one God.[22]

---

14. Bede, Hom. I.11 above, and cf. Aug., *Tract. in Ioh.* 9, 6-17 (CC 36:
    93, 1 - 100, 26)
15. Dn 2:34-35; Aug., *Tract. in Ioh.* 9, 15 (CC 36: 98, 1/14); Jer., *In Dan.*
    (CC 75A: 795, 408/414)
16. Zc 3:9   17. 1 P 2:4-5   18. Jn 1:17
19. Ps 104:24 (103:24)   20. 1 Co 1:24   21. Ps 33:6 (32:6)
22. Greg., *Hom. in evang.* 2, 30, 7 (PL 76: 1225)

But as different as water is from wine is the sense in which the scriptures were understood before the Savior's coming from that [sense] which he himself revealed to the apostles when he came, and which he left to be perpetually followed by their disciples. Of course, the Lord could have filled empty hydrias with wine, since in the elementary stages of the world's creation he created all things out of nothing, but he preferred to make wine from water in order to teach that he had not come to cancel and repudiate the law and the prophets, but to fulfill them,[23] nor to do and to teach other things through the grace of the gospel than what the law and the prophets of scripture had indicated that he would do and teach.

Let us then see, brothers, the six hydrias filled with the saving waters of the scriptures. Let us see this water turned into the most delightful aroma and taste of wine. In the first age of the world, the righteous Abel was killed by his brother out of envy,[24] and on this account he was blessed by the everlasting glory of martyrdom, and received praise for his righteousness, also in the writings of the evangelists and apostles,[25] while the wicked slayer of his brother suffered the penalty of an eternal curse. There are people who, when they hear about this, become apprehensive that they will be damned with the wicked, and, longing to be blessed with the holy, they cast off all that might enkindle hatred and envy[26] and take care to please God through a sacrifice of justice, modesty, innocence, and patience. Such as these unquestionably find in the scriptures a vessel full of water from which they may rejoice that they have been beneficently cleansed and given drink. But if anyone understands the murderer Cain as the Jews' lack of faith, the killing of Abel as the passion of the Lord and Savior, and the earth which opened its mouth and received [Abel's] blood from Cain's hand[27] as the Church (which received,[28] in the mystery of its renewal, the blood of Christ poured

23. Mt 5:17   24. Gn 4:8
25. Mt 23:35; Lk 11:51; Heb 11:4; 12:24
26. Gn 37:8   27. Gn 4:11
28. 'received' (*accepit*); some MSS have 'may receive' (*accipiat*)

out by the Jews), undoubtedly they [who have this under-
standing] find water turned into wine, for they have a more
sacred understanding of the sayings of the sacred law.

As the second age of the world began, the world was destroyed by the waters of the flood because of the great number of sinners, and only Noah, together with his household,
was delivered in the ark on account of his righteousness.[29]
If upon hearing of the horrible devastation of this disaster,
and the marvelous deliverance of a few, one begins to live
more faultlessly, desiring to be delivered with the elect and
fearing to be exterminated with the condemned, one unquestionably has received a hydria of water by which one
may be cleansed or refreshed. But one may begin to see at
a more profound level, and come to an understanding of
the ark as the Church; of Noah as Christ; of the water which
washed away sinners as the waters of baptism, which washes
away sins; of all the animals which the ark contained[30] as
the multifarious differences among the baptized; of the dove
which brought an olive branch to the ark after the flood[31]
as the anointing of the Holy Spirit, with which the baptized
are imbued. [One who has this deeper understanding] unquestionably marvels at wine made from water, for in the
history of the ancient deeds he contemplates his own cleansing, sanctification, and justification being foretold.

In the third age of the world, God, testing Abraham's obedience, commanded him to offer to him as a holocaust his
one and only son, whom he loved.[32] Abraham did not delay in doing what he was ordered, but a ram was immolated in place of his son. Nevertheless, for his virtue of
extraordinary obedience[33] he was granted the inheritance
of an everlasting blessing.[34] Behold, [here] you have the
third hydria, for when you hear that a greater obedience
is repaid by a greater prize, you yourself [will] attempt to
learn and to possess obedience. If in the immolation of his

29. Gn 6-7
30. var.: 'of the human beings and animals'
31. Gn 8:11
32. Gn 22
33. var: 'for his extraordinary virtue of obedience'
34. Gn 22:17-18

one and only son, whom he loved, you understand the passion of the one concerning whom the Father says, *'This is my beloved Son in whom I am well-pleased'*[35] (in him, since his divinity remaining impassible, only his humanity suffered death and sorrow, it is as though a son was offered but a ram was slain); if you understand the blessing which was promised to Abraham about the nations' coming to belief as a gift fulfilled in you — then he has truly made wine out of water for you, since he has opened to you the spiritual sense, by whose new fragrance[2*] you are intoxicated.

At the start of the fourth age, David was alloted the kingdom of the Israelites in place of Saul. He was a humble, innocent and gentle exile, yet he was for a long time tormented by [Saul's] unjust persecution.[36] Behold, [here is] the fourth hydria filled by the saving fountain. Whoever upon hearing these things begins to strive after humility and innocence and to drive pride and envy from his heart, has, as it were, found a draught of the clearest water, by which he may be refreshed. But if he recognizes that Saul signifies the persecuting Jews, and David signifies Christ and the Church; and if he recognizes that on account of the [persecuting Jews'] lack of faith, both their material and spiritual sovereignty has been destroyed, while the reign of Christ and the Church will always remain; [with this understanding] he will perceive a cup of wine made from the water,[37] for he will know that he is reading not only about that king but about his own life and reign, where before he read [the story] as if it were an ancient history about others.

In the fifth age of the world, the sinful people were transported to Babylon,[38] taken into captivity by Nebuchadnezzar; but after seventy years, repenting and reformed, they were led back to their fatherland by Jesus[39] the high-priest. There they rebuilt the house of God, which had been burned

35. Mt 3:17   36. 1 S 15-16; 18-21
37. Var.: 'he will perceive that not only has wine been made from water'
38. 2 K 24-25; 2 Ch 36
39. I.e., Josue, or Jeshua, son of Josedec, high priest at that time; see Ezr 3:2

down, and the holy city, which had been destroyed.[40] If when a person reads or hears these things, he is seized by fear of sinning and flees to the remedy of repenting, he has been cleansed by the water of the purifying hydria. Moreover, one may learn to understand Jerusalem and God's temple as Christ's Church, Babylon as the confusion of sinners,[41] Nebuchadnezzar as the devil, Jesus the high-priest as the true and eternal high-priest Jesus Christ, and the seventy years as the plentitude of good works which are lavishly granted through the gifts of the Holy Spirit (on account of the ten commandments and the seven-fold grace of the same Spirit). And one may see it happen every day that some people are carried off from the Church by the devil through sinning, and others are reconciled by the grace of the Holy Spirit, regaining their senses through Christ and repenting. [One who understands the story in this way] has wine made from water, for understanding that those things which are written pertain to himself, he soon grows warm with the great heat of compunction, as if from new wine, and he earnestly asks to be liberated through Christ's grace from any sort of sin he detects making him a captive.

As the sixth age of the world began, the Lord appeared in the flesh; on the eighth day after his nativity he was circumcised in accordance with the law; on the thirty-third day after this[42] he was brought to the temple, and the offerings stipulated by the law were made for him.[43] Looking at the literal sense of this [story], we clearly learn what great diligence we should have in placing ourselves under the mysteries of the gospel faith, seeing that he, himself the lawgiver in terms of the letter, was careful to be consecrated first by the rites of the ancient ceremonies when he was bringing the blessing of grace, even though he consecrated everything by his divine influence. He thus took care to receive, and at the same time to hand on, the new sacraments of grace.

Behold, [here is] the sixth hydria for cleansing the contagion of sin, for giving drink from the joys of life, and for

40. Ezr 1-6   41. Jer., *Nom.* (CC 72: 138: 13/14)
42. Lv 12:4   43. Lk 2:21-24

bringing cleaner flowing waters to others. But in the circumcision of the eighth day you may understand baptism,
which has redeemed us from the death of our sins into the
mystery of the Lord's resurrection. In [Jesus'] being led into
the temple and the offering of the sacrificial victims of purification, you may recognize a prefiguration of any of the faithful entering from the baptistry to the holy altar and needing
to be consecrated by an exceptional sacrifical victim, the
Lord's body and blood. [If you have this understanding of
the story], you have been granted wine made from the water, and it is a most undiluted wine.

Furthermore, you can interpret the day of circumcision
as [a symbol of] the general resurrection of the human race,
when mortal generation will cease, and all mortality will
be changed into immortality; and you can understand the
leading of the circumcized into the temple with sacrificial
offerings [as a symbol of] the time after the resurrection
when the universal judgment is finished, and the saints,
then made incorruptible, will enter with their offerings of
good works to contemplate forever the form of divine majesty. [If you understand the story in this way], you will unquestionably see wondrous wine made from the water,
concerning which you should testify to its Maker and say,
And your inebriating cup, how splendid it is![44]

The Lord did not choose to make the wine at the marriage celebration from nothing, but, commanding six hydrias
to be filled with water, he marvelously turned this into wine
— for out of his bounty he granted six ages of saving wisdom in the world. When he himself came he made it fruitful by the virtue of a more sublime sense. Those things
which the fleshly are conscious of only in a material way
he unlocked so that they could be perceived spiritually.[45]
Do you wish to hear, brothers, how he made wine from
water? He appeared after his resurrection to two of his disciples walking on the road, and he went with them, and
*starting from Moses and all the prophets, he interpreted those
things in all of the scriptures which were about himself.*[46] Do you

44. Ps 23:5 (22:5)   45. Some MSS add: 'by the spiritual'
46. Lk 24:27

wish to hear next how they were inebriated by this wine?
Afterwards, when they recognized who it was who set before them the word of life, they said to one another, '*Was
not our heart burning in us when he was speaking on the road
and opening the scriptures to us'*?[47]

*Jesus said to the attendants, 'Fill the hydrias with water'. And
they filled them up to the top.* Who are represented by the attendants who were ordered to do this, unless it is Christ's
disciples, who filled the hydrias with water? They did not
do this by filling past ages of the world with the writings
of the law and the prophets, but by understanding [the
scriptures] prudently, and faithfully making them clear.
Scripture, whose attendants the prophets were, is both a
salutary draught of heavenly wisdom, and useful for the
correction of works. They filled them to the top, for they
rightly understood that there was no time among the ages
of the world that was without its holy teachers, who either
by their words or their examples, or by their writings,
opened up the way of life to mortals.

*And he said to them, 'Go and draw out some now and take it
to the chief steward'. And they took it.* The chief steward was
some expert on the law at that time, perhaps Nicodemus
or Gamaliel — or Saul, who was then [Gamaliel's] disciple,
though he is now Paul the apostle, the master of the whole
Church. When the word of the gospel, which was lying hidden in the letter of the law and in prophecy was believed
by such as these, wine made from water was set before the
chief steward.[3*] Hence it is duly reported that the chief
steward called the bridegroom and said, '*Every man puts out
the good wine first, and when* [the guests] *are inebriated, then
he puts out that which is worse. You have kept the good wine
until now'.* It is proper to teachers to recognize the difference between the law and the gospel, between the truth
and the shadow, and to bring forward for all of the earthly
kingdom, as promised by all the ancient teachings, the new
grace of the gospel faith and the everlasting gifts of the
heavenly fatherland.

47. Lk 24:32

Jesus performed this first of his signs in Cana of Galilee, and he manifested his glory. By this sign he made manifest that he was the King of glory,[48] and so the Church's bridegroom. He came to the marriage as a common human being, but as Lord of heaven and earth he could convert the elements as he wished. How beautifully appropriate it is that to begin the signs which he would show to mortals while he was still mortal, he turned water into wine; [but] when he had become immortal through his resurrection, to begin the signs which he would show to those who were pursuing only the goal of immortal life, he first imbued their fleshly and ignorant mind with the savor of heavenly knowledge. At first, when he was lingering[49] on earth, by the gift of his Spirit he opened their understanding, so that they could understand scripture.[50] Later, when the same [Spirit] was sent from heaven, he poured into their hearts the greater fragrance[51] of divine love along with spiritual wisdom, and in addition, he gave them knowledge of all languages[52] with which they would be able to set before the whole earth the grace of the life that they had attained.

Therefore, let us love with our whole mind, dearly beloved brothers, the marriage of Christ and the Church, which was prefigured then in one city and is now celebrated over the whole earth. And let us be joined to the heavenly joys of this [marriage] by an unwearied concentration on good works. Let us take care to celebrate this [marriage] wearing the pure garment of love, for we made our entrance invited by faith; and let us be very solicitous to wash away the soiled spots from our actions and our thoughts before the day of the final judgment, lest perhaps when the king who has made the marriage feast for his son enters, if he sees that we do not have the wedding garment of chastity, he may cast us out and send us into the outer darkness, with our hands and feet tied with respect to the capability of doing good.[53] Let us make the strong vessels of our hearts

---

48. Ps 24:10 (23:10)
49. i.e., between his resurrection and his ascension
50. Lk 24:27, 44-47   51. *flagrantia;* see endnote 2 below
52. Ac 2:1-11   53. Mt 22:2, 11-13

clean by faith, according to the purification [demanded by] heavenly commands, and let us fill them with the waters of saving knowledge by paying attention more frequently to sacred reading. Let us ask the Lord that the grace of knowledge which he has conferred upon us may not chance to puff us up, that it warm us with the fervor of his charity,[54] and that it turn us to seeking and being conscious only of divine things, so that we can become spiritually drunk, and we can ourselves sing with the prophet, *You have given us to drink the wine of compunction.*[55] And so it comes about that to us also, if we are making good progress, Jesus may manifest his glory both now in a partial way, insofar as we are capable of grasping it, and in the future perfectly. In this glory he lives and reigns with the Father in the unity of the Holy Spirit for all ages. Amen.

54. 1 Co 8:1   55. Ps 60:3 (59:5)

NOTES

1. At this point several manuscripts have the following addition: Remembering this hour when he was hanging on the cross, the Lord said to his mother, 'Behold, by my dying now is revealed what I took from you'. Nevertheless, this [human] nature was to be glorified afterwards in the glory of his resurrection. *His mother said to the attendants, 'Do whatever he says to you'.* His mother was aware of her son's humanity, although by what [he had just said] he might seem to have denied what that [humanity] required. Nevertheless, his mother was aware of her son's dutiful nature and that he would not deny what was asked [by her]. Confidently she commanded the attendants to fulfill the orders her son would give. (This is also found in the Ps.-Bede *Exposition on John's Gospel,* (*PL* 92: 658, 1-11).

2. I take *flagrantia* here as the attested spelling variant of *fragrantia* (see Niermeyer, p. 437). It could, however, also be taken as the noun derived from *flagro,* meaning 'a burning heat,' or metaphorically, 'ardor' or 'glow' (Glare, p. 709).

3. At this point two manuscripts have the following addition: And it is good that in the house of this marriage celebration, which is a figure of the sacraments of Christ and the Church, there was a *triclinium* [referring to the word translated 'chief steward,' *architriclinus*], that is, three ranks of those reclining at different heights are referred to, for there are three ranks of the faithful, which make up the Church, namely the married, the continent, and teachers. Hence Ezechiel also attests that only three men are to be delivered on judgment day, Noah, Daniel, and Job [Ezk 14:14, 20]. By Noah, who ruled the ark on the waves, he signifies all the governors of the Church. By Daniel, who in the middle of the royal treasures of Babylon strove after continence in a singular way, he signifies all those who by living continently deride unclean luxury [var. according to one ms.: who by living continently deride the luxury of the world]. By Job, who while leading a married life practiced the work of virtues and patience, which is to be imitated by all, he signifies all married people who are devoted to God. Therefore the first rank of those reclining at the marriage of the heavenly bridegroom, that is, of those spending their life [var.: of those rejoicing] in the faith and workings of the Church, is the rank of the married faithful; the second rank is the continent; and the highest rank is the preachers. [cf. Aug., *Ennar. in Ps.* 132, 5 (*CC* 40: 1929, 1 - 1930, 19)] The first and last parts of this passage are found in the Ps.-Bede *Exposition on John's Gospel,* (*PL* 92: 661, 50 - 662, 1).

homily 1.15

John, the baptist and precursor of our Lord and Savior, with his words had preached to the people for a long time that he was coming, and later he pointed him out with his finger as [Jesus] came to him, saying, as you have heard from the reading of the holy gospel, brothers, which was just now read, *'Behold the Lamb of God, behold him who takes away the sin of the world'*.

'Behold the Lamb of God'—behold one who is innocent and exempt from all sin, inasmuch as he was indeed bone of Adam's bones and flesh of Adam's flesh but derived no soiling stain of fault from sinful flesh.

'Behold him who takes away the sin of the world'—behold one who appears just among sinners, mild among the wicked (that is, like a lamb among wolves), and also has the power to justify sinners and the wicked. The apostle Peter shows how he takes away the sins of the world, and in what way he justifies the wicked, when [Peter] says, *You were not redeemed with corruptible silver or gold from your vain way of life, your fathers' traditions, but with the precious blood of Jesus Christ, as of an uncontaminated and immaculate lamb.*[1]

1. 1 P 1:18-19

And in the Apocalypse, John the apostle, whose gospel this is, says, *Who loved us and washed us from our sins in his blood.*[2] Not only did he wash us from our sins in his blood when he gave his blood for us on the cross, or when each of us was cleansed in his baptism by the mystery of his most sacred passion, but he also takes away every day the sins of the world, and washes us of our daily sins in his blood, when the memory of his blessed passion is reenacted on the altar, when a created thing, bread and wine, is transformed by the ineffable sanctification of the Spirit into the sacrament of his flesh and blood. Thus his body and blood is not poured forth and slain by the hands of the unfaithful to their own ruin, but he is taken by the mouth of the faithful to their salvation.[3]

The lamb in the law of passover rightly shows [us] a type of him, since having once liberated the people from their Egyptian servitude, it sanctified the people every year by being immolated in memory of their liberation, until he came, to whom such a sacrificial offering gave testimony. When he was offered to the Father for us as a sacrificial offering and for a sweet savor,[4] he transformed, by the lamb that was offered, the mystery of his passion into a created thing, bread and wine, having been made *a priest forever according to the order of Melchisedech.*[5]

There follows John's giving testimony to the Lord: 'This is he,' he says, 'about whom I said, "After me comes a man who ranks ahead of me because he was before me." ' [That is to say,] 'After me comes a man who was born in the world after me, who started to preach to the world after me, [but] *who ranks ahead of me*, since he excels me by the power of his majesty [6] as much as the sun excels the morning star, though appearing after it. *He was before me*, because *in the beginning was the Word and the Word was with God, and the Word was God'.*[7]

2. Rv 1:5
3. Greg., *Dial.* 4.58 (*PL* 77: 425)
4. cf. Gn 8:21; Ex 29:41; Lv 2:9, 12; 4:31; 8:28; 17:6; Nb 15:3, 7
5. Heb 7:17; Gn 14:18; Ps 110:4 (109:4)
6. Some MSS add: 'as much as a judge excels a herald'
7. Jn 1:1

Understand *'after me comes a man'* [in reference to] the time
of his human nativity, in which he was later in time than
John. Look at *'who ranks ahead of me'* [in reference to] the
primacy of his royal power, by which he presides over even
the angels. Understand *'because he was before me'* [in reference to] the eternity of his divine majesty, by which he is
equal to the Father. *'After me comes a man who ranks ahead
of me because he was before me'* — 'After me in his humanity
comes one who excels me in dignity because he was prior
to me in his divinity'.

'And I was not aware of him,' he says. It is certain that John
was aware of the Lord, to whom he was sent to give testimony. He was preaching that he was to come as judge
of all, saying, *'His winnowing fan is in his hand, and he will
thoroughly clean out his threshing floor'.*[8] He testified that the
Holy Spirit would have to be given by him, saying, *'He will
baptize you in the Holy Spirit'.*[9] He desired to himself be
cleansed by him, saying, *'I ought to be baptized by you, and
do you come to me'?*[10] How is it then that [John] says, *'And
I was not aware of him,'* unless [in the sense] that now since
[Jesus] had been baptized, [John] acknowledged him more
completely, though he had known him before? He had
known him as Savior and Judge of the world, but when
the Holy Spirit descended upon [Jesus], he recognized at
a more profound level the power of his majesty. For since
blessed John was worthy to see the Holy Spirit (although
in bodily form), and since he was worthy to hear the voice
of the Father (although sounding in a physical way), we
must not doubt that he gained much from what he saw and
heard, and that he received much heavenly knowledge concerning the excellence of [Christ's] divine power, the eyes
of his mind being uncovered, so much so that in comparison with the understanding with which he then began to
be illuminated, it would have seemed to him that he had
been ignorant of him in every possible way.

Diligently giving testimony to the Lord, for which
[purpose] he was sent, [John] continued, *'But so that he may*

8. Mt 3:12   9. Mt 3:11   10. Mt 3:14

be made manifest in Israel — on that account I have come baptizing with water'. That is, to speak clearly, 'I have not come baptizing with water because by baptizing I can take away the sins of the world, but so that by baptizing and preaching I may manifest to the people of Israel the one who, baptizing in the Holy Spirit, is capable of taking away the sins not only of Israel, but also of the whole world, if it would believe in him. On that account I came baptizing unto repentance, so that by so baptizing I may prepare the way for him who will baptize unto the forgiveness of sins'.

And John gave testimony, saying, 'I saw the Spirit descending like a dove from heaven, and it rested on him'. It is good that the Spirit descended upon the Lord in the form of a dove, so that the faithful may learn[11] that they cannot be filled with his Spirit unless they are simple, unless they possess true peace with their brothers, which is signified by the kiss of doves. Ravens also have kisses, but they tear flesh (which a dove does not do at all), signifying those *who speak peace with their neighbor, but wicked things are in their hearts.*[12] A dove, which by nature is innocent of the tearing of flesh,[13] most suitably fits those innocents who pursue peace and sanctity with everyone, *solicitous to keep the unity of the Spirit in the bond of peace.*[14] And so the Spirit, by descending as a dove, does not represent merely its own innocence and simplicity, or that of him on whom it descended, but likewise that of those who *think of* him *in goodness and seek him in simplicity of heart.*[15] The Lord himself says in praise of the piety that they share with one accord, and of the gentleness granted by a spiritual grace, *One is my dove; she is the* [only] *one of her mother, the elect of her progenetrix.*[16] Indeed, he calls the grace of the Spirit 'the mother and progenetrix of the Church'. By that inspiring [grace] she too receives the capacity of being rightly called a dove. Accordingly, in Hebrew, the language in which holy scripture was set forth, 'spirit' is a name that is feminine in gender. On this account, the Church is appropriately given the name 'the one dove

---

11. Some MSS add: 'that they cannot become his members unless'
12. Ps 28:3 (27:3)   13. Aug., *Tract. in Ioh.* 6, 4 (CC 36: 55, 5/11
14. Eph 4:3   15. Ws 1:1   16. Sg 6:8

of Christ,' and 'the elect of her mother and progenetrix,' for undoubtedly it is not because of her own merits, but because of a gift of spiritual grace she has received, that she is gathered into the unity of the Christian faith from many nations, that she is gladdened by a mutual dove-like peace, [and] that she is blessed by her share in election.

'*And I,*' [John] says, '*was not aware of him*'. You understand what is implied: '[I did not recognize him] as sublimely as I recognized him when the Spirit descended upon him'. '*But he who sent me to baptize with water said to me, "The one upon whom you will see the Spirit descending and resting upon him, he it is who baptizes with the Holy Spirit." ' The Lord baptizes with the Holy Spirit, pardoning sins through the gift of the Holy Spirit. For either he would first baptize some of his disciples with water, through whom the river of baptism would flow to the rest of the faithful; he would baptize them too with the Spirit by unloosing them from their sins and administering the gifts of the Spirit — or else his faithful, calling upon his name, would baptize the elect with water and anoint them with sacred chrism. Nevertheless, he himself baptizes them in the Holy Spirit, for no one except him is capable of releasing the bonds of sins or of bestowing the gifts of the Holy Spirit.

Hence when the evangelist John had said, *The Pharisees heard that Jesus was making and baptizing more disciples than John,* he straightaway continued with, *although Jesus did not baptize, but his disciples did,*[17] clearly teaching that Jesus' disciples baptize with water in his name; nevertheless he himself is rather to be understood as baptizing, since he pardons sins.[18] The Lord baptizes in the Holy Spirit when, through the inspiration of the same Spirit, he enkindles the hearts of his faithful ones with the fervor of his charity or of fraternal charity. For, [scripture] says, *The charity of God is poured out in your hearts through the Holy Spirit who has been given to us.*[19] He baptizes in the Holy Spirit when he gives to any of the elect a manifestation of the Spirit for the sake of an

17. Jn 4:1-2
18. Aug., *Tract. in Ioh.* 5, 7-9; 6, 6-7 (CC 36: 44, 1 - 46, 26; 56, 1 - 57, 31)
19. Rm 5:5

advantage in doing works of virtue. Concerning this baptism he said to his disciples when he was about to ascend to heaven, *'You will be baptized with the Holy Spirit not many days hence'.*[20]

But this must be looked at more carefully, because when he had said, *'The one upon whom you see the Spirit descending,'* he added on, *'and resting upon him'.* His Spirit also descends on the saints. But without doubt the Spirit sometimes comes in their hearts and sometimes withdraws, because as long as they are in the body they cannot be without sin, [and] because they are not capable of directing the eye of their mind always to the contemplation of heavenly things, but often they bend it toward concern about their earthly way of life. Hence it is said, *'The Spirit breathes where he wishes, and you hear his voice but you do not know whence he comes or where he goes'.*[21] The Spirit comes to the saints [and] goes from the saints, so that they may be refreshed from time to time by the frequently-recurring light of the return of him whom they are not capable of having always. However, the Spirit remains continually in the only Mediator between God and human beings, the man Jesus Christ,[22] in whom he does not find any stain of unclean thought, which he would shun. [The Spirit] remained wholly in him, not only from that time when John saw [the Spirit] descending upon him, but from the time when he began to become a human being [as] he was conceived by [the Spirit's] instrumental activity.[23] Hence he too has the power of giving to men, no less than the Father does, as he attests, stating, *'The Paraclete, the Holy Spirit, whom the Father will send in my name, will teach you all things'.*[24] And in another place he showed that he himself would send him: *'For if I do not go away, the Paraclete will not come to you. If I go away, I will send him to you'.*[25] The reason for this is that there is one substance [and one] indivisible activity in the divinity of the Father and the Son and the Holy Spirit.

Now concerning the Spirit — that he comes by his own volition where he wishes, and he works what he wishes

20. Ac 1:5   21. Jn 3:8   22. 1 Tm 2:5
23. *ministerio et opere*   24. Jn 14:26   25. Jn 16:7

by his own power — the Son bears witness where he says what I have recorded above, *'The Spirit breathes where he wishes'*.[26] [And] the Apostle says, *All these things are the work of one and the same Spirit, who distributes to each individual as he wishes*.[27] The reason why the Spirit is shown descending upon the one who was baptized, in whom he always remained, was so that the Baptist too might acknowledge in a more lofty way the one whom he had already been preaching, and so that he might give a sign to believers that they could by no means be worthy of the baptism of that same Spirit unless they had been baptized with water.

Next, we must seek how the sign of acknowledgement of the Son of God (that the Spirit descended and rested upon him) was special, since he gave a promise to his disciples, saying, *'And I will ask the Father, and he will give you another Paraclete, to remain with you forever, the Spirit of truth'*. And a little later: *'He will remain among you and he will be in you'*.[28] For if the Spirit remains among God's chosen servants, and if he will be among them, what does it add to the Son of God's greatness that the Spirit remains upon him?

We must note that the Holy Spirit will always remain in the Lord, whereas in holy human beings, as long as they are clothed in a mortal body, [the Spirit] may remain with some forever [but] may withdraw from others to return [later]. He remains among them so that they may devote themselves to good acts, love voluntary poverty, follow gentleness, mourn with desire for eternal things,[29] hunger and thirst after justice, [and] may embrace mercy, purity of heart and the tranquility of peace; but also so that they may not be afraid to suffer persecution for the observance of justice,[30] so that they may desire to devote themselves to almsgiving, prayers and fasting, and the other fruits of the Spirit. [The Spirit] withdraws at times, however, so that they may not always have the capability of curing the sick, restoring the dead to life, [31] casting out demons, or even

26. Jn 3:8   27. 1 Co 12:11   28. Jn 14:16-17
29. *aeternorum*, the reading of several MSS   30. Mt 5:3-10
31. Some MSS add 'cleansing lepers'

prophesying. He remains always so that they can have virtues [and] live in a marvelous way; he comes at times so that what they are internally may shine forth also to others through the signs of [their] miracles.

'And I have seen,' [John] says, *'and given testimony that this is the Son of God'.* Above he had said, *'After me comes a man who ranks ahead of me'.* Now he gives testimony *'that this is the Son of God,'* clearly designating the truth of both natures, namely the human and the divine, in one and the same person of Christ. Let Mani blush when he hears *'a man comes'*; let Photinus fall silent when he hears *'this is the Son of God'. Let the gentle hear and be glad,* [32] for after John came a man stronger than John, who baptizes in the Holy Spirit, and he is the Son of God. Because we human beings have drawn away from God through pride, the Son of God became a human being through mercy, so that as one and the same [person] he might be one with the Father through his divinity and with us through his humanity; so that by a human nature like ours he might struggle with the enemy for us, [and] by a divine nature consubstantial with the Father he might recreate us in the image and likeness of God, which we lost by sinning; so that through death, which is ours in our weakness, he might destroy him who has sovereignty over death, and through the impassibility of his divine nature he might reconcile us to God the Father, with whom he lives and reigns, God, in the unity of the Holy Spirit throughout all ages. Amen.

---

32. Ps 34:2 (33:3)

homily 1.16

The sublimity of divine scripture is so great and of such a sort that not only words reported as having been said by holy people or by our Lord himself are full of spiritual mysteries, but so are even the circumstantial details which seem to be set down simply. For behold, dearly beloved brothers, we have heard the gospel tell us that *John was standing* [there] *and two of his disciples, and turning his gaze on Jesus as he walked by, he said, 'Behold the Lamb of God'.* We immediately recognize (or rather call back to mind as something we already know) the reason why his precursor called Jesus the Lamb of God, namely because he knew that [Jesus] was singularly innocent, beyond other mortals clean, that is, from every sin; because he foresaw that [Jesus] was going to redeem us in his own blood; because of his own volition he was going to lavish [upon us] the gift of his wool, from which we can make for ourselves a wedding garment — that is, he was going to leave us an example of living by which we ought to be warmed in love. This testimony of the Lord's precursor, because it is easily accessible to the faithful, quickly pours into the hearts of those who hear it a fountain of deepest love.

But it should not be supposed that there was no reason, having to do with mystical meaning, for the evangelist's mentioning, when he was about to relate this, the fact that John was standing with his disciples, but Jesus was walking; and particularly [for mentioning] that [Jesus] was walking to the place where he could show John's disciples, who were following him, the lodging in which he was dwelling, and [for the evangelist's mentioning] other things of this sort which the continuation of the gospel reading records. If [these things] are scrutinized with attention to detail, we will find that they redound with heavenly and mystical meanings. *John was standing,* and he turned his gaze on Jesus because he had already ascended that great summit of the soul's perfection from which he rightfully deserved to look upon the eminence of divine majesty. He was standing, because he had climbed up to that stronghold of virtues from which he could not be cast down by any wicked deeds brought about by temptations. And his disciples were standing with him, because with their hearts unshakable they were following his instruction.

The gospel says, *And turning his gaze on Jesus as he walked by,* [John] *said, 'Behold, the Lamb of God'.* Jesus' walking suggests the divinely-arranged plan of his incarnation, by which he deigned to come to us and to present to us an example for living, just as his lodging is a very apt designation of the eternity of his divinity, in which he is always equal to the Father. Turning his gaze on Jesus as he walked by, John said, *'Behold, the Lamb of God'.* Seeing him keeping company with human beings, and demonstrating to them by his deeds and words the source of heavenly life, [John] announced clearly that [Jesus] was not as he had supposed, but that he was the one who was sent by God the Father into the world for the redemption of the human race, [and] he was the one who would give a model of innocence and patience to those who believed in him, concerning whose coming in the flesh the prophet spoke out, saying, *He is led like a sheep to the slaughter, and like a lamb before the shearer he remains silent, without voice.*[1] And again, *He was wounded on account of our sins, and by his bruises we have been healed.*[2]

1. Is 53:7   2. Is 53:5

And the two disciples heard him speaking, and they followed Jesus. When John gave testimony that Jesus was the Lamb of God, the two disciples followed him, desiring to receive the word of grace from Jesus himself rather than from his precursor, so that they might in that way deserve to be counted among the heritage of God's lambs. It is good that we find that the first disciples who followed the Lord were two in number, so that they might also designate mystically that all who follow him perfectly must be devoted by a two-fold love, that is, [they should be] on fire with love of their Redeemer, and at the same time with love of their brothers.

Jesus turned and, seeing them following him, said to them, 'What do you seek'? Jesus could not have been ignorant of what John's disciples who were following him were seeking, but by turning to those who were following, by first inquiring about what they were seeking, [and] by giving them confidence to ask for whatever they wished, he made it clearly known how much he is delighted by our zeal for good, [and] how willingly he goes to meet those who are starting on the journey of truth, in order to bring them help.

They said to him, 'Rabbi' (which interpreted means Master), 'where do you dwell'? They did not wish to enjoy transitory instruction in the truth, but instead they inquired about the lodging where he was dwelling, so that at that time they could more freely be imbued with his words in secret, and thereafter could visit him more often in order to be instructed more fully. Hence, because he saw that they were asking, seeking, and knocking well,[3] he was willing to reserve for them the secret retreat of his hidden mysteries, and as he led them in, he illuminated them with the rudiments of the gospel faith which they desired, for there follows: *'Come and see'.* And at once there is added, *They came and saw where he was staying, and they stayed with him that day.*

If there is a desire to look in a more profound sense into what course of action is suggested for us by the disciples' having come to the Lord when he was walking, but

---

3. Mt 7:7-11

immediately then inquiring about where he was dwelling, [these facts] doubtlessly advise us that whenever we recall to our mind the 'passing over'[4] of his incarnation, we should ask that he may deign to show us his dwelling-place, his eternal lodging which is with the Father, as we say with Moses, 'Lord, show us your glory'.[5] His commanding the disciples to 'come and see' where he was staying shows us the zeal for virtues that we must take on, by which we can come to eternal joys. To come after Jesus means that we are able to see his lodging by our good works, to which he himself pointed out beforehand that we should devote ourselves; and [thus] by daily progress in them we are able to come into possession of the summit of the divine vision.

They came and saw where he was staying, and they stayed with him that day. It was about the tenth hour. Because the law was given in ten commandments, it is usual for the perfection of the law to be indicated by the number ten. It is therefore good that the disciples came at the tenth hour to see Jesus' lodging, for one who desires to see God must surely make himself subject to God's mandates, and one who is trying to reach later the enjoyment of the light of divine contemplation must first, with the Lord's aid, fulfill the ten commandments of the law through works of light, as it were illuminating the ten hours of the day with the sun.[6] And those staying that day with the Lord awaited evening in the most blissful contemplation of truth. But indeed, after bringing to perfection their good works, [and] after fulfilling the Lord's commands, all of the elect are to achieve with him that everlasting day which is subject to no end, with him, namely, to whom the prophet sang, desiring to see him, *for better is one day in your courts than thousands.*[7]

Andrew, the brother of Simon Peter, was one of the two who had heard John and had followed [Jesus]. He first found his brother Simon and said to him, 'We have found the Messiah' (which interpreted is 'the Christ'). And he led him to Jesus. Andrew brought his brother Simon too the good news about the following of the Lord whom he had found. This is truly to find the Lord — to be aflame with true love of him, and to take care also of one's brother's salvation. One follows his Maker's leadership perfectly when he also strives to have the companionship of his neighbor insofar as he can. *'We have found,'* Andrew said, *'the Messiah' (which interpreted is 'the Christ').* 'Messiah' is the same as 'Christ'—'Messiah' in the Hebrew language means 'Christ' in Greek; in Latin it is interpreted 'the Anointed One'. Hence *'chrisma'* in Greek means 'anointing' in Latin.[8] The Lord is named Christ, that is, the Anointed One, because, as Peter says, *'God has anointed him with the Holy Spirit and with power'.*[9] Hence the psalmist also speaks in his praise, *God, your God, has anointed you with the oil of gladness above your companions.*[10] He calls us his companions since we have also been fully anointed with visible chrism for the reception of the grace of the Holy Spirit in baptism, and we are called 'Christians' from Christ's name. He was anointed above his companions since, as John the Baptist bore witness, *'not by measure does God give the Spirit,'* but *'he has given all things into [Jesus'] hand'.*[11]

Concerning [his] companions in the anointing, the Apostle says, *To each of us grace is given according to the measure of Christ's bestowal.*[12] Both priests and kings are called 'christs' in the law, undoubtedly as figures of this King and High Priest, our Lord and Savior, and as a type of him they were also anointed with earthly oil.[13] Not only they, but also the faithful of our own time, as they are called 'Christians' from Christ, so also are they rightly called 'christs'—from the anointing with the sacred chrism, from the grace of the Spirit with which they are consecrated. The prophet testified [to this] when he said, *You went forth for the salvation of your people, so that you might save your christs.*[14] He did indeed go forth for the salvation of his people, so that he might save

---

8. Aug., *Tract. in Ioh.* 7, 13 (CC 36: 74, 6/11)
9. Ac 10:38   10. Ps 45:7 (44:8)   11. Jn 3:34-5
12. Eph 4:7
13. cf.Bede, *Hom.* I.5 (CC 122: 36, 163/167)
14. Hab 3:13 (Vet. Lat.)

his christs, *since on account of us human beings and on account of our salvation, he descended from heaven and became incarnate* so that he might grant to us who have been thoroughly anointed and healed by spiritual grace to be sharers in his holy name.

There follows: *Jesus, looking at him, said, 'You are Simon, son of John'*. Jesus looked at Simon not only with exterior eyes, but also with the internal power of vision of his divinity, in accordance with what [was said] regarding blessed Samuel: *'A human being sees the outward appearance; God looks at the heart'.*[15] He saw the simplicity of [Peter's] heart; he saw the sublimity of his soul, as a consequence of which he was to be given precedence over the whole Church. He saw that when Andrew called, [Peter] rushed quickly to him, aflame with love, and so as he came he addressed him in a familiar manner of speaking: *'You are,'* he said, *'Simon, son of John'*. It is no great thing for the Lord to say the name of any man or of his father, since he holds the names of all the saints inscribed in heaven.[16] But since he was about to bestow upon the disciple a name more sublime in merit, and since he was about to give him an identifying name which would be fitting for the head of the whole Church, he first wished to show that even the [name] which he had received from his parents did not lack signification regarding virtue. Simon means 'obedient,' and John means 'the grace of God'.[17] *'You are Simon, son of John'* — 'You are the obedient son of God's grace'. And rightly is he called by a name [meaning] obedience, since first he took care to [come to] see the Lord as soon as Andrew invited him; and later, when the Lord himself called him to discipleship together with Andrew, whom [the Lord] called at the same time, he did not put off following him immediately, but left behind the nets which he made his living by using.[18]

Andrew's name too carries with it a true image of his mind. For the Greek 'Andrew' means 'manly' in Latin.[19] By willingly following the Lord, either at John's preaching

---

15. 1 S 16:7   16. Lk 10:20
17. Jer., *Nom.* (CC 72: 148, 4; 140, 1/2); *In Matth.* 16, 17 (CC 77: 141, 59/60)
18. Mt 4:18-20; Mk 1:16-18   19. Isid., *Etymol.* 7, 9, 11

or at the order[20] of the Lord himself, he shows [us] that he belonged to the heritage of those who boldly despise temporal possessions out of love for eternal things, [and] who believe that they will *see the good things of the Lord in the land of the living*.[21] Until they attain these things, they strive *to await the Lord* with the psalmist, and *to act in a manly way*, and *to strengthen their heart*.[22]

Simon's being the son of John, that is, of 'the grace of God,' clearly demonstrates that whatever everlasting reward he deservedly got from the Lord for his obedience, [or] whatever way in which he committed himself to obeying the Lord, he undoubtedly received the ability to have it entirely through the prevenient grace of divine benevolence. Behold, you have heard, dearly beloved brothers, why the first of the apostles was at first referred to as Simon, [and] what mystical meaning there was in his being the son of John. It remains to be carefully investigated what hidden mystery may be contained in the name with which the Savior then renamed him.

'*You*,' [Jesus] said, '*will be called Cephas*,' *which interpreted is* '*Peter*'. We have no need to seek another interpretation for the identifying name Peter, as if it were Hebrew or Syriac, but we must know for certain that in Greek and Latin 'Peter' signifies the same thing as Cephas does in Syriac, and in both languages the name is derived from [the word for] rock.[23] He was called Peter by reason of the firmness of his faith; he was called Peter by reason of the invincible toughness of his mind; he was called Peter because with single devotion he clung to that most solid rock, concerning whom the Apostle says: *The rock is Christ*.[24] Thus it was that that same rock, namely Christ, once asked his disciples who they would say that he was, and Peter responded saying, '*You are the Christ, Son of the living God*'.[25]

[Christ] then immediately granted a worthy remuneration for his pure confession according to the signification

20. 'order' = *iussionem*; var.: 'vision' = *uisionem*
21. Ps 27:13 (26:13)   22. Ps 27:14 (26:14)
23. Jer., *Nom.* (CC 72: 142, 14); Isid., *Etymol.* 7, 9, 2-3
24. 1 Co 10:4   25. Mt 16:15

of both men,[26] but the very appellation 'Peter' also made clear what sort of sacramental meaning it carried within it-self.[27] For first concerning 'Simon' he said, *'Blessed are you, Simon Bar-Jona, for flesh and blood has not revealed this to you, but my Father, who is in heaven'.* And then he added concerning 'Peter,' *'And I say to you that you are Peter, and upon this rock I will build my Church'.*[28]—'You are Peter, and upon this rock from which you have received your name, that is, upon me myself, I will build my Church. Upon this perfection of faith which you have confessed I will build my Church, and if anyone turns aside from the society of this confession, even though it may seem to him that he does great things, he will not belong to the building which is my Church'.

So Peter received his name from the firm rock, namely Christ, whom he ardently loved. And indeed Christ is called a rock because he bestowed a stronghold incapable of being captured upon those fleeing to him for protection, [and] because he rendered those hoping in him protected and safe from the snares of the ancient enemy. Nor may we pass over another reason why the Lord is called a rock—because he administers to us flowing streams of spiritual charismatic gifts, [and] because he purifies us with the most sacred communion in his blood.

This is more easily understood, and perhaps it will be retained with more pleasure, if we recall to our memory what, according to the historical sense, the rock is, concerning which the Apostle explains that it mystically signified Christ.[29] The people, after they were liberated from Egyptian servitude, came through the Red Sea into the desert, where they journeyed for forty years until they came to the land of promise. Once, when they were worn out by hunger and thirst in the wilderness, they cried out to Moses.[30]

---

26. 'both men' = *utriusque hominis*; var.: 'both names' = *utriusque nominis,* but not in the best MSS
27. Aug., *Retrac.* 1, 20, 1 (CSEL 36: 97, 15 - 98, 16); *Serm.* 76, 1, 2-3 (PL 38: 479-80); *Serm.* 149, 6, 7 (PL 38: 802); *Serm.* 244, 1 (PL 38: 1148); *Serm.* 270, 2 (PL 38: 1238-39); *Serm.* 295, 1, 1 - 2, 2 (PL 38: 1348-49)
28. Mt 16:17-18   29. 1 Co 10:1-4   30. Ex 14-16

And, as is written, when Moses prayed, the Lord *rained down upon them manna to eat, and he gave them the bread of heaven.*[31] Once again [the Lord] commanded that [Moses] strike a rock with a rod, and when he did it, water came out and the people drank.[32] Hence it is said in the psalm, *He struck the rock, and the waters flowed.*[33]

We, dearly beloved brothers, we are the people of God who, liberated from the yoke of Egyptian servitude, passed through the Red Sea, for when we were baptized by water we received forgiveness of the sins which were oppressing us. In the midst of the hardships of the present life, as though in the dryness of a desert, we await the entry promised us into our heavenly fatherland. In this desert we are in danger of wasting away from spiritual thirst and hunger, if our Redeemer's gifts do not strengthen us, if the sacraments of his incarnation do not renew us. He himself is the manna which refreshes us with heavenly nourishment so that we may not waste away in the journey of this world. He himself is the rock which intoxicates us with spiritual gifts — the rock who, when struck by the wood of the cross, pours forth from his side the drink which is life for us. Hence he says in the gospel, *'I am the bread of life. He who comes to me will not hunger, and he who believes in me will not ever thirst'.*[34] And, fittingly enough in the sphere of figurative meaning, the people were first saved through the sea, and so mystically came to the food, the manna, and to the rock, the drink, for he first cleanses us with the water of regeneration, and then allows us to cross over to a participation in the sacred altar, where we will receive a share in the flesh and blood of our Redeemer.

It has been a pleasure to speak so extensively in explaining these things concerning the mystery of the spiritual rock from which the first shepherd of the Church received his name, and upon which the whole fabric of holy Church continues immovable and unshaken, and through which the Church itself is born and nourished. [This has been a pleasure] because when things sent in advance in the former

31. Ps 78:24 (77:24)   32. Ex 17:6   33. Ps 78:20 (77:20)
34. Jn 6:35

figurative way are at last spiritually clarified by a new explanation, such things have a tendency to be implanted in the hearts of hearers much more firmly, and sometimes more sweetly, than things which we are admonished to believe or to do without any figurative examples, but only by simple telling.

Let us take care, however, dearly-beloved brothers, as we cling always to the stronghold of this Rock, not to be torn away from the firmness of the faith by any frightening hostility, or any soothing serenity of transitory things. With temporal delights put behind us, may only the heavenly gifts of our Redeemer delight us at the present time; among the hardships of the world may only the hope of seeing him console us. Let us attentively recall the illustrious example of David, the prophet and king. Since he could find no comfort for his soul in the many honors and riches of the kingdom which came to him, having finally raised the gaze of his mind to heavenly desires, he was mindful of God, and he was delighted.[35] And so that we may be worthy to come to this vision of his, let us attempt to put away from our body and mind the obstacles of the vices which tend to impede this [vision]. For one does not come to him except by the straight path of [good] works, and his pure face is not seen, except by those who are pure of heart. *'Blessed are the pure of heart for they will see God'.*[36] May he deign to grant us this since it is he who deigned to promise it, Jesus Christ, our God and Lord, who lives and reigns with the Father in the unity of the Holy Spirit through all ages. Amen.

---

35. Ps 77:3 (76:4) LXX   36. Mt 5:8

homily 1.17

John 1:43-51   *After Epiphany*

We have heard in the gospel reading, dearly-beloved brothers, about the generous grace of our Redeemer — that he is wont not only to call us mercifully to follow, but also to receive us gladly when we come, and to bring us along to the recognition of the brightness of his divinity. We have heard about the devout faith, charity, and works of the disciples, and undoubtedly it is in these three virtues of heavenly life that the whole perfection of the Church of the present [age] consists, because *without faith it is impossible to please God*[1] and *faith without works is vain.*[2] And no matter what virtues one is endowed with, or no matter how far one has progressed by faith, if one does not have charity, it avails him nothing.[3] That Philip not only followed Jesus when he called him, but also proclaimed him to Nathanael as one to be followed is unquestionably *faith which works by love*[4]— faith because he did not put off believing in Jesus, whom he recognized to be the Christ; a work of love because by following [Jesus] immediately [Philip] disclosed how much he loved the one whom he recognized; he showed how greatly he was on

---

1. Heb 11:6   2. Jm 2:20   3. 1 Co 13:3   4. Ga 5:6

fire with love of his neighbor by bringing him good news. His neighbor, Nathanael, revealed how much loving care he had for the the Master of truth, to whom he did not delay to come as soon as he was called. He made known the greatness of the faith he had received by its perfection, and immediately with a clear voice he confessed him to be Son of God and King of Israel.

But now that we have briefly gone over these ideas, I would like to run through the whole course of the gospel reading, repeating [it] from the beginning and scrutinizing it more at length. *Jesus wished to go into Galilee. And he found Philip and said to him, 'Follow me'.* From what came before it is evident that the place from which Jesus wished to go into Galilee was Judaea, where John was baptizing and giving testimony to [Jesus], that he was the Lamb of God. From [John's] disciples [Jesus] summoned two to follow him, and one of them, Andrew, led his brother Peter to him also.[5] According to the spiritual sense, it is clear what it means to follow the Lord, and you already recognize this because of frequent explanations to your fraternity. One follows the Lord if one imitates him. One follows the Lord if, insofar as human weakness allows, one does not abandon those examples of humility which, as a human being, the Son of God demonstrated. One follows [the Lord] if, by showing oneself to be a companion of his sufferings, one painstakingly longs to attain communion in his resurrection and ascension.

There must be some reason with respect to the mystical meaning for its being reported that when Jesus was going to say, *'Follow me,'* to Philip, he decided to go into Galilee. Galilee is interpreted as 'an emigration made,' or as 'revelation'.[6] In that it means 'an emigration made,' it designates the progress of the faithful, by which they strive either to 'emigrate' from vices to the eminence of virtues, or to make daily progress in passing gradually from lesser to greater in those virtues. In this way they may go, with the Lord's help, from this vale of tears to the height of heavenly glad-

5. Jn 1:35-41   6. Jer., *Nom.* (CC 72: 131, 2)

ness. In that [Galilee] denotes 'revelation,' it suggests the blessedness of eternal life for which they are laboring in the present. The psalmist includes both interpretations of this name [Galilee] in one verse, when he says, *They will walk from virtue to virtue; the God of gods will be seen in Zion.*[7] This is the vision concerning which the Apostle says, *We, with unveiled faces beholding the Lord's glory, are transformed from glory to glory, as by the Spirit of the Lord.*[8] It is good, therefore, that when Jesus was about to call a disciple to follow him, he wished to go forth into Galilee, that is, into 'an emigration made,' or to 'revelation,' so that, just as he himself (as the gospel bears witness) *advanced in wisdom and age and grace among God and human beings,*[9] and just as he suffered and rose and thus entered into his glory,[10] so also he might show his followers that they should advance in virtues, and should 'emigrate' through transitory sufferings to the gifts of eternal joys.

Philip was from Bethsaida, the city of Andrew and Peter. We must not suppose that it was by chance, and without a mystical reason, that the evangelist wished to point out the name of the city Philip was from, and the fact that it was the same [city as that] of Andrew and Peter. [We must suppose] that by the name of the city he was concerned to point out typologically what sort [of person] Philip was in heart already then, and what sort he was going to be with respect to his ministry, and also what sort Peter and Andrew [were going to be]. Bethsaida means 'the house of hunters'[11]; and certainly they were hunters who heard from the Lord, *'Come after me, and I will make you become fishers of men'.*[12] He too was a hunter who, before he was ordained to the ministry of preaching by the Lord, immediately showed by spontaneously preaching how intent he was on catching souls [to bring them] to life: [Philip] *found Nathanael and said to him, 'We have found him of whom Moses wrote in the law and the prophets, Jesus, the son of Joseph, from Nazareth'.*

Let us see how great [was] the net of his faith, and how, when he found his brother, he encircled him, entwining him

7. Ps 84:7 (83:8)   8. 2 Co 3:18   9. Lk 2:52   10. Lk 24:26
11. Jer., *Nom.* (CC 72: 135, 21/22)   12. Mt 4:19

in the huge mesh of his devout preaching, since he providently longed to capture him for eternal salvation. He said that he who had been found was the one whom Moses and the prophets designated in their writings as the one who was to come.[13] He calls him by the name 'Jesus' because the oracles of the prophets were in agreement that this would be the name of the Christ. Desiring to be saved through his grace, Habakkuk says, *I will glory in the Lord; I will rejoice in God my Jesus.*[14] And Zechariah too, making mention of a temptation, in which temptation [15]he was victorious over the devil, says, *And he showed me Jesus the high priest, and he was standing before the angel of the Lord, and Satan was standing on his right hand to oppose him.*[16] Saluting and awaiting from afar the mystery of his incarnation, the patriarch Jacob says, *'I will await your Salvation, Lord'.*[17] Since in Hebrew Jesus means 'saving' or 'savior' in Latin,[18] the psalmist likewise, promising to the faithful people an eternal vision of him, says in the person of God the Father, *I will fill him with length of days, and I will show him my Salvation.*[19] Also, when that venerable and aged prophet of the New Testament, Simeon, received in his hands one who was small in body, he perceived in his mind that he was great in divinity, [and] instructed by the Spirit gave thanks thus: *'Now, Lord, dismiss your servant according to your word in peace, because my eyes have seen your Salvation'.*[20]

[Philip] called him *'son of Joseph'* not in order to allege that he was born of a union of male and female, since he had learned in the prophets that he was to be born of a virgin, but in order to teach that, in accordance with the oracles of the prophets, he had come from the house and family of David, from which he knew that Joseph had descended. For it should not to be wondered at that Philip called him 'son of Joseph' (whom he knew to be the husband of his

---

13. Some MSS add: 'so that it would consequently be understood by all who followed that it was he whom all the writings of the ancients served by affirming his coming'
14. Hab 3:18 (Vet. Lat.)
15. Several MSS omit the second 'temptation'
16. Zc 3:1   17. Gn 49:18   18. Isid., *Etymol.* 7, 2, 7
19. Ps 91:16 (90:16)   20. Lk 2:29-30

inviolate mother), since we read that even the inviolate and ever-virgin Mother herself, following the custom of the general public, spoke thus: *'Son, why have you done so to us? Behold, your father and I have been seeking you in sorrow'.*[21] [Philip] added also [Jesus'] native place, *'from Nazareth,'* in order to indicate that he was the one about whom they had read in the prophets, *'For he will be called a Nazarene'.*[22] It is therefore no wonder that Philip immediately 'captured' Nathanael into agreeing to believe in and come to Christ, since he spread out from all sides so many nets of truth [to catch] him. *'We have found him of whom Moses wrote in the law and the prophets, Jesus, the son of Joseph, from Nazareth,'*

And not without reason is it alleged that he was born in Bethsaida, that is, in 'the house of hunters,' who is shown to have received such concern about his beloved hunt for God, and at the same time so much grace, for there follows: *And Nathanael said to him, 'Something good can be from Nazareth'.*[1*] Nazareth is interpreted as 'of cleanliness,' or 'his flower' or 'separated'.[23] Assenting then to the words which brought him the good news, Nathanael said to Philip, *'Something good can come out of Nazareth,'* as if he were clearly saying, 'It can happen that from a city with such a great name something of supreme grace may arise for us—namely the very Lord and Savior of the world, who is in a unique way *holy, innocent, undefiled, separated from sins;*[24] who says in the Song of Songs, *"I am the flower of the field and the lily of the valleys;"*[25] and concerning whom the prophet says, *There shall go forth a branch out of the root of Jesse, and a nazareus* (that is, a flower) *will go up from his root*[26]—an extraordinary teacher may be sent [from there] to proclaim to us the flower of virtues and the cleanliness of sanctity'.

We can also understand this place [in the sense] that when Nathanael said to Philip, *'We have found him of whom Moses wrote in the law and the prophets, Jesus, the son of Joseph, from Nazareth,'* he understood the rest well, but he wondered how [Philip] could say that Christ had come from Nazareth,

21. Lk 2:48   22. Mt 2:23   23. Jer., *Nom.* (CC 72: 137, 24/25)
24. Heb 7:26, with the attested var. 'from sins' instead of 'from sinners'
25. Sg 2:1   26. Is 11:1; *nazareus,* for the Vulg. *flos*

since the prophets announced that he was to come from the house of David and the city of Bethlehem, where David had been. And so [Nathanael] responded in astonishment, *'From Nazareth'*? But he immediately called to mind how well the identifying name 'Nazareth' fit the mysteries of Christ, and he carefully assented to the proclamation, saying, *'Something good can be'* [from there].

What follows can fit either [of the above] senses: *Philip said to him, 'Come and see'*. He advised him to come and see, so that if there remained any uncertainty in his heart in regard to the words of the proclamation, actually seeing and talking with the one whom he proclaimed might wipe it all away. The pious hearer did not delay devoting himself to the one who had been proclaimed to him, [but he] eagerly asked and piously knocked [27] that he might be worthy to receive the light of truth.

Hence the Lord, acting quickly to satisfy his desire with good things,[28] repaid with praise the beginnings of his salvation which he foresaw, so that he might bring him gradually to seek and at the same time to grasp higher things: *Now [Jesus] saw [Nathanael] coming to him, and said about him, 'Behold, a true Israelite, in whom there is no guile'*. Here we must note that by praising a human being, God, who knows hearts,[29] did not declare that [Nathanael] was without sin, but without guile.[30] *For there is no just man on earth who does good and does not sin.*[31] We read that many have gone without guile, that is, have conducted themselves with simple and clean hearts. Moreover, all the faithful are taught to live as such, as scripture says, *Experience the Lord in goodness, and seek him in simplicity of heart.*[32] And the Lord himself says, *'Be prudent as serpents and simple as doves'.*[33] Such a model of patience was Job, about whom it is written, *He was a man simple and righteous.*[34] Such a one was the patriarch Jacob, of whom it was said, *Jacob, a simple man, dwelt in tents,*[35] [and] when, because of the purity of his simple

27. Mt 7:7-8   28. Ps 103:5 (102:5)   29. Ac 1:24
30. Aug., *Tract. in Ioh.* 7, 18 (CC 36: 77, 1/28)
31. Qo 7:21   32. Ws 1:1   33. Mt 10:16
34. Jb 1:1   35. Gn 25:27

conscience he was worthy to see God, he was named Israel as well,[36] that is, 'a man seeing God'.[37]

Such a one was Nathanael, since on account of his equally blameless way of life, the Lord reckoned him worthy of the merit of the name of the patriarch, saying *'Behold, a true Israelite in whom there is no guile'*: Behold, one truly descended from the patriarch who saw God; in him, just as in that patriarch, there was proven to be no duplicity. Oh what a beautiful omen for one coming to God and desiring to see him — *'Behold, a true Israelite, in whom there is no guile'*. *'Blessed are the pure of heart for they will see God'*.[38] He who desired to see God was praised as pure of heart by none other than God himself, *'who weighs inmost thoughts and hearts,'*[39] and he was declared to be an Israelite, that is, one begotten by 'a man who saw God'. Oh what a great hope of salvation is opened by this statement of our Redeemer to those of us who have come to the faith from the gentiles! For if he is truly an Israelite who behaves as one ignorant of guile, the Jews, although physically [descended] from Israel, already lost the name of Israelites, as many as have by their guileful hearts degenerated from the simplicity of their patriarch. And we have been admitted among the descendants of the Israelites, since, although according to the flesh we have our origin from other nations, nevertheless by [our] faith in the truth and by [our] purity of heart and mind, we follow in the footsteps of Israel, in accordance with that [saying] of the Apostle: *Not all who are from Israel are Israelites, nor are all who are descendants of Abraham* [his] *children, but 'Through Isaac shall your descendants be called'* — *that is, the children of God are not those who are children of the flesh, but it is those who are the children of the promise who are judged to be posterity.*[40]

There follows: *Nathanael said to him, 'How do you know me'? Jesus answered and said to him, 'Before Philip called you, when you were under the fig tree, I saw you'. Nathanael answered him and said, 'Rabbi, you are the Son of God; you are the King of Israel'.* Because Nathanael recognized that the Lord had seen

36. Gn 32:28   37. Jer., *Nom.* (CC 72: 139, 22)   38. Mt 5:8
39. Ps 7:9 (7:10)   40. Rm 9:6-8

and known things which happened in another place (that is, how and where he was called by Philip, even though [Jesus] was not there physically), [Nathanael], considering here the visionary power of his divine majesty, straightaway acknowledged him not only as 'Rabbi' (that is, 'master'), but also as Son of God and King of Israel (that is, the Christ). And it is pleasing to see how the servant's wise acknowledgment responded to the Lord who was praising him. [Christ] averred that this man was truly an Israelite, that is, 'a man who could see God,' because he had no guile. And [Nathanael] professed with religious devotion that [Christ] was not only a master who commanded profitable things, but also the Son of God, who bestowed heavenly gifts, and the King of Israel (that is, of the people who see God). By this confession [Nathanael] expresses that [Christ] is his king, and that he is a servant of his kingdom.

This statement of the Lord (in which he said that he had seen Nathanael before he was called by Philip, when he was under the fig tree) can also be understood mystically with regard to the choosing of the spiritual Israel, that is, the Christian people, since the Lord mercifully deigned to see them when they did not yet see him, when they had not yet been called by his apostles to the grace of faith, but they were still concealed under the covering of oppressing sin, as Paul attests when he says, *Who has blessed us in Christ with every spiritual blessing in heaven, as he chose us in him before the establishment of the world, that we might be holy and unspotted in his sight.*[41] And sometimes in the scriptures, to be sure, the fig tree suggests the sweetness of divine love — hence it is written: *He who keeps a fig tree will eat its fruit, and he who is his master's guardian will be glorified.*[42] But because our first parents, shamed by guilt for their transgression, made aprons for themselves from fig leaves,[43] the fig tree can fittingly designate the tendency toward sin, which is wrongfully filled with sweetness for the human race.[44] Those placed under it can be his elect, those who do not

41. Eph 1:3-4   42. Pr 27:18   43. Gn 3:7
44. Aug., *Enarr. in Ps.* 31, 9 (CC 38: 232, 17/43); *Serm.* 69, 3-4 (PL 38: 442); *Serm.* 89, 5 (PL 38: 557); *Tract. in Ioh.* 7, 21 (CC 36: 79, 1/19)

yet recognize the grace of their election — just as the Lord
saw Nathanael when he was situated under the fig tree
though Nathanael did not see him. *For the Lord knows who
are his,* [45] and the very name Nathanael is most suitably appropriate to their salvation. For Nathanael is interpreted 'gift
of God,' [46] and unless one is called by the gift of God, one
will never evade the guilt of the first transgression; he will
never evade wrongfully-enticing things under the shelter
of his daily-increasing sins; he will never be worthy to come
to Christ to be saved. Hence the Apostle says, *For by grace
you have been saved, through faith, and not of yourselves. It is
a gift of God, not a result of your works, lest anyone glory.* [47]

There follows: *Jesus answered and said to him, 'Because I said
to you that I saw you under the fig tree, you believe. You will
see a greater thing than these'.* He subsequently discloses what
is the greater thing of which he speaks, by giving his pledge
of a future opening of the kingdom of heaven to believers,
and of a proclamation to the world of both his natures in
one person. This in reality is a much more excellent hidden mystery than the fact that he foresaw us enlightened
by him while we were still placed in the shadow of sin. It
is a greater thing that he imbued us, the saved, with the
grace of knowledge of him, that he disclosed to us the joys
of heaven, [and] that he dispersed preachers of his faith into
the world, than that he knew in advance, before the ages,
that we would be saved by the power of his majesty.

'Amen, amen, I say to you,' he says, *'You will see heaven
opened, and the angels of God ascending and descending upon
the Son of man'.* We recognize that the effect of this promise
is already fulfilled. We see heaven opened, because after
the God-man gained entrance into heaven, we recognize
that in his name an entry into our heavenly home was
opened up for us believers too. We see angels of God
ascending and descending upon the Son of man, because
we know that holy preachers announce the sublimity of
Christ's divinity together with the weaknesses of his humanity. Angels ascend upon the Son of man when

45. 2 Tm 2:19   46. Jer., *Nom.* (CC 72: 83, 14)   47. Eph 2:8-9

preachers teach that *in the beginning was the Word, and the Word was with God, and the Word was God.*[48] Angels descend upon the Son of man when they add[49] [to this], *The Word was made flesh and dwelt among us.*[50] And it is not without reason that holy preachers are typologically called angels,[51] from which fact it is customarily granted that the name of evangelists is derived from [the word] angels, so that just as the latter are heralds, so are the former. Because of their having the duty of the loftiest preaching they may be given the name 'good heralds'.[52]

And we should note that the Lord called himself 'Son of man,' [while] Nathanael proclaimed him 'Son of God'. Similar to this is that place in the other evangelists where [Jesus] himself asks the disciples who people say the Son of man is,[53] and Peter answers, *'You are the Christ, Son of the living God'.*[54] This was done under the guidance of the dispensation of justice, so that when both substances of the one Mediator, our Lord and God, were to be mentioned, by our Lord himself and by one who was purely human, it was the God-man who would declare the weakness of the humanity assumed by him, and the one who was purely human who would declare the power of eternal divinity in him; the former would profess his humility and the latter his high position.

And we should note also that the Lord, who called blessed Nathanael 'a true Israelite,' also recalled to memory the vision of the patriarch Jacob, who through a blessing was called 'Israel,'[55] in that word in which he said, *'You will see heaven opened and the angels of God ascending and descending upon the Son of man'.* Now when Jacob, wishing to rest in a certain place, put a stone under his head, *he saw in his sleep a ladder standing upon the earth with its top touching heaven, and also angels of God ascending and descending on it, and the*

---

48. Jn 1:1
49. *adiungunt,* a well-attested variant to the singular *adiungit*
50. Jn 1:14
51. Aug., *Tract. in Ioh.* 7, 22-23 (CC 36: 80, 16-18)
52. Isid., *Etymol.* 6, 2, 42-43
53. Mt 16:13; Mk 8:27-29; Lk 9:18-20
54. Mt 16:16   55. Gn 32:28; 35:10

Lord resting on the ladder saying to him, 'I am the God of Abraham your father, and the God of Isaac'.[56] And rising in the morning and rendering praise to the Lord with due trepidation, he took the stone *and set it up as a mark, pouring oil on it.*[57]

The Lord made mention of this place and most clearly bore witness in a figurative way concerning himself and his faithful ones.[58] The ladder which he saw is the Church, which has its birth from the earth but its *way of life in heaven,*[59] and by it angels ascend and descend, when evangelists announce at one time to perfect hearers the preeminent hidden mysteries of [Christ's] divinity, and at another time announce to those still untaught the weaknesses of his humanity. Or they ascend when [in their teaching] they pass to heavenly things to be contemplated by the mind, and they descend when they educate their listeners as to how they ought to live on earth. The stone under Jacob's head is the Lord, upon whom we ought to support ourselves with all our concentration, the more so insofar as it is surely clear to us that without him we can do nothing.[60]

Jacob anointed the stone and set it up as a mark, because a true Israelite understands that our Redeemer was anointed by the Father with the oil of gladness above his fellows.[61] From this ointment (that is, 'chrism') Christ received his name, and the mystery of his incarnation is the mark of our redemption.[62] It is good that when the stone was anointed on the earth, and raised up as a mark, the Lord was revealed in heaven, for undoubtedly he appeared in time as a man among men while he remained eternal with God the Father. When death was overcome *he ascended over the heaven of heavens to the east,*[63] remaining with us as a mark of our salvation *for all days, up to the consummation of the world.*[64] He who transferred the body he had assumed from earth to heaven, was the one who filled earth, and heaven as well, with the presence of deity.

---

56. Gn 28:11-13   57. Gn 28:18
58. 'his faithful ones' added in several MSS
59. Ph 3:20   60. Jn 15:5   61. Ps 45:7 (44:8)
62. Cf. Aug., *Tract. in Ioh. 7,* 23 (CC 36: 80, 4-18)
63. Ps 67:34 (LXX)   64. Mt 28:20

Thus, as he explains to us the ancient history of Israel, the Lord demonstrates the figurative simplicity of the faithful people, of whom Nathanael was a member; in the stone upon which angels ascend and descend he reveals that it is he himself who is signified, he whose dual nature spiritual masters announced turn by turn. [It was] as if Israel anointed the stone with oil when Nathanael confessed how God anointed Jesus with the Holy Spirit and with power,[65] saying, *'Rabbi, you are the Son of God, you are the King of Israel'*.

It is already evident from the gospel lesson which has been explained how it is not without great symbolic import that it is first said at the opening [of the reading] that Jesus wished to go forth to Galilee, and then is added how he himself called Philip, and how he received Nathanael, who was called by [Philip], and instructed him by the light of truth. Galilee is interpreted, as we have said, 'an emigration made,' or 'revelation'. It is properly said that he wished to go forth into Galilee when he deigned to reveal to the faithful the sacraments of his majesty. We will ascend to perfect knowledge of these [sacraments] (which is the only blessed life of a human being) in a more sublime way to the extent that now we take care to emigrate more earnestly from earthly to heavenly things, and to advance by degrees in the virtues with the aid of him who is wont to enkindle [in us] desires for good things, to bring [us] to them, and to crown [us], Jesus Christ our Lord, who lives and reigns with the Father in the unity of the Holy Spirit, God for all ages. Amen.

65. Ac 10:38

NOTE

1. Bede's following commentary shows that he takes Nathanael's words in Jn 1:46 as a statement rather than a question. Cf. Augustine, *Tract. in Ioh.* 7, 15 (CC 36: 75, 10 - 76, 21), where Augustine says that the (Latin) text is capable of being read as a question or a statement; after a lengthy discussion Augustine comes down on the side of a statement.

homily 1.18

Luke 2:22-35   *Feast of the Purification*

The sacred reading of the gospel tells us about the solemnity we celebrate today. We venerate it with proper offices on the fortieth day after the Lord's birth. It is dedicated especially to the humility of our Lord and Savior, along with that of his inviolate mother. [The reading] explains that they who owed nothing to the law made themselves subject to the fulfillment of its legal decrees in everything. For, as we have just heard when [the lesson] was read, *After the days of his or her*[1] (either the Lord's or his mother's) *purification were fulfilled according to the law of Moses, they took him to Jerusalem to present him to the Lord, as is written in the law of the Lord: every male that opens the womb shall be called holy to the Lord.*

Now the law commanded that a woman who *had received seed*[2] and given birth to a son was unclean for seven days, and on the eighth day she was to circumcize the infant and present him with a name. And then for another thirty-three days she was to abstain from entry into the temple[3] and from her husband's bed, until, on the fortieth day after the birth, she was to bring her son with sacrificial offerings to

1. *eius*, which is ambiguous as to gender   2. Lv 12:2
3. Lv 12:1-4, 6

179

the temple of the Lord. The firstborn of all of the male sex was to be called holy to the Lord, and for that reason all clean [beasts] were to be offered to God; unclean ones were to be exchanged for clean ones, or killed, and the firstborn of a human being was to be redeemed[4] for five pieces of silver.[5] If, however, a woman gave birth to a female, she was ordered to be [judged] unclean for fourteen days, and to be suspended from entry into the temple for sixty-six more days,[6] until the eightieth day after the birth, which was called the day of her purification. On this [day] she was to come to sanctify herself and her child by sacrifical offerings, and thus at last she would be free to return to her husband's bed.

Dearly-beloved brothers, let us look more carefully at the words of the law which we have set before you, and we will see most clearly how Mary, God's blessed mother and a perpetual virgin, was, along with the Son she bore, most free from all subjection to the law. Since the law says that a woman who *'had received seed'*[7] and given birth was to be judged unclean, and that after a long period she, along with the offspring she had borne, were to be cleansed by victims offered to God, it is evident that [the law] does not describe as unclean that woman who, without receiving man's seed, gave birth as a virgin, [nor does it so describe] the Son who was born to her; nor does it teach that she had to be cleansed by saving sacrificial offerings. But as our Lord and Savior, who in his divinity was the one who gave the law, when he appeared as a human being, willed to be *under the law, so that he might redeem those who were under the law, so that we might receive adoption as sons*[8]— so too his blessed mother, who by a singular privilege was above the law, nevertheless did not shun being made subject to the principles of the law for the sake of showing [us] an example of humility, according to that [saying] of the wise man, *The greater you are, the more* [you should] *humble yourself in all things.*[9]

---

4. Ex 13:2, 12-13   5. Nb 18:15-16   6. Lv 12:5
7. Lv 12:2   8. Ga 4:4-5   9. Si 3:20

*And let them give a sacrificial offering according to what is writ-
ten in the law of the Lord, a pair of turtledoves or two young
pigeons.* This was the sacrificial offering of poor people. The
Lord commanded in the law that those who could were to
offer a lamb for a son or a daughter, along with a turtle-
dove or a pigeon, but one who did not have sufficient wealth
to offer a lamb should offer two turtledoves or two young
pigeons.[10] Therefore the Lord, mindful in everything of our
salvation, not only deigned for our sake to become a human being, though he was God, but he also deigned to become poor for us, though he was rich, so that by his poverty
along with his humanity he might grant to us to become
sharers in his riches and his divinity.[11]

But I would like to look briefly at why it was ordered that
these birds in particular were to be offered as a sacrificial
offering for the Lord. We read that long before the law the
patriarch Abraham offered these [birds] in a holocaust for
the Lord,[12] and in very many ceremonies of the law one
who needed to be cleansed was ordered to be cleansed by
[offering] these [birds].[13] A pigeon indicates simplicity, and
a turtledove indicates chastity, for a pigeon is a lover of simplicity and a turtledove is a lover of chastity[14]— so that if
by chance one loses its mate it will not subsequently seek
another.[15] Hence the Lord says in praise of the Church,
Beautiful are your cheeks like a turtledove's.[16] And again, *Behold, you are beautiful, my friend, behold, you are beautiful, your
eyes are* [like those] *of pigeons.*[17] A soul which has guarded
itself, so as to be chaste and exempt from every infecting
source of unchastity, has cheeks like those of a turtledove.
[And a soul] which, desiring to harm no one, gazes even
on its enemies with simple love, has eyes [like those] of
pigeons.

Both of the birds mentioned, because they are wont to
bring forth a moaning sound in place of a song, indicate

10. Lv 12:6-8
11. 2 Co 8:9; Ambr., *Expos. evang. sec. Luc.* 2, 41 (CC 14: 49, 584/87)
12. Gn 15:9   13. Lv 1:14; 5:7, 11; 12:8
14. Aug., *Tract. in Ioh.* 5, 11 (CC 36: 46, 20/21)
15. Jer., *Adv. Iov.* 1, 30 (PL 23: 252)
16. Sg 1:9   17. Sg 1:14

the lamentation of the saints in this world,[18] which the Lord speaks of when he says, *'Amen, amen, I say to you: you will wail and weep, but this world will rejoice; you will be sorrowful, but your sorrow will be turned into joy'.*[19] And again, *'Blessed are those who mourn, for they will be consoled'.*[20] Therefore rightly are a turtledove and a pigeon offered to the Lord as a sacrificial offering, for the simple and modest way of life of the faithful is to him a pleasing sacrifice of justice, and one who labors in his grief and cleanses his couch with tears every night[21] slays a sacrificial victim most acceptable to God. Although because of their inclination toward grieving, both of these birds designate the saints' mourning in this present life and their heavenly desires, they nevertheless differ in this way, that the turtledove is inclined to grieve as it wanders by itself, but the pigeon in a flock. On that account the first suggests the secret tears of [private] prayers, [while] the other suggests the Church's public gatherings.

It is good that the boy Jesus was first circumcised, and then after some intervening days he was brought to Jerusalem with a sacrificial offering. When still a young man, he first trampled all the corruption of the flesh under his feet by dying and rising, and then, after some intervening days, he ascended to the joys of the heavenly city, with the very flesh, now immortal, which he had made a sacrificial offering to God for our salvation. Each one of us is also first purged by the water of baptism from all sins, as if by a true circumcision, and thus advancing by the grace of a singular light to the holy altar, we go in to be consecrated by the saving sacrificial offering of the Lord's body and blood. Now also since the humanity of our Savior itself is uniquely simple and chaste, and since it is offered to the Father for us, it can fittingly be represented figurally by the immolation of a pigeon or a dove. But the entire Church too will, at the end of the world, first put off all blemish of earthly mortality and corruption in the general resurrection, and then be transferred to the kingdom of the heavenly Jerusalem, there to be commended to the Lord by the sacrificial victims, [her] good works.

18. Aug., *Tract. in Ioh.* 6, 2 (CC 36: 53, 1 - 54, 31)
19. Jn 16:20   20. Mt 5:5   21. Ps 6:6 (6:7)

Simeon and Anna, a man and a woman of advanced age, greeted the Lord with the devoted services of their professions of faith. As they saw him, he was small in body, but they understood him to be great in his divinity. Figuratively speaking, this denotes the synagogue, the Jewish people, who, wearied by long awaiting his incarnation, were ready with both their arms (their pious actions), and their voices (their unfeigned faith), to exalt and magnify him as soon as he came, acclaiming him and saying, *Direct me in your truth and teach me, for you are my saving God, and for you I have waited all the day.*[22] This [interpretation] too must be mentioned, that deservedly both sexes hurried to meet him, offering congratulations, since he appeared as the Redeemer of both.[23]

It is surely with great foreboding, my brothers, that we should listen to the words which this same Simeon, prophesying about the Lord, spoke to his mother, *'Behold, this* [child] *is destined for the ruin and for the resurrection of many in Israel, and for a sign that will be contradicted. And a sword will pierce your own soul, so that thoughts may be revealed from many hearts'.* It is with great yearning that we hear it said that the Lord is destined for the resurrection of many, for *just as in Adam all die, so also in Christ all will be brought to life;*[24] and he himself says, *'I am the resurrection and the life. Whoever believes in me, even if he dies, will live; and everyone who lives and believes in me will not die forever'.*[25] But nonetheless, what is mentioned before [this] sounds frightening: *Behold, this* [child] *is destined for the ruin...* One who falls after having acknowledged the glory of the resurrection is unhappy enough, but worse is one who, having seen the light of truth, is blinded by the oppressive clouds of his sins. Hence we must take the utmost care always to remember to carry out in our works the virtuous good we have recognized, lest what the apostle Peter [said] might be said of us, that *it was better for them not to have acknowledged the way of truth, than after the acknowledgment of it to have turned back*

---

22. Ps 25:5 (24:5)
23. Ambr., *Expos. evang. sec. Luc.* 2, 58 (CC 14: 56, 782)
24. 1 Co 15:22   25. Jn 11:25-26

from what was delivered over to them, that is, *the holy command-ment.*[26]

'*And for a sign,*' [Simeon] says, '*which will be contradicted*'. Many of the Jews and many of the gentiles have often con-tradicted the sign of the Lord's cross externally, and, what is more serious, many false brothers [do so] internally. They follow it superficially in what they profess, but they tram-ple upon it by the reality of their depraved actions, saying that they know God, but denying him in their deeds.[27]

'*And a sword will pierce your own soul*'. [Simeon] uses the word '*sword*' for the effect of the Lord's passion and death on the cross, and this sword will pierce Mary's soul, for she could not without painful sorrow see him crucified and dying. Although she was in no way uncertain about his ris-ing in that he was God, nevertheless, in her fear she sor-rowed that, as he was begotten from her flesh, he died.

'*So that the thoughts of many hearts may be revealed*'. Before the Lord's incarnation the thoughts of many were con-cealed, and it was not fully evident who was on fire with the love of eternal things, [and] who in his mind preferred temporal things to heavenly goods. But when the King of heaven was born on earth, immediately every holy person rejoiced; *Herod,* however, *was upset and all Jerusalem with him.*[28] While [Jesus] was preaching and working miracles, all the crowds feared and glorified the God of Israel; the Pharisees and Scribes, however, with raging mouths criti-cized his saving words and deeds. When he suffered on the cross, the wicked were filled with foolish gladness, [and] the holy with righteous sorrow; when he rose from the dead and ascended into heaven, the gladness of the former was changed into sadness, [and] the unhappiness of the latter was changed into everlasting joy.[29] And thus, in accordance with the prophecy of blessed Simeon, when the Lord ap-peared in the flesh, the thoughts of many hearts were revealed.

We must not believe that this revelation of the different thoughts took place only at that time in Judaea, and not

26. 2 P 2:21   27. Tt 1:16   28. Mt 2:3
29. Jn 16:20

also among us. Now too, with the appearance of the Lord, 'the thoughts of many hearts are revealed' when the word of salvation is read or preached, and some hearers willingly give heed to it, rejoicing to accomplish in their actions what they have learned by hearing, [while] others turn away from what they hear, and do not exert themselves to do these things, but rather struggle against them, reviling them. Hence, brothers, whenever we perceive that the word of heavenly teaching is suffering some hostility from hardened hearers, we should imitate the sorrow of heart of those who, with sorrow befitting their compassion, sustained the Word of God when he suffered in the flesh. On the other hand, whenever we see that very same Word rise through love in the minds of his faithful hearers, and advance, through good works, to the glory of our Maker, we should rejoice with those who beheld Christ with blissful prayers when he rose from the dead and ascended to heaven.

Surely we recognize that it was the custom for birds to be offered to the Lord which were very chaste, simple, and made moaning sounds, and by these [birds] it is signified that the sobriety, simplicity and compunction of our heart must always be offered to our Creator. We should look more carefully at [the fact] that there was a reason why it was commanded that two turtledoves or two young pigeons should be offered, one of these for sin, and the other as a holocaust.[30] Now there are two kinds of compunction by which the faithful immolate themselves to the Lord on the altar of the heart, for undoubtedly, as we have received from the sayings of the fathers, the soul experiencing[31] God is first moved to compunction by fear, and afterwards by love. First it stirs itself to tears because when it recalls its bad [deeds and] becomes fearful that it will undergo eternal punishments for them — this is to offer one turtledove or a young pigeon for sin. When dread has been worn away by the long anxiety of sadness, a certain security is born concerning the anticipation of pardon, and the intellect is

30. Lv 12:8
31. *sentiens*, var.: 'thirsting for' (*sitiens*)

inflamed with the love of heavenly joys.[32] One who previously wept so that he would not be led to punishment presently starts to weep most bitterly because he is separated from the kingdom — this is to make a holocaust of the other turtledove or young pigeon.

A holocaust means something that is wholly burned up, and one makes oneself a holocaust to the Lord if, having rejected all earthly things, one takes delight in burning with the desire of heavenly blessedness alone, and in seeking only this with lamentation and tears. His mind contemplates the choirs of angels, the society of blessed spirits, [and] the majesty of the eternal vision of God, and he sorrows more because he lacks everlasting goods than he wept previously when he was apprehensive about eternal evils. [God] deigns to accept gladly both of the sacrificial offerings of our compunction, he who kindly pardons our mistakes because we have been chastised by mourning for our sins; and for the sake of [our] entry into eternal life he also restores by the light of his eternal vision those who are aflame with the whole concentration of their mind, Jesus Christ our Lord, who lives and reigns with the Father in the unity of the Holy Spirit for all ages. Amen.

---

32. Greg., *Hom. in Ezech.* 10, 4-5, 20-21 (*CC* 142: 381, 95 - 383, 138; 395, 531/57); *Moral.* 32, 3, 4 (*CC* 143B: 1628, 23/33; 1629, 55/68)

homily 1.19

Luke 2:42-52   *After Epiphany*

The holy gospel reading which has been recited is clear to us, dearly-beloved brothers, and there is no need for us to speak in explanation of anything in it.[1] It describes our Redeemer's infancy and childhood, through which he deigned to become a sharer in our humanity, [and] it commemorates the eternity of his divine majesty, in virtue of which he remained and always remains equal to the Father. [This is] so that when the humility of his incarnation has been recalled to memory, we ourselves may take care to practice it as a medicine of true humility against the wounds of all our sins. [We should] recall always with a devout mind, in the interest of our salvation, how greatly we who are earth and ashes should be humbled before divine love,[2] when the highest power did not disdain to be so greatly humbled for our sakes that he came down to adopt the weakness of our frailty.

Likewise, as for the divinity of our Lord and Savior (which we have heard about and believed in and confessed), by which he always continues to be consubstantial and coeternal with the Father and the Holy Spirit, let us hope that

---

1. Several MSS add: 'but to speak instead in admonition'
2. *amore diuino*; var.: 'fear of God' (*diuino timore*)

through the sacraments of his humanity with which we have
been imbued, we may be able to attain the contemplation
of the glory of his divinity, that contemplation which he
himself in his faithful benevolence pledged to his faithful
servants when he said, *'One who has my commandments and
keeps them, he it is who loves me. One who loves me will be loved
by my Father, and I will love him and manifest myself to him'.*[3]
He says, *'I will manifest myself'* — that is, 'Not in such a way
that everyone can look at me, or in such a way that even
the unfaithful can see me and crucify me,[1*] but in such a
way that only the pure eyes of the saints can see *the King*
of ages *in his beauty.*[4] In this way I will show myself to those
who love me, so as to reward them for their love'. Therefore let us hope, as we have said, that through the sacraments of his humanity we may be able to ascend to see the
beauty of his divinity, if we keep these sacraments as we
have received them, unblemished in the worthy honor of
justice and holiness and truth, if we follow his example in
his human way of life, and if we humbly follow the words
of the teaching which he ministered to us through his humanity.

How rash it would be for one who scornfully refuses to
follow the footsteps of his humility to hope to reach the point
of looking upon the joys of his brightness! The Lord's
coming every year to Jerusalem for the Passover with his
parents is an indication of his human humility. It is characteristic of human beings to gather to offer God the votive
offerings of spiritual sacrifices, and by plentiful prayers and
tears to dispose their Maker toward them. Therefore the
Lord, born a human being among human beings, did what
God, by divine inspiration through [his] angels, prescribed
for human beings to do. He himself kept the law which he
gave in order to show us, who are human beings pure and
simple, that whatever God orders is to be observed in everything. Let us follow the path of his human way of life if
we take delight in looking upon the glory of his divinity,
if we want to dwell in his eternal home in heaven all the

3. Jn 14:21   4. Is 33:17

days of our lives,[5] if it delights [us] to see the Lord's will and to be shielded by his holy temple. And lest we be forever buffeted by the wind of wickedness, let us remember to frequent the house, the Church of the present time, with the requisite[6] offerings of pure petitions.

The fact that at twelve years old [Jesus] *sat in the temple in the midst of the teachers, listening to them and asking them questions,* is an indication of his human humility, and moreover it is also an extraordinary example of humility for us to learn. Indeed, the power of God and the Wisdom of God,[7] and the eternal divinity, speaks:[8] *I, wisdom, dwell in counsel, and I am present among learned thoughts. Counsel and equity are mine; prudence is mine; strength is mine. Through me kings reign, and makers of laws determine just things. Blessed is the man who hears me, who watches everyday at my gates, who observes at the posts of my doorway.*[9] Having put on human nature, [Wisdom] itself deigned to come to listen to human beings, so that from men who were undoubtedly gifted with the highest mental ability he might ask the necessary mental procedure of learning, lest, if any were to shrink from becoming disciples of truth they would become teachers of error. And since as a youth he was going to take on the office of teaching, it is good that when still a young boy he listened to his elders and asked them questions. By this provident dispensation he could curb the audacity of those who, when they are not only unlearned but also not yet grown, wish to push themselves forward in teaching rather than submit to the process of learning.

Let us follow the path of his humanity, if the abode of divine vision delight us, as we remember always this command, *My son, listen to the instruction of your father and do not abandon the law of your mother, that grace may be put on your head and a neck-ring on your neck.*[10] Indeed, through listening to paternal instruction and through the observance

5. Ps 27:4 (26:4)
6. 'requisite' (*necessariis*), a well-attested variant for *necessarie*, 'by necessity'.
7. 1 Co 1:24
8. var.: 'the power and the eternal wisdom of God speaks in a divine way'
9. Pr 8:12, 14-15, 34   10. Pr 1:8-9

of maternal law, grace is put on our head and a neck-ring on our neck, for the more one gives heed to divine commands [and] strives to observe with greater diligence what one has learned in the unity of mother Church, the more one may now ascend with greater worthiness to the honor of preaching, and may in the future ascend with greater exaltation to the blessedness of reigning with Christ forever.

But lest anyone should allege that it was on account of ignorance that our Lord and Savior went to masters and listened to them and asked them questions, let us see what follows: *All who were listening to him were amazed at his prudence and his answers, and seeing him they were astonished.* [Jesus] was a true human being and true God. To show that he was a human being he humbly listened to human masters, [while] to prove that he was God, he responded in a sublime way to these same [masters] when they were speaking.

To his mother, who was seeking him, saying, *'Son, why have you done so to us? Behold, your father and I have been seeking you in sorrow,'* he answered, *'Why is it that you were seeking me? Did you not know that I must be about my Father's business'?* This [answer] was an indication of his divine majesty, concerning which he said elsewhere, *'All things that the Father has are mine'.*[11] And so he most rightly bore witness that the temple pertained no less to himself than to his Father. Indeed, when he was found in the temple, he said, *'I must be about my Father's business,'* for as their majesty and glory are one, so also their seat and house are one. It is obvious that not only the material house of God, which it was the custom to build for his temporal worship, but also the intellectual house which is constructed for his eternal praise, are common equally to the Father and the Son, and moreover to the Holy Spirit as well. Accordingly, the same Son who, to one who loves him, makes this promise concerning himself and the Father: *'We will come to him and make our abode with him,'*[12] says of the Spirit, *'And I will ask the Father, and he will give you another Paraclete to abide with*

11. Jn 16:15   12. Jn 14:23

*you forever, the Spirit of truth. . . for he will abide with you and
be in you'.*[13]

Clearly the abode in the hearts of the elect of the holy
Trinity, the nature of whose divinity is one and indivisible, cannot be disparate. Therefore, when he was sitting
in the temple, the Lord said, *'I must be about my Father's business,'* and this is a declaration of his power and glory which
are coeternal with God the Father's. However, when he
returned to Nazareth he was subject to his parents, and this
is an indication of his true humanity as well as an example
of humility. He was subject to human beings in that [human]
nature in which he is less than the Father. Hence he himself said, *'I go to the Father because the Father is greater than
I'.*[14] In that [human nature], he was *made a little less than
the angels.*[15] In that other [nature], however, in which he
and the Father are one,[16] [and] in [virtue of] which he does
not go to the Father only now and then, but is always in
him,[17] *all things were made through him,*[18] and *he is before all
things.*[19] The plan [he arrived at in] his great goodness is
much to be marvelled at, since upon seeing that his parents did not yet grasp the mystery of his divine majesty,
he displayed to them his subjection in human humility, so
that in this way he might educate them gradually to the acknowledgement of his divinity. For when he had said, *'Why
is it that you were seeking me? Did you not know that I must
be about my Father's business'?* the evangelist subsequently
suggests: *'And they did not understand the word which he spoke
to them'.*

*He went down with them and came to Nazareth and was sub-
ject to them.* He spoke of the hidden mystery of his divine
power to the parents of his human weakness — namely to
the mother of his true flesh, and to the most chaste guardian of her chastity. (At that time, when the light of the gospel had not yet been made known, [Joseph] was considered

---

13. Jn 14:16-17   14. Jn 14:28   15. Ps 8:5 (8:6); Heb 2:9
16. Jn 10:30
17. Some MSS add: 'he is always in the Father and the Father in him'
    (cf. Jn 14:10-11)
18. Jn 1:3   19. Col 1:17

by practically everyone who had been able to know them
to be her husband in the full physical sense,[20] and besides,
because he took care of [Christ's] physical needs,[21] he was
called the father of the Lord and Savior.)

As we were saying, [Jesus] said to them, *'I must be about
my Father's business'*. Since they could not by their understanding ascend to the peak of such mystery, and there was
no other way for them to discern that he remained truly
about his Father's business unless they could comprehend
[it],[2]* he went down with them to their lowly way of life
and began to be concerned with their business. In the
benevolent divinely-arranged plan he was subject to them
until, with the assistance of his teaching of humility, they
could acknowledge how far he was above all creatures.

In the light of this, let us, I beseech you, direct our attention briefly to what we in our pride do. Certainly when we
sense that, as we are speaking, some of the simpler brothers
cannot understand the hidden mysteries of the scriptures
(things we do not know from all eternity [as Jesus did] but
have learned with the Lord's help as the occasion offered),
we are inclined to immediately extol ourselves, disdaining
them. We boast about our erudition, as though it were
unique in its magnitude, as though there were not very
many [others] much more learned than we are; and not
wishing to be disdained by the more learned, we ourselves
disdain those who are less learned than we are. Moreover,
we even rejoice to laugh [at them], and we do not care to
call to mind that the right of entry to the kingdom is open
not to those who perceive the mysteries of faith or the commands of their Maker only by meditating, but it is open instead to those who carry out what they have been able to
learn in their deeds. Morever, *he who knows how to do good
and does not do so is guilty of sin.*[22] And, as the Lord himself
bears witness, *'of everyone to whom much has been given, much
will be required'.*[23] That knowledge may not puff us up,[24]
then, but that charity may build [us up] instead, let us follow the example of God's Son when he appeared as a

---

20. *carnali coniunctione*   21. *carnali administratione*   22. Jm 4:17
23. Lk 12:48   24. 1 Co 8:1

human being. With benign humility he subjected himself
to those who, as he observed, were not yet capable of following him to the learning of sublime things. When their
souls were imbued with his example, he rendered them
worthy of heavenly grace and capable of understanding
heavenly hidden mysteries.

And his mother kept all these words, bearing them in her heart.
The virgin mother very carefully retained in her heart everything which she found out about the Lord, whether from
his sayings or his deeds, and she solicitously commended
it all to memory so that, when the time arrived for preaching [about] the Lord and writing about his incarnation, she
would be able to sufficiently explain everything as it had
taken place to those who were seeking to know. Let us too,
my brothers, imitate the Lord's holy mother; and by keeping all of our Lord and Savior's words and deeds in a steadfast heart, let us also, by meditating on them day and night,
drive away the troublesome assaults of empty and harmful thoughts. And by frequent discussion of these [words
and deeds of our Lord], let us take care to rebuke ourselves
and our neighbors about our pointless tales, and chatter
filled with the wicked sweetness of slander, and to enkindle [instead] the frequent offering of divine praises. For if
we desire to dwell in the Lord's house in the blessedness
of the world to come, dearly-beloved brothers, and to praise
him forever, we must eagerly show in this world what it
is that we seek for the future — namely by frequently cross-
ing the threshold of the church, and not only by singing
the Lord's praises there, but also by showing, *in every place
of his dominion,*[25] with our words, and our deeds as well,
whatever may advance the praise and glory of our Maker.

*And Jesus advanced in wisdom and age and grace before God
and human beings.* This indicates the nature of his true humanity, in respect of which he willed to advance through
time, though with respect to his divinity he is the same and
his years have no end.[26] In accordance with his human
nature he did indeed advance in wisdom. He did not

25. Ps 103:22 (102:22)   26. Ps 102:27 (101:28)

[become] wiser by existing through time, since from the first hour of his conception he remained full of the spirit of wisdom, but by demonstrating to others, gradually, through time, the spirit which filled him. In accordance with his human nature he advanced in age, for in terms of the growing which is usual for human beings, from infancy he reached childhood [and] from childhood he reached youth. In accordance with his human nature he advanced in grace. Not that he himself received, through the passage of time, what he did not have, but that he made available the gift of grace that he possessed.

And when it was said that *Jesus advanced in wisdom and age and grace,* it is rightly added, *before God and men,* for the more he disclosed to human beings, as he advanced in age, the gifts of wisdom and grace which were in him, the more he took care to always stir them up to the praise of God the Father, carrying out himself what he commanded others to do, *'Let your light shine before men so that they may see your good works and glorify your Father who is in heaven'.* [27] And so it is not only said that he advanced in grace and wisdom 'before man,' inasmuch as they could recognize his wisdom and grace, but also that he advanced 'before God,' inasmuch as for his praise and glory they gave back the wisdom and grace which they had recognized in him, for whose kindnesses and favors be eternal praise and thanksgiving for all ages. Amen.

27. Mt 5:16

NOTES

1. 'Even the unfaithful can see me and crucify me' (*etiam infideles uidere possunt et crucifigere*). There are several plausible MS variants: 'even the lovers of the world can crucify me' (*etiam mundi amatores possunt crucifigere*); 'even the envious can crucify me' (*etiam inuide possunt crucifigere*).
2. For 'and there was no other way... unless they could comprehend [it],' several MSS have an assortment of readings which, although they vary among themselves, all amount to: 'and it was not proper that they understand how he remained about his Father's business'.

homily 1.20

Matthew 16:13-19   *Chair of St Peter*

Y**ou should think very intently about this reading from the holy gospel which you have just heard, brothers, and you should continually keep it in mind and not forget it, the more so since it sets forth for us the great perfection of faith, and likewise demonstrates that same perfect faith's great firmness against all trials. For if we want to know how we should believe in Christ, what could be plainer than what Peter said to him, *'You are the Christ, the Son of the living God'*. Again, if it pleases us to hear how much this faith is capable of, what could be clearer than what the Lord said concerning the Church that was to be built upon him, *'And the gates of hell will not prevail against it'*. But these things will be more fully explained in their own places.

Turning now, however, to an orderly explanation of the Sunday reading, let us first look at the place where its setting is recounted. *Jesus came into the region of Caesarea Philippi.* Philip, as Luke testifies, was tetrarch of the region of Ituraea and Trachonitis.[1] He established a city in the place where the Jordan arises, at the base of Mount Lebanon, and it was

---

1. Lk 3:1

Judaea's boundary with the northern territory. He named
it Caesarea Philipi.[2]

As he came into the region of this [city], *Jesus asked his
disciples, saying, 'Who do men say the Son of man is'?* He did
not inquire as if he was unaware of what notion either his
disciples or others had about him, but he asked his disciples what they felt about him so that he might repay their
confession of right faith with a worthy reward. Now just
as Peter alone answered for them all, though they were all
asked as a group, so what the Lord answered to Peter he
answered to all of them in Peter. He inquired about what
others felt about him so that by first exposing the notions
of those who were mistaken, he could prove that the disciples had received the truth of their confession not through
popular opinion, but through the hidden mystery of the
Lord's revelation.[3]

'Who,' he says, *'do men say the Son of man is'?* It is very
appropriate that he calls those people 'men' who knew only
how to speak about the Son of man, and who were unaware of the hidden mysteries of his divinity. Those who
do know how to grasp the mysteries of divinity are rightly
said to be more than men, as the Apostle attests when he
says, *Eye has not seen, nor has ear heard, nor has it entered the
heart of man, what things God has prepared for those who love
him.*[4] Since he first mentioned these things as being of 'men'
(that is, of those whose wisdom is only of human heart,
ear and eye), he next adds concerning himself and those
like him who had transcended the general knowledge of
humanity, *But God has revealed* [these things] *to us through
his Spirit.*[5] Similar to this is what [Jesus] said when he had
asked his disciples who men said that he was and they had
told him the opinions of diverse people. *He said to them, 'You,
however, who do you say that I am'?* — setting them apart,
as it were, from the generality of men, and suggesting that
they had then become gods and sons of God by adoption,

2. Jer., *In Matth.* 16, 13 (CC 77: 139, 2/9) Some MSS add here: 'namely
in memory of his own name, and also in honor of Tiberius Caesar,
under whom he reigned'
3. var: 'the Lord's resurrection'　　　4. 1 Co 2:9　　　5. 1 Co 2:10

in accordance with that [saying] of the psalmist, *I have said that you are all gods and sons of the Most High.*[6]

Simon Peter answering said, 'You are the Christ, the Son of the living God'. He called him the 'living' God to distinguish him from the false gods which the [people of the] gentile world, deluded by various errors, had made for themselves out of dead men, or, by a greater madness, had created from insensible matter [gods] whom they could adore. Concerning them it is chanted in the psalm, *The idols of the nations are silver and gold, the work of men's hands. They have mouths but do not speak,* and so forth.[7]

Note, beloved,[8] what a marvelous distinction is made here — that when a statement about the dual nature of our Lord and Savior was to be put forward by the Lord and by his faithful disciple, it is the Lord himself who avows the humilty of his assumed humanity, [while] the disciple discloses the excellence of [Christ's] eternal divinity. The Lord tells of what is inferior about himself; the disciple tells of what is superior about his Lord. The Lord declares of himself what he became for our sake; the disciple declares of his Lord that it was he who had made us.[9] So too in the gospel, the Lord was much oftener inclined to call himself 'Son of man' than 'Son of God,' in order to remind us of the divinely-arranged plan[10] which he had adopted for us. But the more we remember that he descended to the lowliness of humanity for the sake of our exaltation, the more we must venerate with greater humility the heights of his divinity. For if among the mysteries of his incarnation, by which we were redeemed, we always with pious mind recall the power of [his] divinity, by which we were created, it will come about that we ourselves may also, with Peter, be granted the reward of heavenly blessedness.

Now when [Peter] confesses that Christ is the Son of the living God, let us see what follows: *Jesus, answering said, 'Blessed are you, Simon Bar Jona'.* It is a fact that after a true confession of Christ, true rewards of blessedness lie in store.

6. Ps 82:6 (81:6)   7. Ps 115:4-5 (113:4-5)   8. *dilectio uestra*
9. Ps. 100:3 (99:3)
10. var.: 'divinely-arranged plan for the flesh'

But let us attentively observe the nature and worth of that name which glorifies the perfect confessor of [Christ's] name, so that by truthfully confessing him we also may be worthy to be his comrades.

'*Blessed are you,*' he says, '*Simon Bar Jona*'. 'Bar Jona' in Syriac means 'son of a dove' in Latin.[11] The apostle Peter is rightly called 'son of a dove,' for a dove is a very simple animal, and Peter followed the Lord with a prudent and pious simplicity, mindful of that command which he along with his fellow-disciples received from the Master of simplicity and truth: '*Be prudent as serpents and simple as doves*'.[12] Or, since the Holy Spirit descended on the Lord in the form of a dove, one who is shown to be full of spiritual grace is properly given the name 'son of a dove'. The one who loves and confesses him is repaid by the Lord with very just praise when he testifies that [Peter] is the son of the Holy Spirit, since it is [Peter] who says that [Jesus] himself is the Son of the living God — although none of his faithful would doubt that the situation was much different. Christ the Lord is the Son of God by nature; Peter, just like the other elect, is the son of the Holy Spirit[13] because he was reborn of him through grace. Christ is the Son of God before time, for he is the power of God and the wisdom of God,[14] who says, *The Lord possessed me from the beginning of his ways, before he made anything from the beginning.*[15] Peter is the son of the Holy Spirit from the time when he is enlightened by him and receives the grace of divine cognition.

And because the will and the operation of the holy Trinity is one and the same, when he had said, '*Blessed are you, Simon Bar Jona*' (that is, 'son of spiritual grace'), he properly added straightaway, '*for flesh and blood have not revealed* [this] *to you, but my Father, who is in heaven*'. The Father indeed revealed [this] to the 'son of a dove,' for the grace of the

---

11. Jer., *In Matth.* 16, 17 (CC 77: 141, 53/54); *Nom.* (CC 72: 135, 22/24); Isid., *Etymol.* 7, 9, 4
12. Mt 10:16
13. Some MSS add: 'through grace. Christ is the Son of God because he was born of him; Peter is the son of the Holy Spirit'.
14. 1 Co 1:24   15. Pr 8:22

Father and of the Holy Spirit is one, and the same grace is also the Son's. This will be proven by very ready examples from sacred scripture. For the Apostle says this concerning the Father, *God sent the Spirit of his Son into our hearts.*[16] The Son himself says this concerning the Holy Spirit, *'When the Paraclete comes whom I will send to you from the Father'.*[17] The Apostle says this concerning the Holy Spirit, *One and the same Spirit works all these things, distributing to each one as he wishes.*[18] The Father therefore sends the Spirit, and the Son sends the Spirit, and *the Spirit* himself *breathes where he wills,*[19] for, as we have said, unquestionably there is one will and operation of the Father, the Son and the Holy Spirit.

And on that account it is appropriately said that the Father, who is in heaven, has revealed to the 'son of a dove' the mystery of faith which flesh and blood was unable to reveal to him. 'Flesh and blood' are properly understood as [standing for] human beings who are puffed up by the wisdom of the flesh, ignorant of dovelike simplicity, and therefore turned entirely away from the wisdom of the Spirit. Concerning these we were told above that some without understanding said that Christ was John the Baptist, others that he was Elias, and others that he was Jeremiah or one of the prophets. Concerning these the Apostle says, *The natural man does not perceive the things which are of the Spirit of the Lord.*[20]

There follows: *'And I say to you that you are Peter, and upon this rock I will build my Church'.* Peter, who before this was referred to as 'Simon,' received from the Lord the name Peter, because of the strength of his faith and the constancy of his confession, for he clung with a stable and tenacious mind to him concerning whom it was written, *and the Rock was Christ.*[21] And upon this Rock the Church is built — that is, upon the Lord and Savior. To his faithful one who recognized him, and loved him, and confessed him, he granted

---

16. Ga 4:6 17. Jn 15:26 18. 1 Co 12:11
19. Jn 3:8 20. 1 Co 2:14
21. 1 Co 10:4; Aug., *Tract. in Ioh.* 7, 14 (*CC* 36: 74, 8 - 75, 11); Bede, *Hom* I.16 (*CC* 122: 116, 178ff.)

a share in his own name, so that he was called Peter from [the word for] 'rock'. [22] Only through faith in and love of Christ, through the reception of Christ's sacraments, and through observing Christ's commandments does one reach the lot of the elect, and eternal life, as the Apostle attests when he says, *For no one can lay any other foundation except that which has been laid, which is Christ Jesus.*[23]

'And the gates of hell shall not prevail against it'. The gates of hell are depraved teachings, which by seducing the imprudent draw them down to hell. The gates of hell are also the torments and blandishments of persecuters, which, either by frightening or by cajoling any of the weak away from the stability of the faith, open to them the entrance into eternal death. But also the wrong-headed works of the unfaithful, or their silly conversations, are surely gates of hell, inasmuch as they show their hearers and followers the path to perdition. For *faith, if it does not have works, is dead in itself;*[24] and *evil conversations corrupt good morals.*[25] Many are the gates of hell, but none of them prevails over the Church which has been founded upon the rock. One who has received the faith of Christ with the inmost love of his heart very easily scorns whatsoever tempting danger threatens him from outside. But as for any twisted person who ruins the faith of believers either by his works or by his denial,[26] we must not believe that such a one has worked with the Lord to build the house of his profession upon a rock, but in accordance with the parable of another place [in the gospel], we must believe that he has placed it upon sand, without foundation,[27] that is, that he is not following Christ with a simple and true intention, but that he has put forward an earthly, and for that reason a very fragile, posture of a Christian.

There follows: *'And I will give you the keys of the kingdom of heaven'*. The one who confessed the King of heaven with a devotion above that of others was himself rightly

---

22. *petra*   23. 1 Co 3:11   24. Jm 2:17
25. 1 Co 15:33
26. var.: 'who betrays the faith or works of believers by his denial'
27. Mt 7:24-26; Lk 6:48-49

enriched[28] by the conferral upon him beyond the others of
the keys of the heavenly kingdom, so that it might be obvious to all that without this confession and faith no one could
enter into the kingdom of heaven. He names 'the keys of
the kingdom of heaven' that knowledge and power of dis-
cernment with which [Peter] was to receive the worthy into
the kingdom, and to exclude the unworthy from the
kingdom.

Hence he adds clearly, *'And whatsoever you bind upon earth
will be bound also in heaven, and whatsoever you loose upon earth
will be loosed also in heaven'*. Although it may seem that this
power of loosing and binding was given by the Lord only
to Peter, we must nevertheless know without any doubt
that it was also given to the other apostles, as [Christ] himself testified when, after the triumph of his passion and
resurrection, he appeared to them and breathed upon them
and said to them all, *'Receive the Holy Spirit. Whose sins you
forgive, they are forgiven them, and whose sins you retain, they
are retained'*.[29] Indeed even now the same office is committed to the whole Church in her bishops and priests, so that
when she has come to know sinners' cases, she considers
which are humble and truly penitent, and in compassion
she may then absolve them from the fear of perpetual death.
But she may suggest that those whom she recognizes to be
persisting in the sins which they have committed, should
be assigned to everlasting punishments.

Hence in another place the Lord directed concerning a
brother who has been rebuked once and again and a third
time, but does not repent, *'If, however, he does not listen to
the Church, let him be to you as a pagan and a publican'*.[30] And
lest anyone should think it is a light thing to be condemned
by the Church's judgment, [Christ] continued with the terrible saying, *'Amen I say to you, whatever things you bind on
earth will be bound also in heaven, and whatever things you loose
on earth will be loosed also in heaven'*.[31] Thus to each church
of the elect is given the authority of binding or loosing,

---

28. 'enriched' = *ditatus*; var.: 'granted' = *donatus*
29. Jn 20:22-23; cf. Cyprian, *De unitate* 4 (CC 3: 251, 79 - 252, 96)
30. Mt 18:15-17   31. Mt 18:18

according to the measure of guilt or repentance. But since blessed Peter confessed Christ with true faith and followed him with true love, he received in a special way the keys of the kingdom of heaven and preeminence in the power of judging, so that all believers throughout the world might understand that any who separate themselves in any way from the unity of faith or of this fellowship cannot be absolved from the bonds of their sin, nor can they enter the gate of the heavenly kingdom.

Hence we need to direct our whole intention, dearly-beloved brothers, to learning the mysteries of the faith which he teaches, and we need to show that our works accord with our faith. With all vigilance we need to beware of the multifarious and subtle snares of the gates of hell, so that, in accordance with the word of the psalmist, we may be worthy to be snatched from these [snares] by the Lord's aid and to announce his praises at the gates of the daughter of Zion,[32] that is, to enter into the joys of the heavenly city. And we should not think that it is sufficient for our salvation if either in our faith or our acts we [merely] come up to the level of the undiscerning and untaught crowd, for whom there is prescribed in the sacred literature only one rule of believing and of living. But as often as the examples of those who have gone astray are made known to us, let us immediately turn away the eyes of our mind so that they may not see vanity,[33] and instead with attentive heart let us examine what truth itself discerns, following the example of blessed Peter. He rejected the false ideas of those who were in error, and with unhesitating words he delivered his confession of the hidden mystery of the faith he had come to recognize, and he kept [it] with unconquerable care in his heart.

We have come to recognize in this text the trustiness of his confession; elsewhere he himself bears witness concerning the power of his unique love for Christ. When certain disciples were withdrawing from Christ, and he said to the twelve, *'Will you also go away'?* [Peter] answered him, saying,

32. Ps 9:14 (9:15)   33. Ps 119:37 (118:37)

'Lord, to whom shall we go? You have the words of eternal life, and we have believed and recognized that you are the Christ, the Son of God'.[34]

Therefore, my brothers, if we attempt to imitate his example to the best of our abilities, we also will be capable of being called blessed with [Peter], and of being blessed with him. The name Simon, that is, 'obedience'[35] to Christ, also fits us on account of the simplicity of an unfeigned faith[36]; and on account of the gift of the virtues we have received from the Lord, we will be called 'sons of a dove,' and [Peter] himself, rejoicing with [us] in the spiritual progress of our souls, will say, 'How beautiful you are, my friend, how beautiful you are. Your eyes are those of doves'.[37] Thus it will happen that the fire of tribulations may bear us no harm, and no whirlwinds of temptation may prevail over us, since we build upon the rock of faith with gold, silver and precious stones,[38] that is, with the perfect works of the virtues. Instead, when we have been proved by adversities, we will receive the crown of life which he promised us[39] before the ages, he who lives and reigns with the Father in the unity of the Holy Spirit throughout all ages. Amen.

34. Jn 6:67-69   35. Jer., *Nom.* (CC 72: 148, 4)   36. 1 Tm 1:5
37. Sg 4:1   38. 1 Co 3:12   39. Jm 1:12

homily¯ 1.21

We have read, as the Apostle says, that *all have sinned and stand in need of the glory of God. They are justified freely through his grace.*[1] And again, setting forth the greatness of his inestimable grace, he says, *Where sin abounds, grace does more abound.*[2] When the Lord cures the more serious illnesses of the sinners among his chosen ones, he [thereby] demonstrates to all the more ample power of his healing grace. We have heard in the gospel reading that [Jesus] felt compassion for Matthew as he sat at the tax-collector's place intent upon temporal concerns, and suddenly called him. He made a just man of a publican, a disciple of a tax-collector. As he progressively increased in grace, [Jesus] promoted him from the ordinary group of disciples to the rank of an apostle, and not only committed to him the ministry of preaching, but also that of writing a gospel, so that he who had ceased to be an administrator of terrestrial business matters might start to be an administrator of heavenly currency. Doubtlessly the reason why heavenly providence arranged for this to happen was so that neither the enormity of one's wicked deeds nor

1. Rm 3:23-24   2. Rm 5:20

their great number should dissuade anyone from hoping for pardon, since one could look at this man [Matthew], who had been freed from such bonds of the world and made heavenly in order to become, in fact and in name, an evangelist, sharing this name with the angelic spirits.[3]

Jesus saw a man named Matthew sitting in the tax-collector's place, and he said to him, 'Follow me'. He saw him not so much by virtue of corporeal vision as by inner compassion. By this he also deigned to turn his gaze on Peter as he was denying him,[4] so that he would be able to acknowledge his crime and weep over it. This was also the way in which he beheld his people when they had been brought low by Egyptian servitude, so that he might rescue them,[5] as he said to Moses, *'Seeing I have seen the affliction of my people who are in Egypt, and I have heard their groans, and I have come down to liberate them'.*[6] [Jesus] saw the man, [and] felt compassion for him because he was devoted only to human concerns and he was not yet worthy of an angelic name.

[Jesus] saw him sitting in the tax-collector's place, with his stubborn intellect avid for temporal gain. His name was Matthew, [the gospel] says. [The name] Matthew in Hebrew means 'granted' in Latin,[7] a name aptly corresponding to the one who received such a favor of heavenly grace. But we must not pass over the fact that Matthew had two names, for he was also called Levi, and that name too bears witness to the grace granted to him. [Levi] means 'added' or 'taken up,'[8] signifying that he was 'taken up' through being chosen by the Lord, and 'added' to the number of the apostlic band. Mark and Luke in this reading chose to use this name instead, so as to not render their comrade in the work of the gospel glaringly conspicuous for his former way of life.[9] When they come to setting down the list of the twelve apostles, they are silent about the name Levi, and clearly call him by the name Matthew.[10] Matthew

---

3. Bede, *In Luc.* 5, 27/29 (CC 120: 122, 890 - 123, 914); *In Marc.* 2, 14 (CC 120: 457, 814 - 458, 817); Jer., *In Matth.* 9, 9-10 (CC 77: 55, 1272 - 56, 1293); Isid., *Etymol.* 6, 2, 43
4. Lk 22:61   5. Ex 3:7-8   6. Ac 7:34
7. Jer., *Nom.*. (CC 72: 147, 1)
8. Jer., *Nom.* (CC 72: 68, 7/8)
9. Mk 2:14; Lk 5:27   10. Mk 3:18; Lk 6:15

himself, on the other hand (in accord with what is written, *The just man is the first accuser of himself; his friend came and searched him out*[11]), calls himself by his ordinary name when telling of being called from his tax-collector's place, but in his list of apostles he names himself with the addition 'publican'—*Thomas*, he says, *and Matthew the publican.*[12] In this way he offers to publicans and sinners greater confidence about their securing salvation. Paul too, following this teaching formula, says that *Jesus Christ came into this world to save sinners, of whom I am the first. But for this reason I secured mercy, that in me first Christ Jesus might show forth all patience, as an example for those who will believe in him unto eternal life.*[13]

[Jesus] saw a publican, and because as he saw [him] he felt compassion for him and chose him, *he said to him, 'Follow me'*. By 'follow' he meant imitate; by 'follow' he meant not so much the movement of feet as the carrying out of a way of life. For *one who says that he abides in* Christ *ought himself to walk just as he walked,*[14] that is, not to aim at earthly things, not to eagerly pursue perishable gains, [but] to flee base honors, to willingly embrace all contempt of the world for the sake of heavenly glory, to do good to all, to inflict injuries upon no one in bitterness and to patiently suffer those brought upon oneself, and to implore pardon from the Lord for those bringing [these injuries], never to seek one's own glory but always that of our Maker, and to uphold whatever helps one toward love of heavenly things. To do these and other like things is to follow Christ's tracks.

And he arose and followed him. We should not marvel that a publican, upon first [hearing] the Lord's voice ordering him, left the earthly gains that he cared about. Disregarding his property, he attached himself to the band of followers of one whom he perceived to have no riches. For the Lord himself, who outwardly called him by a word, taught him inwardly with an invisible impulse so that he followed [him]. He poured into his mind the light of spiritual grace, by which he could understand that the one who was calling

11. Pr 18:17   12. Mt 10:3   13. 1 Tm 1:15-16
14. 1 Jn 2:6

him from temporal things on earth was capable of giving him incorruptible treasures in heaven.

He arose and followed him. He arose in order to follow. He dismissed the perishable things in which he was involved in order to secure the eternal things to which Truth was inviting him, as in that [saying] of Isaiah, *Arise, you who are asleep, and rise from among the dead, and Christ will enlighten you.*[15]

And it happened as he was reclining at table in the house, behold many publicans and sinners came, and reclined at table with Jesus and his disciples. The conversion of one publican gave many publicans and sinners an example of repentance and forgiveness. For we must not doubt that those who reclined at table with Jesus and his disciples had ceased being publicans and sinners; if they had determined to persevere in their sins, they would not have dared to take food with one who was without sin. They are called publicans who are either publicly tainted by wicked deeds, or who are implicated in public business matters which can scarcely if at all be conducted without sin. And in a beautiful and true foreshadowing, one who was to be an apostle and the teacher of the nations draws after him in his earlier way of life[16] a company of sinners to salvation and to the office of bringing the good news. By the growing merit of his virtues he was to perfect what he already began from the first stages of his faith. For it is not only one who instructs a brother by word who carries on the ministry of a teacher, but also one who by his example turns him to better things. Accordingly these publicans rejoiced to follow him, in imitation of Matthew, not only at that time when they reclined at table with the Lord, but also henceforth, by casting off their secular business concerns, as the evangelist Mark bears witness saying, *Many publicans and sinners were reclining at table with Jesus and his disciples, for there were many and they followed him.*[17]

15. Eph 5:14; Bede was perhaps thinking of Is 60:1. Some MSS read 'the Apostle'.
16. *prima sua conuersatione*; var.: 'first in his conversion' (*prima sua conuersione*)
17. Mk 2:15

We must note, however, that when Luke refers to this he says that the Lord reclined at table with publicans in Matthew's house, and that [Matthew] himself prepared a great feast for him.[18] And it was Matthew who made such a fitting recompense for heavenly benefits, as far as the general judgment is concerned, in that he hoped for everlasting goods from the one for whom he provided his temporal goods, and he restored with an earthly meal the one from whom, as he was giving [the meal], he had received a taste for spiritual sweetness.

On the other hand, if we long to search out what these happenings are at a more profound level of understanding, it was not only in his earthly house that he produced a bodily feast for the Lord, but with great gratitude in the house of his breast he prepared a feast for him through faith and love, [19] as [Christ] himself attests saying, *'Behold, I stand at the doorway and knock. If anyone listens to my voice and opens the gate, I will come in to him and sup with him and he with me'.*[20] The Lord stands at the doorway and knocks when he pours into our heart the memory of his will, either through the mouth of a man who is teaching [us] or through his own internal inspiration. When his voice is heard we open the gate to receive [him] when we willingly present our assent to [his] counsels, whether secret or open, and devote ourselves to accomplishing those things which we recognize are to be done. He comes in order to sup with us and we with him, for he dwells in the hearts of his elect through the grace of his love in order to restore them always by the light of his presence, so that they may advance more and more to heavenly desires, and so that he himself may feed their zeal for heaven, as it were, with a most pleasing banquet.

There follows: *And when they saw it, the Pharisees said to his disciples, 'Why does your master eat with publicans and sinners'?* The Pharisees were bound by a double error when they found fault with the Master of truth for receiving sinners:

18. Lk 5:29
19. Ambr., *Expos. evang. sec. Luc.* 5, 16 (CC 14: 140, 162/63)
20. Rv 3:20

they thought of themselves as just, though they had long departed from justice by the arrogance of their pride, and they denounced as unjust those who by repenting of their sins were already drawing fairly near to justice. Blinded by envy of their brothers' salvation, they recalled that Matthew was a publican, and [that] many others who were reclining at table with the Lord were publicans and sinners, but they were unwilling to keep in mind that, as Luke writes, this same Matthew left everything that he was doing and followed [Jesus].[21] Likewise the other publicans and sinners — the disposition [that led them to] recline at table with him disposed them to attach themselves to him henceforth. The Pharisees were mistaken because they did not know the hearts of the others, or even their own hearts.

He who knew the hidden things of the heart is the one who *came to seek and to save what was lost*,[22] He both strengthened further in faith those he had already accepted as they repented, and stirred up to the grace of humility and piety those whom he put up with when they were still proud and wicked, for there follows: *But Jesus hearing it said, 'The healthy need no physician, but those with a sickness'*. In that he bore witness that he came as a physician to those with a sickness, he increased the hope of obtaining healing and life for those who, roused from the illness of their sins, had already begun to follow the instruction of the Savior and Lifegiver. In that he said that the healthy need no physician, he confuted the rashness of those who, counting upon their own justice, were scornful of seeking the help of heavenly grace. Who could be so just as not to stand in need of divine aid, since he than whom none born of women was greater,[23] John, said most clearly about himself, *'No human being can receive anything of himself unless it be given to him from heaven'*?[24]

By adding, *'Go and learn what this means: I want mercy and not sacrifice,'*[25] [Jesus] also pointed out a counsel of improvement to these Pharisees who were puffed up about their false justice. He advised them that through works of mercy

21. Lk 5:28   22. Lk 19:10   23. Mt 11:11; Lk 7:28
24. Jn 3:27   25. Ho 6:6

they might search out for themselves the rewards of heavenly mercy, and that not despising the needs of the poor, they might be confident of pleasing the Lord by offering themselves as sacrifices. He placed before them testimony from the prophet and ordered them to learn it as they went—as they went from the rashness of their foolish vituperation to a more diligent meditation of holy scripture. [He did this] in order that they, who were accusing him of acting against the decrees of the scriptures in receiving sinners, might instead understand that they themselves did not know what God's commands were and had not made them known.

It is evident that people who, as they devote themselves to daily offerings in the temple, are not moved by any compassion for transgressors, seek sacrifice rather than mercy, contrary to the prophetic utterance. But the Lord, as it is written, *went about doing good and healing all who were oppressed by the devil,*[26] and as often as he went into the temple, he there strove rather to cure the ailing, to guide the unknowing, and to convict the insolent or even drive them out, than to offer sacrificial victims. And it is clear that he carried out the commands of the divine will as the prophet advised, by performing works of mercy and not by celebrating sacrifice.

He did not disdain to give his critics a reason why he was eating with publicans and sinners, so that he might restrain them from their pointless grumbling and stir them up to pursue the gifts of his benevolence: *'For I have not come to call the just,'* he said, *'but sinners'.* The reason why the Lord visited sinners' feasts was so that by teaching [them] he might invite those who invited him to heavenly banquets.

Perhaps it may disturb someone that the Lord said he had not come to call the just but sinners, since it is obvious to all readers that he called to the heights of gospel preaching many too of those he found to be just according to the principles of the mosaic law. If he called only sinners, and not also the just, Nathanael would not have been a sharer in

26. Ac 10:38

his discipleship. When [Nathanael] was first coming toward him, [Jesus] thought him worthy of such praise that he said, *'Behold a true Israelite, in whom there is no guile'.* [27] If he did not call the just, he would not have had Peter and Andrew in the stronghold of the apostolate, since they taught [us] how great the love of justice was with which they were on fire when they rejoiced to see and hear the Lord immediately upon hearing the testimony of the precursor. [28]

How was it, then, that he did not come to call the just but sinners, unless it was because, as Luke says more clearly when he refers to this, *'I have not come to call the just but sinners, to repentance'?* [29] The Lord calls all the elect to the heavenly kingdom, but he calls to repentance only those he finds enveloped in more serious sins. Those he discovers to have devoted themselves to works of justice he does not invite to repentance for their past way of life, but he invites them to progress in a more perfect life. He calls sinners so that they may be corrected through repentance; he calls the just so that they may become more and more just.

His saying *'I have not come to call the just but sinners,'* can also be properly understood thus: that he has not called those who, wishing to establish their own justice, *have not been made subject to the justice of God,* [30] but those who, being conscious of their weakness, are not ashamed to confess that *we have all offended in many things.* [31] If from the hypocritically just he calls to pardon those too who have been corrected, in them too is fulfilled his utterance that he had not come to call the just but sinners — not, that is, the exalted but the humble; not those puffed up about their own justice, but those showing themselves devotedly subject to the one who justifies the wicked. Such people, when they are converted, bear witness with a sincere heart that they must not be [regarded as] just, but sinners.

It is a pleasure to remember, dearly-beloved brothers, to what a height of justice the Lord fetched Matthew, whom he chose out of his publican activities in order to increase

27. Jn 1:47   28. Jn 1:35-42   29. Lk 5:32
30. Rm 10:3; Ambr., *Expos. evang. sec. Luc.* 5, 22 (CC 14: 142, 225/29)
31. Jm 3:2

for sinners their hope of forgiveness. The apostolic band
into which he was incorporated teaches what kind of person he became. The nation of the Ethiopians teaches [this]
too. By his preaching he converted this [nation] from the
farthest ends of the earth to the fellowship of holy Church,
and in the font of baptism he restored them from swarthi-
ness to beauty, for he removed the blackness of their vices,
and adorned them with a covering of virtues.[32] His own
gospel teaches [this]. By writing it he sanctified the beginning of the New Testament. To him it was granted by special privilege to be the first of all to describe what happened,
and to transmit for believers to read the mysteries of the
Lord's incarnation, which all the prophets for ages past foretold would come to be. He composed [his] gospel in the
Hebrew language, to build up the faith of the primitive
Church which was gathered mostly from the Hebrew
people.[33] As the Church was spread widely through the
world, and Greeks and barbarians flowed together into the
unity of the same faith, the leaders of the faithful took care
to have this [gospel] translated into Greek and Latin speech,
as they also soon had translated into the Latin language the
gospels of Mark, Luke, and John (which one after another
had been composed in the Greek tongue), so that everyone throughout the nations of the world could read and
understand them.

Ezechiel the prophet also testified how Matthew would
shine forth among the preeminent members of holy Church,
when under the figure of four animals he described in a
very full discourse the admirable virtues of all the evangelists, which he had learned about in a heavenly vision.[34]
John the apostle too, who was one of them, and who himself was taught by a spiritual vision, mentions these evangelists among the first mysteries[35] of the Church.[36] Those
who handed on to memory in writing the deeds and words

---

32. Eusebius/Rufinus, *Hist. Eccl.* (*GCS* 9: 189, 4)
33. Jer., *De vir. ill.* 3 (*TU* 14: 8, 30/33)
34. Ezk 1:5, 10; Aug. *De cons. evang.* 1, 6 (*CSEL* 43: 9, 3/8); Jer. *In Matth.*,
    Praef. (*CC* 77: 3, 55 - 4, 75)
35. *sacramenta*   36. Rv 4: 6-7

of our Redeemer were indeed of such great dignity that they were pointed out not only by prophetic but also by apostolic testimony. So great were they in dignity that the scriptures of both testaments rightly gave testimony to them, and the citizens of heaven called to memory their glory and pointed out how great they were considered [to be] before God, not only before the beginning of the gift of their most holy work to men, but also after it was begun and carried to completion.

Ezechiel records many things about them, and John, who was outstanding among them, records many things,[37] but for the present, because this sermon must be concluded, it is sufficient for us to record one of John's testimonies: *And when the four animals,* he says, *gave glory and honor and blessing to him who was sitting upon the throne, who lives for ages and ages, the twenty-four elders fell down before him who was sitting on the throne and adored him who lives for ages and ages, and they cast their crowns before his throne.*[38] Whenever we recognize that the magnificence of the eternal King is proclaimed in the books of the holy evangelists, we should fall down humbly before him, implore his mercy with devout prayers, and attribute whatever sort of good work we are able to have not to our own merits, but always to his grace, who sitting on the throne of the Father with the Holy Spirit lives and reigns for all ages and ages. Amen.

37. var.: 'many hidden things'   38. Rv 4:9-10

homily 1.22

Matthew 15:21-28   *In Lent*

I n the reading from the holy gospel which has just been
read, dearly-beloved brothers, we have heard about
the great faith, patience, constancy and humility of a
woman.[1] What those of devout mind find most to admire
about her is the fact, that although as a gentile she was completely separated from the teachings of the divine thoughts,
she was nevertheless not deprived of the virtues which
those thoughts proclaim.

She had a great perfection of faith, since, imploring the
Savior's benevolence, she said, *'Show me mercy, o Lord, son
of David'*. She named the Lord 'son of David,' so it is evident that she believed that he was true human being and
true God. Though she was asking on behalf of her daughter, she did not bring her along, and she did not entreat
the Lord to come to [her daughter], so it is clear that she
trusted that he could give her health by his word, his bodily
presence not being required. And also, after many tears,
finally she prostrated herself and adored him, saying, *'Lord,
help me'*. This teaches us that she had no uncertainty concerning his divine majesty, since she said that his power
was to be adored as God's.

1. Jer. *In Matth.* 15, 25 (CC 77: 133, 1569/73)

215

She had no small measure of the virtue of patience. Although the Lord did not answer a word to her first request, she did not cease entreating him, but with a fuller earnestness she implored the help of his benevolence as she had begun. The reason the Lord kept her waiting for an answer was not that he, the pitying physician of the pitiful, disdained her petitions. Of him it was written most truthfully: *The Lord has heard the desire of the poor.*[2] He kept her waiting for an answer in order to demonstrate to us the perseverence of this woman that we can always imitate. The more she seemed to be disdained by the Lord, the more ardently she persisted in the entreaties she had begun. He kept her waiting for an answer in order to declare that the minds of his disciples should also be merciful. As human beings they were ashamed of the clamor of the woman as she pursued them publicly; but he himself knew the character of his mercy, since he *disposed all things in measure and number and weight.*[3] He kept her waiting for an answer lest an occasion be given to the Jews for finding fault with him for giving preference in teaching or healing to the gentiles over them,[4] so that they might justly refuse to adopt faith in him.

And this is what he said: *'I have not been sent except to the lost sheep of the house of Israel'.* He alone, by himself, was teaching the Jews; through his disciples he called the gentiles also to the grace of faith. Concerning them he said elsewhere, *'And other sheep I have which are not of this fold, and them also I must bring, and they will hear my voice, and there will be one fold and one shepherd'.*[5] This is why when in his own person he was going to heal the body of a gentile girl, he did not carry this out before her mother's incomparable faith had been proven to everyone.

This mother also had the characteristics of constancy and humility surpassing all others. When the Lord compared her to dogs, she did not desist from the earnestness of her entreaty, and did not draw back her mind from hoping for

2. Ps 10:17 (9:38)   3. Ws 11:21
4. Jer., *In Matth.* 15, 23-24 (CC 77: 133, 1553/66)
5. Jn 10:16

the favor of [his] benevolence. Having willingly embraced the indignity she had received, she not only did not deny that she was like dogs, but even continued with a comparison of herself to young dogs. With this prudent argument she confirmed the Lord's statement, but nevertheless she did not rest from the audacity of her request. She confirmed the Lord's statement in which he said to her, *'It is not good to take the children's bread and to give it to dogs'*, as she answered, *'Yes, Lord'*—that is: 'Truthfully, it is as you allege, that it is not good to take the salvation divinely intended for the people of Israel and to give it to gentiles'. But when she said, *'For even the young dogs eat of the crumbs which fall from their masters' table,'* she very prudently demonstrated what great humility and what constancy she bore within her inmost heart. Being unworthy to be refreshed by the meal of the Lord's entire teaching, which the Jews had for their use, she nevertheless supposed that however small the grace imparted to her by the Lord might be, it could be sufficient for her salvation.

Hence from the benevolent Savior, who kept her waiting for a time, not out of lofty disdain for her entreaty, but by provident dispensation, she rightly deserved to hear: *'O woman, your faith is great. Let it be done to you as you wish'*. Indeed, she had great enough faith, since she knew neither the ancient miracles, commands and promises of the prophets, nor the more recent ones of the Lord himself. In addition, as often as she was disregarded by the Lord, she persevered in her entreaties, and she did not cease knocking by asking him, though she knew only by popular opinion that he was the Savior. On account of this she secured the great object for which she implored when, as the Lord said, *'Let it be done to you as you wish,'* her daughter *was healed from that hour.*

This woman, by nature a gentile, but constant and believing in her heart, rightly signifies the faith and devotion of the Church gathered from the nations, which holy preachers expelled from Judaea inspired with the word and the mysteries of heavenly grace. Now let us take a look at the preceding reading from the holy gospel. We will find

that scribes and Pharisees, coming from Jerusalem, assailed
the Lord and his disciples, making a great outcry because
of their lack of faith, and [Jesus] soon left them, having rebuked them with the invective they deserved.[6]

And *going on from there he entered into the regions of Tyre
and Sidon.*[7] Clearly it is prefigured here that after his passion and resurrection the Lord, in his preachers, was going to leave behind the faithless hearts of the Jews and move
on to the regions of foreign nations. Tyre and Sidon, which
were gentile cities, indicate the strongholds of gentile teaching and life, in which the foolish trust. Hence it is good that
the woman, who in her belief entreated the Lord, is reported
to have come out from those territories, for unless the
Church had left the vain dwelling-places of her preceding
way of life, she would never have come to Christ; unless
she had denounced the dogmas of her old error, she would
never have known to adopt the new grace of faith.

The daughter beset by a devil, for whom [the woman]
entreated, is any soul in the Church that is delivered up
to the deceptions of malign spirits rather than to her Maker's commands. The Church, as a solicitous mother, must
intercede for this [soul] so that since [the Church] is not
capable of [converting] such a one by warning, entreating
and rebuking her outwardly, [Christ] may convert her by
inspiring her interiorly, and, when she has been turned from
the darkness of error, he may rouse her to the acknowledgement of the true light. But if the Lord keeps the Church waiting for an answer as she asks in tears — that is, if he keeps
those who wander waiting before giving them the deliverance of mind for which she has entreated — it is not that
she should desist from asking, seeking and knocking, nor
that there should come over her a despair of having her
request granted. Instead she should persevere with great
earnestness; she should resort to the Savior crying out obsti-
nately, and among her petitions she should seek to obtain
the support of his saints until they too offer supplications
to the Lord from heaven that the Church might be heard.

6. Mt 15:1-14   7. Mt 15:21

And thus it will happen that, if she does not turn aside her mind from its proposed intention, she will by no means be deprived of the fruit of her request. One who intervenes, either for the sake of his own weakness or for the sake of others, will obtain the desired effect.

Also, if one of us has a conscience polluted by the stain of avarice, conceit, vain-glory, indignation, irascibility, or envy and the other vices, he has a daughter badly troubled by a demon. He should hasten to the Lord, making supplication for her healing because undoubtedly she is being dominated by thoughts born of the devil's heart and maddened by [his] craft. Moreover, [one with such a conscience] should frequently beg, with continual lamentations and petitions, that she be cleansed by her benevolent Maker. If one has perhaps polluted the good one has done with the plague of false swearing, robbery, blasphemy, detraction, brawling, and also of uncleanness of the body and other things of this sort, he has a daughter disturbed by the frenzy of an unclean spirit. The conduct which he had brought forth by laboring well he has now lost by stupidly serving the devil's deceptions. And so as soon as such a one has recognized his crime, he must flee to petitions and tears; he must seek the frequent intercessions and help of the saints, so that asking for the salvation of his soul, they may say to the Lord, 'We entreat you, Lord [who are] *compassionate and merciful, patient and full of compassion,*[8] pardon her because she is crying after us. Pardon [her] crimes and give [her] grace, because, prostrate with inmost feeling, she seeks our support'.

Being submissive with due humility, [such a person] must not judge himself to be worthy of the company of the sheep of Israel (that is, souls that are pure), but instead he must be of the opinion that he should be compared to a dog and that he is unworthy of heavenly favors. Nevertheless, let him not in despair rest from the earnestness of his entreaty, but with his mind free of doubt let him trust in the goodness of the supreme Benefactor, for the one who could make

---

8. A conflation of Ps 86:15 (85:15) and Ex 34:6.

a confessor from a robber,[9] an apostle from a persecutor,[10] an evangelist from a publican,[11] and who could make sons for Abraham from stones,[12] could turn even the most shameless dog into an Israelite sheep. He may even bestow upon him, as a reward for chastity attained, the pasture of eternal life—that is, he may deign to make righteous a sinner who has turned from his evil way, and as a reward for his good action he may lead him to the heavenly kingdom. Seeing how great is the ardor of our faith, and how tenacious is the perseverance of our praying, the Lord will show mercy. And may he also grant to us what we wish may come to be, namely that with the tumults of our depraved thoughts expelled and the bonds of our sins loosed, both the pure serenity of our mind and the perfection of [our] good works may be restored.

Meanwhile, we must note that this tenacity in praying can only deserve to bear fruit if what we ask for with our mouth we also meditate on in our mind, and if the crying of our lips is not cut apart in another direction from the focus of our thoughts. For there are some who, upon entering a church, stretch out their psalm-singing or their prayer with many words, but because their heart is directed elsewhere, they do not even reflect upon what they are saying. They pray, to be sure, with their mouths, but they deprive their mind, which is wandering outside, of all the fruit of their prayer. They suppose that their prayer is heard by God, when not even those who pour it forth hear it— [there is] no one who cannot perceive that it has been done at the instigation of the ancient enemy. He is aware of the benefit of praying, and he envies human beings the gift of having their requests granted, so he sends upon those who are praying many kinds of frivolous thoughts, and sometimes too phantasms of things that are shameful and harmful. By these he can interfere with prayer in such a way that occasionally, when we are prostrated in prayer, we may endure great surges of thoughts which run every which way, [thoughts] such as we have not known ourselves to endure even when we were lying flat on our backs in bed.

9. Lk 23:40-42   10. Ac 9:1-30   11. Mt 9:9-13   12. Mt 3:9

Hence, dearly-beloved brothers, we must take care to triumph over the acknowledged malice of the devil, clearing our mind, as far as we can, of every sort of cloud which the enemy rejoices in sprinkling about, and begging for the continuing protection of the benevolent Defender, who is able to grant to those entreating him, no matter how unworthy they are, both the grace of praying in a pure way, and that of having their requests granted completely. The purity of our prayer will help us a great deal[13] if in every place and time we restrain ourselves from forbidden acts, if we always check our hearing along with our speaking with regard to idle conversation, if we habituate ourselves to walking in the law of the Lord and scrutinizing his testimonies with all our heart.[14] Whatever things we are accustomed to do, speak, or hear most often, these same things will necessarily return to our mind most often as though to their accustomed and proper place. And just as pigs are accustomed to frequent marshy wallowing places, and doves to frequent clear flowing streams, so too impure thoughts disturb an unclean mind, and spiritual thoughts sanctify a chaste one. If, after the example of the Caananite woman, we continue resolutely in our praying, and remain of fixed purpose, certainly the grace of our Maker will be with us to correct everything in us which is wrong, to sanctify everything unclean, and to make serene everything which is turbulent. He is faithful and just, so that he will forgive us our sins and cleanse us from every iniquity, if with the attentive voice of our mind we cry out to him who lives and reigns with the Father in the unity of the Holy Spirit, God for all ages and ages. Amen.

13. var.: 'it will help the purity of our prayer a great deal'
14. Ps 119:1-2 (118:1-2)

homily 1.23

John 5:1-18   *In Lent*

oday's reading from the holy gospel tells us of two
miracles of human healing at the same time, one displayed invisibly through an angel's ministration, the
other visibly through our Lord's presence. But we must explain the mystical meaning[1] of both briefly, lest a lengthy
explanation of the reading[2] may perhaps be oppressive to
some.

The pool [called] Probatica, which was surrounded by five
porticoes, is the Jewish people, protected on all sides by
the guardianship of the law so that they would not sin. And
indeed the law, which was written down in the five books
of Moses, is properly symbolized by the number five.[3] The
people who used to preserve purity of life in certain respects,
but to be stirred up in certain other respects by the temptations of unclean spirits, are properly designated by the
waters of the pool, which at times used to be calm from the
winds, but then were stirred up as they rushed in.

And it is good that this pool was called 'Probatica'. *Probata*
in Greek means sheep. There were undoubtedly among that
people some who knew how to say to the Lord, *We your*

1. *mysteria*   2. var.: 'of the lengthy reading'
3. Aug., *Tract. in Ioh.* 17, 2 (CC 36: 171, 12/26)

222

people and the sheep of your flock confess you forever.[4] 'Probatica,' though, is commonly taken as 'pool of cattle,' called that because the priests used to wash the sacrificial offerings in it.

The multitude of ailing people who were lying in the aforementioned porticoes, awaiting the movement of the water, signify the throngs of those who, upon hearing the words of the law, were sorrowful because they could not fulfill it by their own powers, and so with all the devotion in their soul they besought the help of the Lord's grace. The blind are those who did not yet have the perfect light of faith. The lame are those who were unable to fulfill by their steps the good things they knew they were to do; the shriveled are those who, no matter how much they may have had the eye of knowledge, nevertheless lacked richness of hope and love. Such as these were lying in the five porticoes, but only those in the pool when the angel came were healed: recognition of sin happens through the law but the grace of forgiveness [comes] only through Jesus Christ.[5]

'Angel' designates the one who descended invisibly into the pool and moved the water to provide the power of healing. Clothed in flesh, [Christ] descended into the water as *an angel of great counsel,*[6] that is, as a herald of the Father's will to Jewish people. By his deeds and his teaching he moved sinners, so that he would be killed — he who, by his bodily death, was able not only to heal those who were ailing spiritually, but also to bring the dead back to life. The movement of the water, then, suggests the Lord's passion, which occurred by the nation of the Jews being moved and stirred up. And because through his passion those who believed were redeemed from the curse of the law, [it is] as if they were healed as they descended into the troubled water of the pool, though up until then they had been lying diseased in the porticoes. The letter of the law taught the ignorant what was to be done and what avoided, yet it did not aid those taught to fulfill its decrees — so it is as if it

4. Ps 79:13 (78:13)   5. Jn 1:17   6. Is 9:6 (LXX)

contained in its porticoes those led from their places of previous ignorance, but did not heal the enfeebled.

The grace of the gospel, however, through faith and the mystery of the Lord's passion, heals all the illnesses of our iniquities, from which we could not be justified in the law of Moses. Thus it is as if it sends the diseased, cast out[7] from the porticoes of the law, into the stirred-up water of the pool so that they can be healed. Through the water of baptism it cleanses [people] from the sins which the law pointed out. The Apostle bears witness *that all we who have been baptized in Christ Jesus have been baptized in his death. We have been buried with him through baptism into death in order that, as Christ has risen from the dead through the glory of the Father, so we also may walk in newness of life.*[8] It is good that the one who first went down after the movement of the water was healed of whatever illness had him in its grip, for [there is] *one Lord, one faith, one baptism,*[9] and a person who in catholic unity is imbued with the mysteries of Christ is healed from whatever illness [caused by] his sins that holds him fast. Whoever is out of harmony with [that] unity is not capable of securing salvation, since it is from One.

Now that we have spoken about the first miracle in the gospel reading which the Lord granted, let us speak to you of the brotherhood about the second, which he would grant. In this [miracle story] it is set forth that one person was healed, not because the benevolence of the almighty Savior was unable to heal everyone whom he found ailing there, but so that he might teach that there is no place of salvation accessible to anyone outside the unity of the catholic faith.

A certain man was there who had been under his infirmity for thirty-eight years. This man, held fast by an infirmity of many years, signifies any sinner weighed down by a huge magnitude or number of wicked deeds. The amount of time during which he was ailing was fitting to his crime by what it signifies. He had been under his infirmity for two years less than forty. This number forty which is produced by

---

7. 'cast out' = *eiectos*; var.: 'chosen' = *electos*
8. Rm 6:3-4   9. Eph 4:5; some MSS add: 'one God'

multiplying the number ten by four, is usually taken in scripture for the perfection of a right way of life, for anyone who does the works of a perfect way of life fulfills the decalogue of the law through the four books of the holy gospel. One who behaves in a way devoid of the love of God and neighbor, which scripture commends equally in the law and in the gospel,[10] has two less than this perfection.[11]

The Lord taught this mystically as he healed the weak man, when he said, *'Rise, take up your pallet and walk'. 'Rise'* means: 'Shake off the sluggishness of the vices in which you have been ailing for a long time, and rouse yourself to the practice of virtues, by which you will be eternally saved'. *'Take up your pallet'* [means]: 'Lovingly carry your neighbor,[12] patiently tolerating his weaknesses, since he patiently put up with you for a long time when you were still weighed down by the burden of temptations'. *Bear one another's burdens, and thus you will fulfill the law of Christ;*[13] and as he says elsewhere, *bearing with one another in charity, being solicitous to keep the unity of the Spirit in the bonds of peace.*[14] *'Walk'* [means]: 'Love God with your whole heart, your whole soul, and your whole strength,[15] so that you may be worthy to reach the vision of him; go forward by making daily strides of good works from virtue to virtue.[16] Do not desert a brother whom by your support you are directing on account of the love of the One toward whom you are proceeding, nor turn [aside from] the right direction of your path, on account of the love of a brother, away from your quest for the One with whom you desire to abide'. But so to be perfectly saved, *'Rise, take up your pallet and walk,'* that is: 'Leave behind your earlier sins, and come to the aid of your brothers' needs. In everything you do, see to it that you do not fix your mind upon this world, but that you hurry to see the face of your Redeemer. "Rise" by doing good works. "Carry your pallet" by loving your

---

10. Dt 6:5; Lv 19:18; Mt 22:37-39
11. Aug., *Tract. in Ioh.* 17, 6 (CC 36: 173, 1 - 174, 3)
12. Aug., *Tract. in Ioh.* 17, 7-8 (CC 36: 174, 13 - 175, 33)
13. Ga 6:2   14. Eph 4:2-3   15. Mk 12:30
16. Ps 84:7 (83:8)

neighbor. And "walk" by awaiting *the blessed hope and coming of the glory of the great God'.*[17]

But amazing is the madness of a faithless people. They should have believed in the unexpected healing of a person who had long been ailing, and should have been spiritually healed [themselves]. Instead they were scandalized, and they fabricated a false accusation against both the man healed and his healer. [They accused] the man healed because he carried his pallet on the sabbath; [they accused] his healer because on the sabbath he had commanded him both to be healed and to take up his pallet. It is as if they paid more attention to the sabbath than to such divine power.

The Jews said to him who had been healed, 'It is the sabbath. It is not lawful for you to take up your pallet'. They were stupidly defending the letter of the law, ignoring the divinely-arranged plan of the One who formerly announced his edicts through a servant, but who now came himself, determined to change the law by grace, so that what the fleshly had long observed in a fleshly way according to the letter, henceforth the spiritual might recognize as requiring observance in a spiritual way. Indeed by the fleshly sabbath, which was kept according to the letter, the people were ordered to keep free from all servile work on the seventh day.[18] [The meaning of] the spiritual sabbath, in the light of the sevenfold spiritual grace which we have received, is that we should remain on holiday from the unrest of vices not only on one day, but every day. For if, according to the Lord's voice, *'Everyone who commits sin is a servant of sin,'*[19] it is clear that sins are properly understood as servile works, and we are ordered to walk free of them, as it were on the seventh day, in the partaking of spiritual grace. [We are ordered] not only to keep from wrong deeds, but also to devote ourselves to good deeds.[20]

The Lord also shows us something typologically in this reading, when he commanded one who had been ailing for

17. Tt 2:13   18. Ex 20:10; 31:15; Lv 23:7   19. Jn 8:34
20. Aug., *Ennar. in Ps.* 91, 2 (*CC* 39: 1280, 2/23); *Serm.* 270, 5 (*PL* 38: 1242); *Tract. in Ioh.* 20, 2 (*CC* 36: 203, 12/26)

two years less than forty not only to rise up on the sabbath day, but also to take up his pallet and walk. He thereby suggested that people who are wasting away from a long illness of vices, and who, being devoid of love of God and neighbor, have, as it were, two less than the perfect sumtotal of virtues — that they can now rise again from their vices through the gift of the Holy Spirit, and that when they have shaken off their sluggishness they should hasten with the burden of brotherly love to the vision of their Maker.

The one who was healed did not recognize Jesus when he was still situated in the crowd, but [only] afterwards in the temple. Mystically this instructs us that if we desire to truly recognize the grace of our Maker, if we desire to be strengthened by his love,[21] if we desire to come to the vision of him, we should eagerly flee the crowd — not only the crowd of wrong thoughts and feelings — but also the crowd of depraved people. They can make it difficult for us to achieve the objective of our sincerity, either by showing us their bad example, or by deriding or even preventing our own good works. Let us be prompt to take refuge in the house of prayer, where, invoking the Lord in secret liberty, we may both give thanks for the kindnesses we have received from him, and entreat [him] with humble devotion for those which are yet to be received. Moreover, let us take care to be the holy temple of God in which he may deign to come and make his abode. We hear from the Apostle that *your bodies are the temple of the Holy Spirit, who is in you.*[22]

Among the things that we must look at very carefully, my brothers, is the fact that as the Lord came into the temple he said to the one whom he had healed, *'Behold, you are healed. Sin no more lest something worse should happen to you'.* With these words he clearly pointed out that it was on account of his sins that the man was ailing; that he could not have been healed except by their being forgiven; and that the one who healed him outwardly from his infirmity was the very one who also healed him inwardly from his

---

21. *amore confirmari*; var.: 'to be conformed to his love' (*amori conformari*)
22. 1 Co 6:19

wicked deeds. Hence [Jesus] cautiously forewarned him not
to draw down upon himself the sentence of a graver damnation by further sinning.

This is not to be understood as though [it meant that] if
anyone suffer infirmity, it is on account of sins that he
suffers infirmity. In the scriptures we discover that there
are five ways in which physical infirmity is given to human
beings. [It is given] to sinners either that they may be corrected through repentance, or, if they do not deserve to be
corrected, that it may be apparent even in this life how they
are going to be condemned to eternal death. To the just,
on the other hand, [it is given] either that they may receive
the greater palm of patience, or that, having been alerted
by their infirmities, they may with greater humility keep
the merit of their justice. To a great many, however, fleshly
infirmity is many times given for this reason, that the glory
and power of either the Lord and Savior, or of his saints,
may be made more widely known through their being
healed.

Now today's reading bears witness to the fact that sinners are punished by infirmity of the body in the interest
of their seeking unimpaired health of the mind. There, when
the man who had been ailing was healed, he heard, *'Behold, you are healed. Sin no more lest something worse should
happen to you'*. [Another reading] that also bears witness [to
this] is the one where the Lord said to the paralytic who
was to be healed, *'Trust, my son; your sins are forgiven you'*.[23]
The fact that those enveloped in graver shameful acts may
not deserve to come to pardon, and very often may receive
the beginning of their undying damnation even in the present time, is brought out by the penalty of King Herod. On
account of his crime of blasphemy, *he was consumed by worms
and expired*[24] before the eyes of the living. After his death
he doubtless hastened to that place where his worm does
not die and his fire is not extinguished.[25]

The story of blessed Job indicates that the just may be
visited by physical pain in order to enlarge their reward for

23. Mt 9:2   24. Ac 12:23   25. Is 66:24; Mk 9:43

their patience. It was not for the sake of washing away his crimes, but for the sake of increasing his merits, that he triumphed by a wonderful practice of constancy over very serious pains of the body which, since there was no one like him upon the earth,[26] the fierce adversary was able to devise against him. In the same way the Apostle shows that the just may be struck by the discipline of sickness in the interest of preserving their humility, when he says, *And lest the greatness of the revelations should puff me up, there was given me a thorn for my flesh, a messenger of Satan, to buffet me.*[27] Hence, again, he says, *Gladly therefore will I glory in my infirmities, so that the power of Christ may dwell in me.*[28] [Christ] himself revealed that often some are ailing in order to show the glory of their Maker, or of his saints, when he said to the disciples inquiring about the man who was born blind, *'Neither has this man sinned nor his parents, that he should be born blind: but in order to manifest God's works in him'.*[29] And concerning the ailing Lazarus, [Jesus] affirmed to his sisters, *'This infirmity is not unto death, but for the glory of God, that through it God's Son may be glorified'.*[30]

But because we are uncertain whether we are being punished for the sake of augmenting our good deserts, or for the sake of decreasing our bad deserts, we must take care to the utmost that whenever we are assailed by physical trials we straightaway turn back to scrutinizing the inner reaches of the mind. And if we discover that we have done anything against the will of our Creator, we should purge it from us by the worthy correction of repentance. Nor should we seek a remedy for the body before we recognize that we have arrived at a pure state of the inner man, lest perhaps after we take care of curing the flesh, the bad health of the mind, which lies hidden within, may be an obstacle to us. Let us learn how to bow humbly before the scourges of [our] benevolent Maker, aware that we suffer less than we deserve, and always mindful of the statement that *blessed is the man who is rebuked by the Lord.*[31] He him-

---

26. Jb 1:8   27. 2 Co 12:7   28. 2 Co 12:9
29. A conflation of Jn 9:2 and 9:3.   30. Jn 11:4   31. Jb 5:17

self says in the Apocalypse, *Those whom I love I rebuke and chastise.*[32]

[The man] who had been ailing for a long time was healed interiorly and exteriorly, that is, he was snatched away from the scourges of open correction, and from the sins for which he deserved them. The Jews, on the other hand, who were very ill interiorly, began to grow more seriously sick by persecuting Jesus because he had done these things on the sabbath. In persecuting him they were following, as they believed, the authority of the law, and at the same time the example of divine work. When the creation of the world had been accomplished in six days, on the seventh day the Lord rested from all his works,[33] and he commanded the people to work for six days and to be free of work on the seventh.[34] They did not understand that the fleshly decrees of the law were to be gradually changed, by spiritual interpretation, with the appearance of the one who was not only the Maker of the law, but also *the Christ, the end of the law unto justice for everyone who believes.*[35] Nor did they attend to the fact that on the seventh day the Maker did not cease from the work of governing the world, and from the annual and even daily replacement of created things, but [only] from the new production of creatures. And they did not recognize the most profound spiritual meaning of the sabbath: either that the Lord, having been crucified and having worked out our salvation on the sixth day of the week, *in the middle of the earth*[36] (that is, the flesh which he had assumed), would rest on the seventh day in the sepulcher, until he would rise again on the eighth day;[37] or that his saints, after the six ages of this world in which they labor in the doing of good works, attain in another life a seventh [age] of rest for their souls, until in the eighth [age] of the resurrection of bodies they too are granted the reception of what is incorruptible.[38]

But let us listen to what he himself, who was the Author of grace as well as of the law, answered the unlearned

32. Rv 3:19   33. Gn 2:2   34. Ex 20:9-10
35. Rm 10:4   36. Ps 74:12 (73:12)
37. Aug., *Tract. in Ioh.* 17, 15 (CC 36: 177, 1 - 178, 27)
38. Bede, *Hom.* I.11 (CC 122: 77, 149)

defenders of the law in order to bend their necks by the power of reason: *'My Father,'* he said, *'works even until now, and I work'.* In saying this he did not mean that while the Father had so far been working, he himself was then starting to work after the Father; rather that as the Father had always been working, from the beginning of creation, he himself had always been doing the same works together with him.

That you may be aware that God the Father worked not only on those first six days but *'even until now,'* read the [saying] of the prophet, *Before I formed you in the womb, I knew you;* [39] and in the psalm, *He who shaped the hearts of every one of them;* [40] and elsewhere, *Who covers the heavens with clouds and prepares rain for the earth, who produces hay on the mountains,* [41] and other things of this sort. We must indeed note that [the psalmist] did not put the verb in the past tense, saying, 'who covered and prepared and produced,' but in the present, 'he covers, prepares, produces,' in order to demonstrate that the Father works every day, no less on the sabbath than on other days. So that you may not doubt that the Son works all things equally, recall that [saying] of the psalmist: *He spoke, and flies and gnats came; he spoke, and the locust and the grasshopper came; he spoke, and there stood forth the wind of a storm.* [42]

If *he spoke, and they were made,* [43] beyond doubt it was through his Word that he made [them]. The Father's word is the Son, about whom John said, *All things were made through him.* [44] Likewise, since the psalmist relates to the praise of the Creator not only the primordial creation of the world, but also the daily governing of his creation, he says, among other things, *You have made all things in wisdom.* [45] If we rightly confess that *Christ* [is] *the power of God and the wisdom of God,* [46] and God made and rules all things in wisdom, it is undoubtedly a fact that the Father *'works even until now,'* and the Son too. Therefore, *'my Father,'* he says,

39. Jr 1:5   40. Ps 33:15 (32:15)   41. Ps 147:8 (146:8)
42. Ps 105:31, 34; 107:25 (104:31, 34; 106:25)
43. Ps 148:5   44. Jn 1:3   45. Ps 104:24 (103:24)
46. 1 Co 1:24

'worked not only on the first six days, as you suppose, but
he works even until now,' not by producing a new kind of
creation, but by propagating those which he created in the
beginning so that they do not come to an end. *'And I work'*
('even until now' is understood) 'with him disposing, ruling and enhancing all things'.[47] And if he were to speak
clearly, [he would ask], 'For what do you envy me? Why
do you blind readers[48] of the law find fault with me because
in the form of a human being, I have brought health to one
human being, since in the nature of my divinity, which is
one with God the Father, I am always quietly at work
[governing and maintaining] the whole human race, and
moreover the whole fabric of the world and all things visible and invisible'?

But they had little capacity for understanding a great mystery of such a sort,[49] and *therefore they sought all the more
to kill him, because he not only broke the sabbath, but also said
that God was his Father, making himself equal to God.* What
especially aggrieved them was that he wanted people to believe that he was God's true Son,[50] that is, not [a son]
adopted by grace like the rest of the saints, of whom the
prophet speaks, *I have said: You are gods, and all of you are
sons of the Most High,*[51] but [a Son] in all things equal to the
Father by nature; [a Son], that is to say, of whom the Father
himself said in the sight of his sons (that is, the prophets,
who were adopted by grace as his sons): *He has cried out*[52]
*to me, 'You are my Father: my God, and the support of my
salvation'. And I will make him my firstborn, high above the kings
of the earth.*[53]

Christ's Jewish killers understood what the Arians, who
were confessors of Christ's name, were unable to understand: that inasmuch as Christ said, *'My Father works even
until now, and I work,'* he proclaimed himself equal to God

47. Pr 8:30   48. *lectores*; var.: 'proposers' (*latores*)
49. var.: 'such a great spiritual mystery'
50. Some MSS add: 'though they knew from the infirmity of his flesh
    that he was true man'
51. Ps 82:6 (81:6)
52. Some MSS have 'will cry out,' the Vulgate reading
53. Ps 89:26–27 (88:27–28)

the Father,[54] for those whose working is one and the same are also equal in majesty. But the impiety of both [Jews and Arians] leads to one end. The one group understood what the Lord said, but denied that what he had said was true. The other group admits the truth of those matters to which the Lord bore witness about himself, but recoils from following and comprehending the sense of the truth in these matters. So that we can avoid the most abominable end of these [two groups], dearly-beloved brothers, we must believe the words of our Savior with respect to their truth,[55] and also take care to understand them properly. In addition, we must strive to place all hope of our salvation in these [words of Christ]. Let us believe that he has truthfully proclaimed himself equal to the Father in the glory of his power, in his eternity and his reign; and by doing well let us attempt to come to one vision[56] of them both. Concerning this [one vision], when Philip asked and said, *'Lord, show us the Father and it is enough for us,'* the Lord answered, saying, *'One who sees me sees the Father also'*.[57]

We must certainly note that the statement *'making himself equal to God'* was said by a Jewish person, who supposed that our Lord Jesus Christ, by his proclamation, made himself what he was not, and did not truthfully tell what he was. We, brothers, being imbued with the sacraments and teaching of the catholic faith, should believe and confess that our Lord Jesus Christ was by nature made equal to us in his humanity while always remaining equal to the Father in his divinity. In neither nature did he make himself by shaping what he was not, but in both he revealed [himself] truthfully by proclaiming what he was. May he deign to introduce us to the perpetual sight of the glory of his majesty, in which he lives and reigns one God with the Father and the Holy Spirit through all ages. Amen.

---

54. Aug., *Tract. in Ioh.* 17, 16 (CC 36: 178: 8/15)
55. var.: 'their full truth'
56. var.: 'to the one life and vision'
57. Jn 14:8-9

homily 1.24

Matthew 16:27-17:9   *In Lent*

O ur Lord and Redeemer was disposed to lead his chosen ones through the labors of this life to that life
of future blessedness which knows no labor, so, by
his gospel, at times he describes the exertions of temporal
strife, and at other times he describes the palm of eternal
rewards. [He did this] so that, having heard about the
difficulties of the struggle, [his chosen ones] will remember that they are not to seek rest in this life; and, having
heard besides about the delights of future reward, they may
more easily bear the passing evils which they hope will be
recompensed by everlasting goods.[1]

Since a little before [the present reading] he had mentioned his own sufferings and those of his [followers],[2] he
immediately continued with what we have just heard when
[his words] were read, which said: *'For the Son of man is to
come with his angels in the glory of his Father, and then he will
render to each one according to his work'*. Here he clearly refers
to the day of the final reckoning, when he, who formerly
had come in humility and dejection to be judged by the
world, will come in great power and majesty to judge the

---

1. Ambr., *Expos. evang. sec. Luc.* 7, 1 (CC 14: 214, 2 - 215, 19)
2. Mt 16:21,24-26

234

world.[3] Then, with the severity of a judge, he will seek the perfection of their works from those to whom, in the lavishness of his mercy, he had granted the gift of his favors. Then, rendering to each according to his works,[4] he will lead his chosen ones into his Father's kingdom; the condemned, however, he will cast with the devil into undying fire.[5]

And it is admirably said that *'the Son of man is to come in the glory of his Father'*. The Son of man is indeed to come in the glory of God the Father, for though in his human nature he is less than the Father, in his divinity he is of one and the same glory with the Father, being in all things true man and true God.

What follows, however, rightly gladdens the pious, and it rightly frightens the contumacious: *'and then he will render to each according to his work'*. Those who, as they now do good works, are afflicted by unjust oppression caused by evil people, undoubtedly await with a glad spirit that time when they will not only be freed by the just Judge from the injurious treatment of the unjust, but they will also receive a reward for their justice and patience. But those who, living in an evil way, suppose that the Judge's patience is negligence, and repent too late, will be struck down with the just sentence of eternal damnation. The psalmist, in agreement with this statement of the gospel, says, *Mercy and judgment I will sing to you, O Lord.*[6] He testifies that he will first sing mercy, and then judgment, for surely whatever deposit the Lord generously conferred upon us in his first coming, he will as a strict [judge] demand [back] in his second coming.[7] Any perverse person, who despises the Lord's mercy when he grants it, will rightfully be terrified of the Lord's judgment when he scrutinizes [him]. One who gratefully remembers that he has received the grace of mercy will rejoice as he awaits the separation at the judgment, and so, with unrestrained melody, he will sing mercy and judgment to his Judge.

3. Lk 21:27; Greg., *Moral.* 17, 32, 53 - 17, 33, 54 (*CC* 143A: 883, 57 - 885, 52)
4. Rm 2:6   5. Mt 25:31-46
6. Ps 101:1 (100:1); Aug., *Ennar. in ps.* 100, 1-3 (*CC* 39: 1403, 1 - 1408, 37)
7. Greg., *Hom. in evang.* 1, 1, 2 (*PL* 76: 1079)

For everyone the time of the universal judgment is uncertain; for each and every person the hour of passing away
is uncertain. To those unaware of when their promised rest
may come, the present affliction could seem long. So the
benevolent Master willed to point out in advance the joys
of the eternal promise to some of his disciples while they
were still living their lives on earth, in order that those who
had seen [him], and everyone who was able to hear [about
him], would the more easily tolerate present adversities if
they often recalled to their minds the gift of the future reward for which they were waiting.

Hence there follows: *'Amen I say to you, there are some of
those standing here who will not taste death until they have seen
the Son of man coming in his kingdom'.* The disciples indeed
saw him coming in his kingdom, for on the mountain they
saw him shining in that brightness with which he will be
seen in his kingdom by all the saints when the judgment
has been brought to completion.[8] But since the eyes of the
disciples were still mortal and corruptible, they were then
unable to sustain what the whole Church of the saints will
have the power to look upon when she has become incorruptible through resurrection. Concerning this it is written,
Their eyes will see the king in his beauty.[9]

*And after six days Jesus took Peter, James and his brother John,
and led them up a lofty mountain by themselves.* When he was
about to show his glory to the disciples, he led them up
a lofty mountain in order to teach everyone desiring to see
this [glory] not to rest in base pleasures, not to serve fleshly
allurements, not to become attached to earthly avarice, but
to be always raised by the love of what is eternal toward
the things of heaven; and [to teach] that as far as is possible for mortals, they should always imitate the angelic life
of purity, piety, peace, love and justice, like the one who
said, *But our way of life is in heaven, from which we also await
a savior, our Lord Jesus Christ.*[10]

When he was about to show his disciples the glory of his
majesty, he led them up a mountain so that they might

8. Jer., *In. Matth.* 16, 27 - 17, 1 (CC 77: 146, 204 - 147, 230)
9. Is 33:17   10. Ph 3:20

learn, and so that everyone who thirsts to see this [glory] may learn, that they should not seek it in the depths of this world, but in the kingdom of heavenly blessedness. And when [the evangelist] says that *he led them up a lofty mountain*, it is good that he adds *by themselves*. Although the just are now oppressed by the proximity of the perverse, they are nevertheless separated from them by their whole heart and the intention of their faith. And in the future [the just] will be led away from them completely *'by themselves'* when he hides *them in the secret of his presence from the disturbance of men, and* shields *them in* his *tabernacle from the contradiction of tongues.*[11]

[Jesus] showed his disciples the brightness of his appearance six days after the time when he had promised it. This signifies that on judgment day the saints will receive the kingdom which *God, who does not lie, promised before the times of the world.*[12] The *'times of the world'* consist of six ages,[13] upon the completion of which they will hear him say, *'Come, blessed of my Father. Come into possession of the kingdom prepared for you from the foundation of the world'.*[14] The six days of the promised vision of the Lord and his glory can designate the perfection of good works, without which a person will not be capable of coming to contemplate his Maker's majesty, though he may be capable of achieving something else. Since the Lord formed created things in six days, and rested from his works on the seventh, the good works by which we are to come to our rest are aptly represented by six days.[15] And because one who eagerly desires to see God, and to reach the glory of the blessed resurrection, should do those things which he knows are good, after six days the Savior showed his disciples the glory of his kingdom, as he had promised them.

There follows: *And he was transfigured before them, and his face was resplendent as the sun. His garments became white as snow.* The Lord was transfigured before his disciples, and

11. Ps 31:20 (30:21)   12. Tt 1:2
13. Bede, *Hom.* I.11 (CC 122: 77, 149); I.14 (CC 122: 98, 103)
14. Mt 25:34
15. Ambr., *Expos. evang. sec. Luc.* 7, 7 (CC 14: 217, 87/92)

he gave them a sign of the glory of his body, which was
to be made illustrious through [his] resurrection. He also
made manifest the fact that the bodies of all of the chosen
would be of great brightness after their resurrection.[16] Of
them he said elsewhere, *'Then the just shall shine as the sun
in the kingdom of their Father'.*[17] Here, as a proof of his own
future brightness, his face was resplendent as the sun. Not
that the Lord's brightness and glory and that of his saints
could be equal, since the Apostle says to the saints, *Star
differs from star in brightness; so also [is] the resurrection of the
dead.*[18] But because we can see nothing brighter than the
sun, not only the Lord's glory, but also that of the saints
in the resurrection, is compared to the appearance of the
sun; he could not find anything brighter than the sun to
give as an example to human beings.

However, it should not be supposed that at the judgment
any of the condemned will see this glorified majesty of the
Lord's body, or this brightness of the bodies of the saints.
They will only *look upon him whom they have pierced, and all
the tribes of the earth will sorrow over him.*[19] And when, with
the bringing to completion of the judgment, the wicked are
taken away lest they see God's glory, then the just will go
in to contemplate forever the glory of his kingdom, and in
keeping with their state they will be transfigured by the light
of incorruption. Hence the Apostle says, *He will refashion
the body of our humility, conforming it to the body of his brightness.*[20]

If anyone asks what the Lord's garments, which became
white as snow, represent typologically, we can properly understand them as pointing to the Church of his saints.[21] Of
them Isaiah said, *You will be clothed with all of these as though
with an ornament.*[22] And the Apostle affirmed, *For as many
of you as have been baptized in Christ have put on Christ.*[23] At
the time of the resurrection they will be purified from every

16. Leo, *Serm.* 51, 3 (*CC* 138A: 299, 76/81)
17. Mt 13:43   18. 1 Co 15:41-42
19. A conflation of Jn 19:37 and Rv 1:7.
20. Ph 3:21   21. Aug., *Serm.* 78, 2 (*PL* 38, 490-91)
22. Is 49:18   23. Ga 3:27

blemish of iniquity and at the same time from all the darkness of mortality. Concerning the Lord's garments the evangelist Mark says beautifully that *they became as splendid as snow, such as no fuller on earth can make them white.*[24] It is evident to everyone that there is no one who can live on earth without corruption and sorrow; and it is evident to all who are wise, although heretics deny it, that there is no one who can live on earth without being touched by some sin. But what a fuller (that is, a teacher of souls or some extraordinary purifier of his body) cannot do on earth, that the Lord will do in heaven. He will purify the Church, which is his clothing, *from all defilement of flesh and spirit,*[25] renewing [her] besides with eternal blessedness and light of flesh and spirit.

There follows: *And behold there appeared to them Moses and Elijah speaking with him.* Luke writes more clearly of how they appeared, and what they spoke about with him. [Luke] says, *Moses and Elijah were seen in majesty, and they spoke of his passing away, which he was about to fulfill in Jerusalem.*[26] Moses and Elijah, who talked with the Lord on the mountain, and spoke about his passion and resurrection, represent the oracles of the law and prophets which were fulfilled in the Lord. They are now evident to everyone who has been taught, and will be more clearly evident to all of the elect in the future.[27] It is well said that they were 'seen in majesty,' for then it will be seen more clearly with what great merit of truth not only the sense, but even the words of divine eloquence will have been brought forward.

Although by Moses and Elijah we can rightly understand everyone who is going to reign with the Lord, by Moses, who died and was buried, [we can understand] those who at the judgment are going to be raised up from death. By Elijah, on the other hand, who has not yet paid the debt of death, [we can understand] those who are going to be found alive in the flesh at the Judge's coming. At one and the same moment, both of them, having been caught up

24. Mk 9:2   25. 2 Co 7:1   26. Lk 9:30-31
27. Aug., *Serm.* 78, 2, 4 (*PL* 38: 491); Jer., *In Matth.* 17, 3 (*CC* 77: 148, 258/62)

in clouds to meet the Lord in the air,[28] will be led into eternal life, as soon as the judgment is brought to completion.

It is appropriate that Moses and Elijah are reported to have been 'seen in majesty'. The mark of the favor with which they are to be crowned is shown by the preeminence of their majesty. It is also appropriately recorded that they spoke about his passing away, which was to be fulfilled in Jerusalem. The Redeemer's passion has become a unique subject for praise to his faithful, since the more they remember that they could not have been saved apart from his grace, the more they should always ponder in a faithful breast the greater memory of this grace, and bear faithful witness [to it].

The more fully one tastes the sweetness of heavenly life, the more fully will one turn away from everything that used to please here below. When Peter has seen the majesty of the Lord and his saints, at once he rightly forgets all the earthly things that he knew, and he delights in clinging uninterruptedly only to those things which he sees, saying, *'Lord, it is good that we are here. If you are willing, let us make three tents here, one for you, one for Moses, and one for Elijah'.*

As another evangelist bears witness, Peter did not know what he was saying,[29] insofar as he supposed that tents would have to be made in the heavenly way of life. No house will be needed in the glory of heavenly life, where, with the light of divine contemplation making all things peaceful, no breeze of adversity will remain to be feared, as the apostle John bears witness. Describing the brightness of the heavenly city, he says, among other things, *And I saw no temple in it. For the almighty Lord and the Lamb are its temple.*[30] But [Peter] knew well what he was saying when he said, *'Lord, it is good that we are here,'* for in reality the sole good of a human being is to enter into the joy of his Lord[31] and to attend upon him by contemplating him forever. Hence if it has happened to someone that, as a consequence of his guilt, he never sees the face of his Creator,

28. 1 Th 4:17   29. Lk 9:33   30. Rv 21:22
31. Mt 25:21

it is proper to suppose of such a one that he has never had any true good.

If when blessed Peter had contemplated the glorified humanity of Christ, he was affected by such joy that he did not wish to be separated from sight of him, what, dearly-beloved brothers, may we suppose is the blessedness of one who will be found worthy to see the heights of his divinity? And if seeing the transfigured form of the man Christ on the mountain, with only two of the saints, namely Moses and Elijah, led to the greatest good, what word is capable of explaining or what sense is capable of comprehending how great will be the joy of the just when they come *to Mount Zion and to the city of the living God, Jerusalem, and to the throng of many thousands of angels,*[32] when they look upon God, the producer and maker of this city, not *through a glass darkly* as now, but *face to face?*[33] Concerning this vision Peter himself, speaking of the Lord, says to the faithful, *Even now when you do not see him, you believe in him. When you do see him, you will exult with a gladness that is indescribable and glorified.*[34]

There follows: *And as he was still speaking, behold a bright cloud overshadowed them, and lo, a voice from the cloud said, 'This is my beloved Son in whom I am well-pleased. Hear him'.* Because they were seeking to make tents, a covering of bright cloud admonished them that houses are not necessary there, in the dwelling of heavenly life, where the Lord protects everything with the eternal overshadowing of his light. When the people were making their way through the desert, for forty years *he spread a cloud for their protection,*[35] lest the sun should scorch them by day or the moon by night.[36] How much more does he protect with the covering of his wings those who dwell in the tent of the heavenly kingdom forever?[37]

We know, as the Apostle says, that *if our terrestrial house in which we dwell should be dissolved, we have a building from God, a house not made by hands, eternal in heaven.*[38] Because

32. Heb 12:22   33. 1 Co 13:12   34. 1 P 1:8 (Codex Amiatinus)
35. Ps 105:39 (104:39)   36. Ps 121:6 (120:6)   37. Ps 61:4 (60:5)
38. 2 Co 5:1

they longed to perceive the resplendent face of the Son of man, the Father was present in his voice, teaching that this was his beloved Son, in whom he was well-pleased. From the glory of his humanity upon which they were looking, they were to learn to long to contemplate the presence of his divinity, which was equal to [the Father's] own.

[Regarding] the fact that the Father's voice said of the Son, *'in whom I am well-pleased,'* this is what the Son testified elsewhere: *'And he who sent me is with me, and he will not leave me*[39] *alone because I always do what is pleasing to him'.*[40] And the fact that [the Father's voice] continued, *'Hear him,'* admonished [them] that [Christ] was the one concerning whom Moses foretold to the same people to whom he gave the law, *'Your God will raise up a prophet for you from your brethren, as he did me. You will listen to all things whatsoever he will speak to you'.*[41] [The Father's voice] did not forbid [them] to listen to Moses and Elijah (that is, to the law and the prophets), but it suggested to all of them that listening to his Son was to take precedence, since he came to fulfill the law and the prophets.[42] It impressed upon them that the light of gospel truth was to be put before all the types and obscure signs of the Old Testament. By the benevolent divinely-arranged plan, lest the disciples' faith should falter when the Lord was crucified, it was strengthened when the moment of the cross was drawing near. There was revealed [to them] how his humanity too was to be lifted up by heavenly light through his resurrection. And the heavenly voice of the Father gave assurance that the Son was coeternal to the Father in his divinity, so that as the hour of the passion approached, they would be less sorrowful at his dying when they remembered that after his death he would soon be glorified as a human being, though in his divinity he had always been glorified by God his Father.

The disciples, inasmuch as they were fleshly and still fragile in substance, were afraid when they heard God's voice, and fell upon their faces. The Lord, inasmuch as he was

39. Var.: 'has not left me'   40. Jn 8:29   41. Ac 3:22 (Dt 18:15)
42. Mt 5:17

a benevolent master in everything, consoled them by his word, and at the same time by his touch, and he lifted them up.

And as they were coming down from the mountain, Jesus charged them, saying, 'Tell the vision to no one until the Son of man rises from the dead'. He charged them to be silent for a time about the vision of his majesty which was shown [to them], lest, if it were generally divulged to the people, either these people might obstruct the divinely-arranged plan of his passion by resisting their rulers, thus hindering the achievement of human salvation which was to come through his blood; or those who had believed when they heard about this vision might be scandalized upon seeing the opprobrium of the cross.[43] [The vision] was proclaimed more opportunely when his passion, resurrection and ascension were completed, and the apostles were filled with the Holy Spirit. Then everyone who wished to be initiated into his sacraments could not only believe in the achievement of his resurrection, but they could also learn from those who saw [the vision of the transfiguration], about the way in which the resurrection happened. They might also proclaim to everyone, as something to be believed as well as loved, the eternity of his divine birth, which they had heard about from the Father.

Now that the reading about the Lord's transfiguration has been explained to us, dearly-beloved brothers, let us return to our conscience and, if it delights in seeing the Lord's glory, let us ascend the mountain of virtues when we have passed beyond our fleshly desires. If we wish to attain the Lord's whitest of garments, *let us make ourselves clean from all defilement of flesh and spirit, perfecting* [our] *sanctification in the fear of God.*[44] If we desire to hear the voice of God the Father, [and] if we desire to look upon the majesty of his consubstantial Son, let us eagerly strive to turn away from perverse and unprofitable mortal things, and let us strive to avert our eyes from the pointlessness of this deceiving world. Then, as the glory of our resurrection glistens, we

43. Jer., *In Matth.* 17, 9 (CC 77: 150, 317/20)
44. 2 Co 7:1

also may be worthy [to do] what we are now unable to do, to see as well as tell of the wonders of our Maker,[45] as he himself grants us, who lives and reigns with the Father in the unity of the Holy Spirit, God for ages and ages. Amen.

45. Ex 14:13; Ac 2:11

homily 1.25

We ought to consider the present reading from the holy gospel, dearly-beloved brothers, especially attentively and always call it to mind, since it commends to us our Maker's greatest gift. Behold, as we have heard, a sinful woman was presented to him by her wicked accusers. He did not command that they stone her, in accordance with the command of the law, but he commanded her accusers first to consider themselves, and then to pass sentence upon the sinner accordingly. Then, from consideration of their own weakness, they might recognize how they should show mercy to others.

It is customary for the scriptures to signify the sort of things that are going to be told about later, sometimes by a circumstance of time, sometimes by a circumstance of place, and sometimes by both. So when the evangelist was about to refer to tempering of the severity of the law by our Redeemer's mercy, he first mentioned that Jesus made his way to the Mount of Olives, and that at daybreak he came again to the temple. The Mount of Olives designates the height of the Lord's benevolence and mercy, for in Greek 'mercy' is called *oleos*, and an olive plantation is called *oleon*,[1]

---

1. Some MSS spell *eleos* and *eleon*. Cf. end note 1 to *Hom.* II.4.

and also because anointing with oil usually soothes weary and aching limbs. But oil is preeminent in power and purity too, and it tends to make its way up and float on the top of any liquid that you choose to pour into it. This fact not inappropriately suggests the grace of heavenly mercy, concerning which it was written, *The Lord is gracious to everyone, and his compassion is over all his works.*[2] The time of daybreak stands for the dawn of the grace by which the light of the gospel truth was to be revealed when the shadow of the law was taken away. Jesus made his way to the Mount of Olives to announce that the peak of mercy consists in himself; he came again at daybreak to the temple to signify that, as the radiance of the New Testament was beginning, that same mercy was to be disclosed and presented to the temple, namely to his faithful ones.

And all the people came to him, and sitting down he taught them. The Lord's sitting suggests the humility of his incarnation, through which he deigned to show mercy to us. Hence we also are commanded, *Rise after you have sat down,*[3] or if it were said clearly, 'Hope to receive the reward of heavenly exaltation not before but after you have chastened yourself with true humility'.

It is good that we are told that when Jesus taught sitting down, all the people came to him. After he became a neighbor to human beings by the humility of his incarnation, his words were more readily received by many,[4] [but] they were despised by more people because of their proud wickedness. The gentle heard and were glad, magnifying the Lord with the psalmist, and exalting his name to each other.[5] The envious heard, and they were destroyed *and not moved to compunction*; they tempted him and scoffed with scorn; they gnashed their teeth at him.[6] Accordingly, testing [him], they brought a woman who had been apprehended in adultery, asking what he would order to be done with her in view of the fact that Moses had given a mandate to stone such a one. If he also determined that she was to be stoned they

2. Ps 145:9 (144:9)   3. Ps 127:2 (126:2)
4. Some MSS add: 'by many, I say, his words were received'
5. Ps 34:2-3 (33:3-4)   6. Ps 35:16 (34:16)

would scoff at him inasmuch as he had forgotten the mercy
which he was always teaching; if he forbade stoning, they
would gnash their teeth at him, and, as they saw it, rightly
condemn him as a doer[7] of wicked deeds contrary to the
law. But far be it from earthly stupidity to find out what
he would say, and from heavenly wisdom to fail [to know]
what he would answer; far be it from blind wickedness to
stand in the way of *the Sun of justice*[8] to keep him from giving light to the world.

Bending down, Jesus wrote with his finger on the ground. Humility is represented by Jesus' bending; subtlety of discern-
ment is represented by the finger, which is flexible because
of the physical arrangement of its joints. Besides, by the
ground we are shown the human heart, which customarily
produces the fruits of good or bad acts. When the Lord had
been implored to make a judgment concerning the sinful
woman, he did not immediately give judgment, but first
bending down he wrote with his finger on the ground, and
then at last he made a judgment on what he was being ob-
stinately asked about. Typologically this teaches us that
when we look at any of our neighbors' errors, we should
not judge by censuring them before we turn humbly back
to our own conscience and meticulously clear it of guilt with
the finger of discretion, and before we discriminate by pains-
taking examination between what in [our conscience] is
pleasing to [our] Maker and what is displeasing, in accordance with that [saying] of the Apostle, *Brothers, even if a
person is caught in some moral fault, let you who are spiritual
instruct such a one in a spirit of* [9] *gentleness, considering yourselves lest you also be tempted.*[10]

*When they continued to ask him, he raised himself up and said
to them, 'Let one who is without sin among you be the first to
throw a stone at her'.* From this side and that, the scribes and
pharisees spread traps and snares for the Lord, supposing
that in judging he would either be unmerciful or unjust.
He foresaw their treachery, and as it were passed through
the threads of their net. And as in all things he showed the

7. 'doer' = *factorem*; var.: 'promoter' = *fautorem*
8. Ml 4:2   9. Some MSS add 'his'   10. Ga 6:1

judgment of justice and the gentleness of benevolence, in them was fulfilled that [saying] of the psalmist to which we have referred, that they were destroyed *and not moved to compunction*.[11] Now 'they were destroyed' lest they hem in the Lord with snares; and 'not moved to compunction' so as to follow him with offices of love.

Do you want to hear about his restraint as he shows mercy?—*'Let one who is without sin among you'*. Again, do you want to hear about his justice in judging?—*'be the first to throw a stone at her'*. He said, 'If Moses gave you a mandate to stone such a woman as this, see that he did not command sinners to do this, but the just. First fulfill the justice of the law yourself, and, with this done, being *innocent in hands and clean of heart*,[12] come together to stone the guilty woman. First carry out the spiritual edicts of the law, faith, mercy and charity, and with this done turn aside to judge fleshly things'.

When the Lord had given judgment, *bending again, he wrote on the ground*. In accordance with our usual human manner, we can understand that the reason why the Lord might wish to bend before his unprincipled tempters and to write on the ground was that by directing his look elsewhere he might give them the freedom to go away. He foresaw that as they had been astounded by his answer, they would be more inclined to depart quickly than to ask him more questions. Accordingly, *hearing this, one by one they went away, starting with the eldest*.

Figuratively speaking, the fact that both before and after he gave his opinion he bent and wrote on the ground admonishes us that both before we rebuke a sinning neighbor and after we have rendered to him the ministry of due correction, we should subject ourselves to a suitably humble examination, lest perhaps we be entangled in the same things that we censure in [our neighbors], or in any other sort of misdeeds. For it often comes about, for example, that people who publicly judge a murderer to be a sinner may not perceive the worse evil of the hatred with which they

11. Ps 35:16 (34:16)   12. Ps 24:4 (23:4)

themselves despoil someone in secret; people who bring
an accusation against a fornicator may ignore the plague
of the pride with which they congratulate themselves for
their own chastity; people who condemn a drunkard may
not see the venom of envy with which they themselves are
eaten away. In dangers of this sort, what saving remedy
is left for us except that, when we look at some other sinner, we immediately bend down — that is, we humbly observe how we would be cast down by our frail condition
if divine benevolence did not keep us from falling? Let us
write with a finger on the ground — that is, let us
meticulously ponder with discrimination whether we can
say with blessed Job, 'For our heart does not censure us
in all our life,'[13] and let us painstakingly remember that *if
our heart censures us, God is greater than our heart and he knows
all things.*[14]

We can also understand [the story] rightly as meaning
that, when the Lord was about to give pardon to the sinful
woman, he wished to write with his finger on the ground,
in order to point out that it was he himself who once wrote
the ten commandments of the law on stone with his finger, that is, by the action of the Holy Spirit. And it is good
that the law was written upon stone, since it was given to
subdue the inmost hearts of a hard-hearted and defiant people.[15] It is good that the Lord wrote on the ground when
he was about to give the grace of forgiveness to the con-
trite and humble of heart, who would be able to bring forth
the fruit of salvation. It is good that, bending down, he
wrote with his finger on the ground, who once upon a time,
showing himself to be sublime, wrote on a stone on the
mountain.[16] Through the humiliation of the humanity which
he had adopted, he poured out the spirit of grace upon the
fruitful hearts of the faithful, though once he appeared exalted in [the form of] an angel and gave hard mandates to
a hard-hearted people. It is good that he was bent over when
he wrote on the ground [but] upright when he uttered the

13. Jb 27:6   14. 1 Jn 3:20
15. Aug., *Tract. in Ioh.* 33, 5 (CC 36: 308, 15/17)
16. Some MSS add: 'with his finger'

words of mercy, since through his unity with human infirmity he promised the gift of his benevolence, [but] through the power of his divine might he delivered it to human beings.

Raising himself, Jesus said to her, 'Woman, where are they who were accusing you? Has no one condemned you'? She said, 'No one, Lord'. No one dared to condemn the sinful woman, for they all began to discern in themselves what they recognized to be more damnable.

But let us see the great gift of mercy with which he encouraged the accused woman [after] he put to flight the crowd of her accusers with the authority of the justice he brought forward. There follows: *Jesus said, 'Nor will I condemn you. Go and sin no more'.* Here was fulfilled the statement of the psalm-writer, who chanted in the Lord's praises, *Proceed prosperously and reign on account of truth and gentleness and justice, and your right hand will lead you in a marvelous way.*[17] He reigns *on account of truth,* for by proclaiming the way of truth to the world he spreads the glory of his kingdom to bands of believers. He reigns *on account of gentleness and justice,* for many make themselves subject to his kingdom because they recognize that he is gentle in liberating from sin those who repent, and he is just in condemning the defiant for their sins; he is gentle in bestowing the gift of faith and the heavenly virtues, and just in giving an everlasting reward in the contest of faith and heavenly virtues. His *right hand* led him *in a marvelous way,* for when God was dwelling in human nature, it showed him to be marvelous in everything that he did and taught, but it also pointed out that by a marvelous prudence he always eluded the snares which crafty enemies were able to devise.

'Nor will I condemn you,' he said. *'Go and sin no more'.* Since *he is merciful and benevolent,*[18] he released [her] from her past sins; since *he is just and has loved justice,*[19] he forbade [her] to sin any more. But because some could doubt whether Jesus was able to forgive sins, since they knew that he was a true human being, he deigned to show more clearly what he was capable of in his divinity.

17. Ps 45:4 (44:5)   18. Si 2:13   19. Ps 11:7 (10:8)

After he had fended off the villainy of his tempters and removed the sinful woman's guilt, he again spoke to them saying, *'I am the light of the world. One who follows me does not walk in darkness, but he will have the light of life'*. Here he clearly taught, not only by what authority he had forgiven the woman's sins, but also what he himself had expressed figuratively by making his way to the Mount of Olives, by coming again at daybreak to the temple, and by writing with his finger on the ground: that he himself is the summit *of mercies and the God of all consolation,*[20] the herald as well as the bestower of unfaltering light,[21] the source of the law as well as grace.

'I am the light of the world,' he said, and it is as if he were to say clearly: 'I am the true light which enlightens every human being coming into the world;[22] I am the Sun of justice who rises for those who fear God,[23] even though for a time I seem to be covered over by the cloud of [my] flesh. I am covered by a cloud of flesh not that I may be hidden from those seeking [me], but that I may be less bright for the sake of the weak.[24] Let them heal the eyes of their minds, let them purify their ears, with faith, so that they may be worthy to look upon me. For *Blessed are the pure of heart since they will see God'*.[25]

'One who follows me does not walk in darkness, but he will have the light of life'. [This means]: 'One who follows my orders and example now will not fear the darkness of condemnation in the future. Instead he will have the light of life, where he will never ever die'.

Let us, brothers, now pursue the light of justice, by the faith[26] which works through love,[27] so that we may then be found worthy to reach it by that appearance[28] with which he both repays and increases the merit of love, as he himself attests, saying, *'One who loves me is loved by my Father, and I will love him and manifest myself to him'*.[29] Let us come

---

20. 2 Co 1:3   21. Si 24:6   22. Jn 1:9   23. Ml 4:2
24. Aug., *Tract. in Ioh.*, 34, 4 (CC 36: 313, 41)
25. Mt 5:8
26. 'by the faith' (*fide*), a well-attested variant for 'the faith' (*fidem*)
27. Ga 5:6   28. *specie*   29. Jn 14:21

with all our concentration of mind to him who has his place on the invisible Mount of Olives. God, his God, has anointed him with the oil of gladness above his companions[30] in order that he may deign to make us also companions of that anointing of his, that is, sharers of spiritual grace.

We will not be worthy to gain this in any other way than by loving justice and hating iniquity. The psalm which says this prefaces it with, *You have loved justice and hated iniquity*,[31] so that in proclaiming the glory of the head it may show how the members who are able to belong to him ought to conduct themselves. Let us also call to mind that he came at daybreak to the temple, and while occupied in teaching he loosed a sinful woman from her crime, and let us also strive to show ourselves to be our Maker's temple. When the darkness of our vices has been dispelled, let us strive to go forward into the light of the virtues, so that the Lord may visit our inmost hearts and instruct us with heavenly discipline. If he discovers in us any uncleanness, may he propitiously deign to cleanse us of it, he who lives and reigns with the Father in the unity of the Holy Spirit, God for all ages. Amen.

Scriptural and patristic indices will appear in Book Two.

30. Ps 45:7b (44:8b)　　　　　31. Ps 45:7a (44:8a)

Lightning Source UK Ltd.
Milton Keynes UK
UKHW010617101120
373097UK00003B/861